ADVENTURE TRAVEL NORTH AMERICA

Other books by Pat Dickerman
(1986 editions)

Adventure Travel Abroad
Farm, Ranch & Country Vacations

ADVENTURE TRAVEL NORTH AMERICA

by
PAT DICKERMAN

Adventure Guides, Inc.
New York

An Owl Book
Henry Holt and Company
New York

COVER PHOTO CREDITS (clockwise from upper left):

Sportyaks on the Green River in Utah—*Bill Belknap for Fastwater Expeditions, Utah (and Nevada).*

Packing into Wyoming's highcountry—*Lynn Johnson for Rimrock Dude Ranch, Wyoming.*

Learning to climb jagged peaks—*Colorado's Outward Bound School, Colorado.*

Cycling in the Cascades—*Bicycle Adventures, Washington.*

Ski touring in the Tetons—*Peter Koedt for Timberline Tours, Wyoming.*

COVER AND BOOK DESIGN: Dennis Wheeler.

DESIGN IMPLEMENTATION: Doreen Maddox.

Designed and produced by
Adventure Guides, Inc.
36 East 57 Street
New York, New York 10022

Published by Henry Holt and Company, Inc.,
521 Fifth Avenue, New York, New York 10175.

Published simultaneously in Canada.

Library of Congress Catalog Card Number: 86-260

ISBN 0-03-008563-2 (pbk.)

First Edition

Printed in the United States of America

10 9 8 7 6 5 4 3 2 1

ISBN 0-03-008563-2

CONTENTS

A NOTE OF APPRECIATION. . .

An extraordinary amount of careful double-checking is required to research, write, and publish a book with as many facts and recommendations as this one includes. Special thanks are due to June Rogoznica for her painstaking efforts, and to Connie Smith and Betsy Baumgardner for all their help. My thanks also to Debbie Joost, Barbara Lyons, Doreen Maddox, Gay Northrup, Judith Orringer, Rick O'Shea, Susan Roy, and Dennis Wheeler for their special contributions.

I also appreciate the quantities of information and excellent photos provided by the outfitters and services about whom the book is written, as well as the valuable insight which vacationers have generously shared with us.

And my thanks in advance to the readers who will catch the spirit we have attempted to convey. We hope each participant in these adventures will reap joy along with the jouncing.

Gratefully,

Pat Dickerman

INTRODUCTION

Fifteen years ago we produced a brochure reporting on some 40 outfitters and services for adventurous trips. They took vacationers on horsepacking, rafting, jeeping, canoeing, mountaineering, jet boating, hiking, and covered wagon excursions. It was the first such information ever published, and it opened with the comment: "There's a growing new vacation trend in this country."

What an understatement! Even before the brief manuscript was off the typewriter, I realized it should be a book. We expanded it into a book the following year after months of research, and have come out with new editions every other year or so since. This edition marks its fifteenth anniversary.

Explosion of adventure travel

Although no reliable statistics exist, probably at least 5,000 individuals are involved today in providing outings in North America for people who are discovering the great outdoors. Wherever there is a runnable river, an old wagon trail, a scenic wilderness to explore, or wildlife to study, services have sprung up to provide the guides and equipment and expertise for special journeys.

The whole spectrum of adventure travel has grown with amazing speed. An outfitter for bicycle trips who planned for 100 customers his first season found himself operating trips for 3,000 cyclists seven years later. A rafting service considered five rafts sufficient for 500 or so people per summer on a one-day river run in Pennsylvania. Five years later, his fleet had expanded to 350 rafts, and he was servicing 25,000 customers.

In ever-growing numbers vacation plans involve sailing schools or windjammer cruises, a trek on horseback or on foot, riding with the cowboys on a cattle drive, rafting a remote river, kayaking into icy fjords, jeeping, van camping, exploring, cross country skiing, or floating under a giant nylon bubble filled with hot air. Activities that few vacationers knew how to arrange 15 years ago are almost—but not quite—commonplace today.

The adventurers

Outdoors enthusiasts seem to fit no stereotype. They are doctors, librarians, professors, lawyers, accountants, nurses, secretaries, salesmen. Some are in top echelons of companies, while others pride themselves on never having held a full-time job.

But whoever they are, they want far-from-routine vacations—challenging or soft, expensive or not. They want to participate actively in whatever they do. The are achievers when they're on a holiday—exhilarated to discover they can climb a mountain or raft a river or sail a boat or cycle a given route without having to resort to the sagwagon.

Perhaps you know nothing of navigating, orienteering, topographical map reading, campcraft skills, how to steer a boat, how to read a river or how to mount a horse. You have never spent a night in a sleeping bag camped under the stars, or in the rain. You have never journeyed on treks powered by horse, mule, burro, paddle, pole, wind, water current, or your own two feet. Still, you can safely venture on these expeditions into the wilds. Outfitters and other services make it possible.

That is what this book is all about. It tells of the experts who can guide you and teach you what you need to know to become a genuine adventurer. It tells what their trips are like, the areas they explore, their rates, and what is required of participants. Trips are open to neophytes as well as experts.

Demands and rewards

Adventure travel is for anyone with an adventurous and inquisitive spirit. Depending upon the ruggedness of the expedition, you may have to put up with blistering sun or chilling cold, with drought or drenching rain, with bouncing, jostling, dunking, bruising, and both predictable and unpredictable hazards. It's not that adventurers yearn for discomforts. It's more a question of their being sporty enough to endure them along with gaining the rewards.

What they gain is experiencing the beauty of an isolated canyon, or seeing the world from the top of a high peak. They camp beside an alpine lake, watch a black bear eat berries, spot deer at the water's edge, or wake to the bugling of an elk or the honking of geese. They master a difficult climb, navigate a turbulent river, or achieve some other goal that did not seem within reach. They have the thrill of being surrounded with unbelievable beauty, and the camaraderie of sharing a rugged experience with others—a special reward when it's shared with friends or family. The hazards are insignificant in comparison with rewards.

Age requirements

We are frequently asked about minimum and maximum ages for adventure vacations. We find that a rugged little six-year-old can do as well on a not-too-difficult pack trip as any neophyte adult. And we hear of youngsters aged nine who outhike their parents on the exhausting climb up the Bright Angel Trail at the Grand Canyon. Though twelve years is considered the minimum by most outfitters for a difficult river run, some even younger participate in these trips. It's more a matter of being a good sport and willing to fit in with the basic requirements.

That holds true at the other end of the age scale as well. A California vacationer wrote us several years ago: "In June I will journey to the Arctic, flying to Yellowknife, then down the MacKenzie in a cruiser for 1,200 miles to where it empties into the Arctic Ocean. I'll visit Eskimo villages, then fly into Dawson City. Once again I will be floating down the Yukon River for several days with my outfitter friends for my annual dip into the Fountain of Youth!" This trekker's age? Somewhere into her eighties—we didn't ask how far.

Finding the outfitters and services

Along with the desire for active vacations come many questions. How do you find these trips? Where? During what months? Who operates them? What is the choice? What expertise do they require? What do they cost? How do you make reservations?

Providing the answers is the purpose of this book. To the best of our ability we have reported accurately on every page. Most of the outfitters we cover belong to regional associations which establish standards of service and safety. We have known many of them through our years of publishing, have participated in many of their trips, and have carefully researched still others. A nominal service fee from each helps to support our research. Each service is prepared to provide complete.

"Best vacation ever"

Sometimes it's the simple things that give the greatest pleasure. One trekker writes of "the display of Northern Lights as we came up the icy home stretch—the frost in the mornings, the sunsets at night—the stillness, and knowing that the ten of us were the only humans in that vast, beautiful valley."

For one packtripper, four days in the saddle meant fulfilling a dream he had had since his childhood days of watching *Rawhide* and *Gunsmoke* on TV.

Another adventurer flew to Alaska for an exceptionally rugged river trip. She was "pooped—physically, mentally, spiritually" when she joined eight others for the demanding expedition. "I went with an imagined love for the wilderness," she writes. "I came away with the real thing. I went alone, I came back with eight friends. The scenic overdose was totally rejuvenating. It was the best vacation I've ever had."

For couples, families, and solo travelers, we hope this book will open the way to a whole new world of rewarding vacations.

Happy adventuring!

Pat Dickerman, *President*
Adventure Guides, Inc.
36 East 57 Street
New York, New York 10022
(212) 355-6334

READER'S GUIDE

Chapter Coverage

The chapters cover adventures on land, water, snow, and in the air, with introductions to give an overview of each activity, and reminders of things to check when making reservations. *Wilderness Living/Nature Expeditions* recommends excursions which focus on natural history, basecamp explorations, overland treks, wilderness courses, workshops, and seminars, and *Youth Adventures* reports on programs especially for teens. New in this edition is *Van Camping*, and the *Combos* chapter.

Format

Within each chapter we list services alphabetically (with a few exceptions), first by state, then by Canadian province, with those in the Caribbean or Mexico following. Listings are cross-referenced from one chapter to another for services which offer more than one type of trip.

If a service offers trips in widely separated regions, the listing generally appears under the state where its headquarters are located.

Abbreviations

Throughout the book we have used abbreviations for states, as recommended by the U.S. Postal Service:

AL—Alabama	KY—Kentucky	ND—North Dakota
AK—Alaska	LA—Louisiana	OH—Ohio
AZ—Arizona	ME—Maine	OK—Oklahoma
AR—Arkansas	MD—Maryland	OR—Oregon
CA—California	MA—Massachusetts	PA—Pennsylvania
CO—Colorado	MI—Michigan	RI—Rhode Island
CT—Connecticut	MN—Minnesota	SC—South Carolina
DE—Delaware	MS—Mississippi	SD—South Dakota
DC—District of Columbia	MO—Missouri	TN—Tennessee
FL—Florida	MT—Montana	TX—Texas
GA—Georgia	NE—Nebraska	UT—Utah
HI—Hawaii	NV—Nevada	VT—Vermont
ID—Idaho	NH—New Hampshire	VA—Virginia
IL—Illinois	NJ—New Jersey	WA—Washington
IN—Indiana	NM—New Mexico	WV—West Virginia
IA—Iowa	NY—New York	WI—Wisconsin
KS—Kansas	NC—North Carolina	WY—Wyoming

Abbreviations for Canadian Provinces and Territories are as follows:

Alta.—Alberta	Nfld.—Newfoundland	P.E.I.—Prince Edward Island
B.C.—British Columbia	N.W.T.—Northwest Territories	Que.—Quebec
Man.—Manitoba	N.S.—Nova Scotia	Sask.—Saskatchewan
N.B.—New Brunswick	Ont.—Ontario	Y.T.—Yukon Territory

Rates

The rates given for each service are somewhat generalized. They are for one person in a group unless otherwise noted, and usually do not include state taxes. It is inevitable that rates will change, and that some excursions will be canceled whereas new ones will be offered. All of this should be checked with the outfitters and services (or with our office) when making reservations.

Policies concerning deposits, full payment, and cancellations vary and should be clarified when making reservations. One way of protecting vacation funds where prepayment is required is through low-cost cancellation insurance, available through insurance companies and travel agencies.

Dates

Dates of operation are abbreviated and indicated on a month-to-month basis—Jun.-Sep., for instance, rather than indicating whether the early, middle, or end of each month applies. Each service's brochure includes dates and costs, as well as trip descriptions, what to bring, and other details.

Brochures

Each service will forward a brochure on request with detailed trip descriptions, current trip dates and rates, and what-to-bring information.

Safety

Safety measures—such as wearing lifejackets on rivers—are not to be taken lightly. Once a trip is launched, the outfitter's word is law, and potential dangers will be reduced if it is obeyed. Some services require participants to sign waivers releasing the outfitter from liability in case of accident or loss of personal possessions.

Reservations

We have given the name, address, and telephone number of each outfitter and service so that you may contact them directly for reservations. You also may get in touch with the advisory and partial reservations service at our office. The number is (212) 355-6334.

Our Sourcebooks

For years unusual travel has been our specialty. We started several decades ago with *Farm, Ranch & Country Vacations*, a book which has sent thousands of vacationers to the rural spots it tells about.

That led to *Adventure Travel North America*—which in turn has spawned a new book this year, *Adventure Travel Abroad*. These publications are available at bookstores or may be ordered from our office.

1 ON FOOT

BACKPACKING/HIKING

Amble along through cypress swamps beneath the sultry Florida sun. Or traverse frozen tundra and suddenly find yourself face-to-nose with an Alaskan moose—as surprised to see you as you are to see him. Your own two feet, and either a light daypack or provisions crammed into a backpack, are your passports for trips with expert guides into spectacular wilderness areas throughout North America—and in Hawaii.

The joys are deceptively simple. Stop a few minutes to savor a blue Colorado columbine. Pause beside a waterfall in the Canadian Rockies. Gaze for several hours at a clear, twinkling sky from your campsite in Mexico's Copper Canyon. You've left the world of civilization behind. It's a time to absorb the beauty of here and now.

Whether you're a tenderfoot or a trooper, outfitters for backpacking and hiking treks serve as your ambassadors to the wilderness. They teach you to read a map and compass. They demystify the skills of camping and introduce you to the flora and fauna, and to the techniques of wilderness living.

Novices may want to start with a series of day hikes, spending daylight hours exploring and discovering, and reaching shelter and food by nightfall. The hiker, carrying at most a light daypack, can cover more ground in a day than a backpacker.

But the packer can trek deep into the wilderness with everything needed for housekeeping right on his (or her) back—perhaps 40 pounds of gear, sometimes more. The essentials include a sleeping bag, pad, and plastic ground cloth, dehydrated or freeze-dried foods, toilet articles, clothing, cooking gear, raingear, first aid kit, flashlight, trail map, and perhaps a tent.

Backpackers develop a fetish for traveling light. They tear labels off teabags, cut towels in two, and chop the handle from a toothbrush. On the trail every ounce counts.

The outfitters for backpacking treks provide a list of the equipment and clothing you will need for a specific trip. Most agree that the right shoes are a hiker's best friends. For day hikes over uncomplicated terrain, well-made sneakers will suffice. For more serious hiking, get a good pair of lightweight hiking boots for many needs. They're easy to break in, and less expensive than medium or heavyweight boots. But the latter are essential for treks over rough terrain and in wet and cold weather. Wearing two pairs of socks is important to take the friction off your feet—a wool outer sock and either a cotton or silk liner.

As for clothing, one practical expert advises that most of what you'll need is probably already in your closet. Wool and cotton are the preferred fibers; comfort is the key. Casual shirts, pants, a sweater and a windbreaker will get you started. Beyond that, check your outfitter's list.

A trip itself is easy to arrange. Contact any of these outfitters for scheduled departures, or ask about custom trips which can be designed to your specifications. Would you like to explore Glacier Bay or the Admiralty Islands? The Appalachian or the Pacific Crest Trails? A subtropical swamp in Georgia or the Na Pali Coast in Hawaii? Would you prefer a rugged adventure on Vancouver Island's west coast, or walking Vermont's trails with overnights at comfortable inns?

The possibilities are unlimited. Go wherever your feet will take you. The longest journey, you know, begins with a single step.

Refreshing moments in the West Kootenay Mountains—*Kootenai Wilderness Recreation, B.C., Canada.*

Reminders

What equipment will your outfitter supply and what should you bring? How heavy a pack must you carry? How many miles will you cover each day? Is the terrain rugged or easy? Will you have some layover days? What do the rates include?

Where will you meet and how will you get there? Will you need a fishing license? Ask about elevations and weather, and where you will stay the nights before and after the trip. Is this a custom trip, or are you joining a group?

ALASKA

ALASKA DISCOVERY, INC., P.O. Box 26, Gustavus, AK 99826. Att.: Hayden & Bonnie Kaden. (907) 697-2257.

The Kadens are dedicated to "exposing people to the truly unique wilderness of Alaska." They arrange custom backpack trips to almost any areas of the state, especially the Panhandle and environs: Chicagof, Admiralty, Pleasant and Lemesurier Islands, Glacier Bay National Monument, Juneau, and Sitka. Trips of 1-10 days generally run about $100/day/person; for 6 or more they'll custom-tailor to meals a day, camping gear, and expedition equipment. Individuals and group's wishes. Cost includes guide service, all charters, insurance, 3 meals a day, camping gear, and expedition equipment. Individual and couples may sign up for scheduled trips. This highly personalized service has been cited by the Alaskan legislature for "excellence in pioneering tours sensitive to the environment." Instruction is given on low-impact camping so each area remains in the virgin state in which it was found. (See *River Running, Ski Touring, Wilderness Living.*)

BROOKS RANGE WILDERNESS TRIPS, P.O. Box 40, Bettles, AK 99726. Att.: Dave Schmitz. (907) 692-5312.

"If it hadn't been for the tussocks, the caribou, the windstorm over Ernie Pass, the 'Gates of the Arctic,' the 20 to 30 river crossings, the air drops, etc., this would have been a dull trip," quips a backpacker from Princeton, NJ. Dave guides hikers into the spectacular, trail-less wilderness of the Brooks Range. In the Noatak River Drainages they explore little known side valleys and backpack to the Continental Divide—"an unheralded gem of the Brooks Range," says Dave of this trip. Another challenging exploration takes you from Anaktuvuk Pass over the Divide, or in the western Brooks Range through "rugged and breathtaking scenery" to a tiny hot springs. On the North Slope you explore isolated valleys surrounded by un-named mountains where "the grandeur is majestic, the atmosphere religious." For those not wishing to carry a heavy pack, Dave plans a basecamp trip at a lake. You'll have time to observe Dall sheep, wolves, grizzlies, birdlife, and to fish, relax and have fun. All trips start at Dave's lodge in Bettles. Most trips 7-10 days. Rates from $140-$170 and up/day including bush flights to and from wilderness. (See also *Canoeing/Kayaking, Dog Sledding.*)

CAMP DENALI, Box 67CA, Denali National Park, AK 99755. Att.: Wally & Jerri Cole. (907) 683-2290. [Winter: (907) 683-2302.]

For guided and unguided hiking, Camp Denali offers an unsurpassed wilderness headquarters from which to make daily sorties over taiga trails and gravel bars to observe wildlife, birds, wildflowers, or just to enjoy the majestic scene. Located at the end of the road near Wonder Lake in the geographical heart of Denali National Park, 90 miles from the entrance. Camp Denali offers a full view of the snow-capped 14,000-foot peaks of the Alaska Range, and when the clouds lift to reveal Denali, towering above at 20,320 feet, it's a picture you won't forget. No rough camping here. You stay in cabins with views, wood stoves, and private privies. Family-style meals are a treat, and natural history and interpretive programs at the lodge in evenings add to your store of knowledge of the Alaskan environment and history. Minimum stay 4-5 nights, $160/person/night. (See also *Wilderness Living*.)

HUGH GLASS BACKPACKING CO., P.O. Box 110796-AT, Anchorage, AK 99511. Att.: Chuck Ash. (907) 243-1922.
   "Wilderness living is much more 'here and now' than our normal social setting," says outfitter Chuck Ash. What better way to experience the Alaskan wilderness on a down-to-earth basis than by trekking? His "high-quality adventures through the finest roadless wilderness in Alaska" are led by experienced Alaskan guides. Hike the Arrigetch Peaks with their granite spires—the most dramatic

Trekking in the Wrangell Mountains— *Hugh Glass Backpacking Co., AK.*

mountains in the Brooks Range. Take the Gates-of-the-Arctic Trek north of the Arctic Circle along the Koyukuk River, where the rim of a canyon is so steep the sheep use it as a mountain face. Traverse the majestic, remote eastern Brooks Range from Fort Yukon to Prudhoe Bay. On the Wrangell Mountains Trek see volcanoes, blue ice, and a "natural beauty so rugged, vistas so sweeping, that the mind can not contain it all." This is the land of Dall sheep and grizzly bear, of wolf and moose. Trips 8-10 days. Average: $115/day. Only 6 backpackers per trip to reduce impact on the environment. (See also *Canoeing/Kayaking, Wilderness Living*.)

ALASKA   **SOURDOUGH OUTFITTERS,** Box 18-AT, Bettles, AK 99726. Att.:
David Ketscher. (907) 692-5252.
     Sourdough takes small groups of backpackers on 5- to 14-day trips
into spectacular areas of the Central Brooks Range—the Arrigetch
Peaks, Boreal Mountain and Frigid Crags peaks in the Gates of the
Arctic, the headwaters of the Noatak River, and other areas. You
follow game trails, creeks, and ridges because there are no established
hiking trails in these remote and beautiful areas. "We supplement our
diets with tasty Arctic grayling and tangy blueberries," Dave Ketscher
says, "and we see Dall sheep, moose, grizzlies, and wolves." The
terrain can be rugged; be prepared to carry enough food for the
duration of the trip or between air drops. Some trips may be
combined with still more adventure—canoeing out on the Alatna,
North Fork, or Noatak rivers. Bring pack and sleeping gear. Rates:
include bush flights from Bettles to remote lakes, and back. (See also
Canoeing, River Running, Dog Sledding, Ski Touring.)

CALIFORNIA **ALL-OUTDOORS ADVENTURE TRIPS,** 2151 San Miguel Dr.,
Walnut Creek, CA 94596. Att.: George Armstrong. (415) 932-8993.
     "Beginners come home feeling like experts," promises George
Armstrong, "and experienced backpackers share their skills with
novices and collect new trekking tips." His 5-day backpacking trip in
the high Sierra allows ample time for fishing, photography, and
pursuing personal interests. "They are well organized and
well-equipped," writes one participant. "The food is super and the
guides exceptionally well trained." With camping gear and transport
to/from trailheads, $155/5 days. For a Teen Special they combine
backpacking and river rafting—7 days/$275. Charters, equipment
rentals. (See also *Cycling, River Running.*)

MOUNTAIN TRAVEL, 1398-AG Solano Ave., Albany, CA 94706.
(800) 227-2384 or (415) 527-8100.
     Mountain Travel specializes in wilderness treks to all parts of the
globe. Backpack in Alaska's Arrigetch Peaks of the Brooks Range and
raft the Alatna River (14 days, $1,575). Or hike the glaciers of Mt.
McKinley with commanding views of the Alaskan plains and peaks
(14 days, $1,490). To scale the highest peak in the eastern U.S., try Mt.
Washington on a demanding 60-mile hike in New Hampshire's White
Mountains (10 days, $750). MT also guides sojourns in Hawaii to see
the exotic beauty of the outer islands—Kona and Maui. Hike in
Waipio Valley, swim at Hapuna Beach, and visit volcanoes (15 days,
$1,150). Or hike in Kokee State Park, backpack the spectacular Na
Pali Coast, and see volcanoes on Hawaii, (15 days, $950). Rates
include sleeping gear, some meals; air extra. (See also
*Mountaineering, Canoeing—AK, River Running—AK, Wilderness
Living—AK.*)

SIERRA WILDERNESS SEMINARS, Box 707, Arcata, CA 95521.
Att.: Marie Toombs or Tim Keating. (707) 822-8066. [Jul.-Sep.: Box
1048, Lone Pine, CA 93545. (619) 876-5384.]
     Participants always discover something new about themselves on
our seminars," says leader Keating. "I enjoy watching the tension of

the city melt away as the trip progresses." On both scheduled and custom seminars Toombs and Keating teach individuals how to backpack through the wild, natural beauty of the High Sierra in Sequoia and Kings Canyon National parks and the John Muir and Golden Trout wilderness areas. Teaching includes route finding, scrambling, pack loading, energy conservation, outdoor cooking, proper fire making, mountain emergencies, safety, backpacking comfort, and other techniques. For all levels of experience, age 14 up, 2 days/$195 to 14 days/$485 including equipment and food. Pack and sleeping bag rentals. Arrival: Lone Pine, CA. Jul.-Sep. (See also *Ski Touring*.)

COLORADO

COLORADO ADVENTURE NETWORKS, INC., 194 S. Franklin St., Denver, CO 80209. Att.: Brooke and Eric Durland. (303) 722-6482.

"Vancouver Island's West Coast Trail must rate as one of the top 10 outstanding backpacks in North America," Brook Durland claims. Originally built as a lifesaving trail for shipwreck survivors, the recently reconstructed remote path includes countless wooden ladders up and down the cliffs, two crossings on ferries operated by local Indians, and suspension bridges and hand-pulled cable cars over deep ravines. You camp on the beach, walk at low tide, and hike the trail through otherwise impenetrable rainforests. "You see bald eagles, fascinating tidal pools, sea lions, otters, and hear grey whales sounding offshore," Brooke describes. "You cross sea chasms on fallen tree trunks (or jump across), talk with lighthouse-keepers, sit beside a majestic waterfall. It's the rugged adventure of a lifetime!" For up to 8 packers, 8 days, Jun.-Jul., $580 including airport pickup in Seattle and transfer to put-in point. (See also *Ski Touring, Canoeing*—Quetico Canoe Adventures MN.)

OUTDOOR LEADERSHIP TRAINING SEMINARS, P.O. Box 20281-A Denver, CO 80220. Att.: Rick Medrick. (303) 333-7831 or 942-4362.

"Our 5-day courses are planned for those with little experience who wish a gentle and supportive introduction to the Colorado wilderness," Rick Medrick writes. You learn the basics of backpacking—everything from navigation to first aid—in the beautiful Sangre de Cristo Range. "We believe that each of us has tremendous, untapped potential which can be unleashed through personal, transformative experiences in the outdoors," says Medrick. "It changed my whole life," comments one hiker. Food and equipment are included in the $275 fee; bring or rent packs and sleeping gear. Also 3- to 10-day custom trips, outdoor education courses for academic credit, and leadership workshops. Jun.-Aug. Arrival: Denver or Colorado Springs, CO. (See also *Mountaineering, River Running, Ski Touring, Wilderness Living*.)

PARAGON GUIDES (The Mountaineering School at Vail), P.O. Box 3142-A, Vail, CO 81658. (303) 949-5682.

You are invited to "experience the pleasure of outdoor living and a rare combination of beauty, inspiration, and new friendships" on these trips in Colorado's Gore Range. You hike 6 hours a day and learn about campcraft, orienteering, and "open-air" cooking. "You're

COLORADO

probably safer on the mountain with Paragon's staff than you are walking those blocks next to your home," says one hiker. "The guides' patience in teaching my children to climb will be remembered by the entire family," writes another. Specialized trips for backpacking, family adventure, and fly fishing. Rate for 6-day trips, $60-$90/day, family and group discounts. Rate includes all but pack and sleeping bag. Arrival: Denver. (See also *Mountaineering, Ski Touring*.)

UNIVERSITY OF THE WILDERNESS, P.O. Box 1687, Evergreen, CO 80439. Att.: DAT Trips. (303) 674-9724.

This nonprofit environmental organization sponsors trips in the Colorado Rockies, Utah's Canyonlands and slickrock country, and the Snowy Range of Wyoming's Medicine Bow National Forest. The focus, according to Director Bill Mounsey, is on "wilderness as a place to enjoy and a source of understanding." Activities include wildlife identification, birding, discussions of local ecology and archaeology. Sample trips and rates: Rocky Mountain/Hot Springs (CO), 9 days, $345; Four Falls Canyon (UT), 9 days $345; Snowy Range Beyond the Gap (WY), 5 days, $275. Bring or rent packs and sleeping gear. For 5-10 hikers. (See also *Wilderness Living—WY*.)

FLORIDA

FLORIDA TRAIL ASSOCIATION, INC., P.O. Box 13708, Gainesville, FL 32604. Att.: Member Services Coordinator. (904) 378-8823.

Quoting Jean Craighead George in the *American Walk Book*, "When the sun shines...the Florida Trail is a glistening and fascinating path. It winds past cypress swamps and over bright 'islands'—elevations in the terrain. A rise of no more than 12 inches will support an entirely different community of plants." Willows flourish here, and pine, cypress, ferns, flowers, orchids, bromeliads "which erupt like fountains from the ground" and primitive birds. Many miles of the trail are open to the public, but where it crosses private land, membership in FTA is required. Membership fees: $23/single, $28/family. *Walking the Florida Trail* (FTA's guidebook for members and permit holders), $12. Non-resident permit, $17 for 60 consecutive days (give dates.) Prime hiking: Oct.-Apr. (See also *Canoeing*.)

GEORGIA

WILDERNESS SOUTHEAST, 711-AG Sandtown Rd., Savannah, GA 31410. Att.: Dick Murlless. (912) 897-5108.

One veteran of a WS expedition writes: "The working together—sharing difficulties as well as joys—is a great experience for families, including single-parent familes like mine. Our trip was beautifully planned. Even the cooking and cleanup were fun." Participants can hike in the footsteps of Indians and pioneers and climb to the top of a rocksummit in the soft green Smokies; or explore slave cabin ruins, high dunes, and miles of unspoiled beach on Cumberland Island. Some are base camp trips with a special focus, such as wild edible plants. For 3-7 days, 10-16 hikers. Rates average $45/day, including guides, all food, tents. Group and youth discounts. Bring or rent day pack and sleeping gear. All year (See also *Canoeing, Scuba—FL, Wilderness Lving, Youth Adventures*.)

HAWAII

HIKE MAUI, P.O. Box 10506, Lahaina, HI 96761. Att.: Kenneth Schmitt. (808) 879-5270.

The island of Maui has everything—primeval jungle, rugged mountains, hidden waterfalls, dramatic seacoasts, blow holes, and volcanic craters that look like the moon. Ken Schmitt—"a well-read,

Edging their way toward Hanawi Falls in Maui—*Ken Schmitt for Hike Maui, HI.*

athletic, knowledgeable man," according to hikers—leads groups of 2 to 6 on 50 different day hikes to explore the island's enticing secrets. Choose something easy like a short jaunt to a marine preserve—perfect for snorkeling. Or test your fitness with an all-day hike up the high ridges of West Maui that jut 4,000 feet into the tropical sky. Whatever your choice, Schmitt discusses the flora, fauna, geology, and history of each rewarding area. He also provides a picnic lunch, day packs, rain ponchos, and round-trip transportation from your residence anywhere in Maui. Rates for day trips: adult, $45-$85; child, $25-$45. Longer trips for 4 or more: $100/day per person, bring sleeping bag and backpack frame. Year round.

MINNESOTA   **BEAR TRACK OUTFITTING CO.**, Box 51, Grand Marais, MN
55604. Att.: David & Cathi Williams. (218) 387-1162.
 "Personalized service and instruction and the finest equipment are
the strong points of our business," remarks David Williams, your
outfitter for backpacking adventures in the Boundary Waters Canoe
Area, Superior National Forest, and Isle Royale National Park. The
Isle Royale trip begins with a ferry ride on Lake Superior. From there
you hike, study the predator-prey relationship of wolf and moose,
identify wildflowers, and learn about local geology. You cover a
primitive region of lakes, forests, rivers, and high ridges. BWCA trips
start along the famous Gunflint Trail. Rates begin at $25/person/day.
Group & family rates. Complete outfitting. Max. 10 people, 3-14
days, May-Oct. Arrival: Grand Marais, MN, via Duluth or Thunder
Bay, Ont. (See also *Canoeing, Ski Touring*.)

NEW YORK   **MOHONK MOUNTAIN HOUSE**, New Paltz, NY 12561. (914)
255-1000 or (212) 233-2244.
 The Mohonk resort property lies at the heart of the 22,000-acre
Shawangunk Mountain natural area with 110 miles of trails and
carriage roads ideal for hiking and jogging. During Hikers Holiday
packages overnight guests have a choice of naturalist-guided hikes.
Some require a brisk pace—bushwhacking and climbing—over 10-12
miles of rough terrain; others involve leisurely hikes of 6-8 miles on
carriage roads and trails; or, for downright sauntering, there are 2- or
3-mile easy loops. In fact, Mohonk has enough paths and trails to
keep pedestrians on the move for weeks without retracing a single
step. Hikers Holiday, spring or fall, starts at $90/person for room with
private bath and 3 meals or $70/person with non-private bath.
Day-only admissions, $5/adult, $2/child. (See also *Ski Touring*.)

NORTH   **NANTAHALA OUTDOOR CENTER**, US 19 West Box 41, Bryson
CAROLINA   City, NC 28713. (704) 488-2175.
 With the Appalachian Trail just outside its door and other trails
nearby, NOC has become a popular gathering place for hikers year
round. Weekend clinics with 2 days and 1 night on the trail ($120, all
inclusive) emphasize the basics of backpacking. Maximum group is 10
students and 2 instructors. Private instruction, outfitting, trip
planning, and guide service can be arranged to meet the needs of
almost any group. NOC treks into the Joyce Kilmer Memorial Forest,
Great Smoky Mountains National Park, Shining Rock and Slick Rock
Wilderness areas, and Shining Rock Mountain. Arrival: Asheville,
NC, or Chattanooga, TN (See also *Mountaineering, Cycling,
Canoeing, River Running*.)

OREGON   **PACIFIC CREST OUTWARD BOUND SCHOOL**, 0110 S.W.
Bancroft, Dept. AT86, Portland, OR 97201. (800) 547-3312 or (503)
243-1993.
 "Many people consider this the most exciting, worthwhile
adventure they've ever experienced," writes Outward Bound. "Superb
instructors provide safe wilderness training in small groups. You need
not be an athlete to have fun." This non-profit school with 20 years of

dicated to helping each person try his hardest—and
s one hiker: "I reached new heights of adventure and
bilities beyond my wildest dreams." Learn
rock climbing skills in the alpine wilds of Oregon,
California, (May-Oct.) or in the world-renowned
Springs, CA, (Oct.-Mar.). Courses run 4-22 days,
p) and adults. Cost: from $350-$1,250. Financial aid
River Running, Youth Adventures.)

TEXAS ITIONS, P.O. Box 44, Terlingua, TX 79852. Att.:
s. (915) 371-2490.
e since 1971, Larry Humphreys arranges custom
ckpackers in some of the greatest primitive
hgre Plateau and San Juan Wilderness in CO;
WY; Beartooth Wilderness, and Cabinet
end National Park, TX; and Copper Canyon in
area is different—some with lakes, waterfalls, desert
canyons, natural springs, Indian caves and pictographs, and rock
climbing opportunities, but it's the Copper Canyon trip in Mexico
which he considers the best, though little known. "It's the poor man's
Nepal without the snow-capped mountains," he says. "You hike over
precipitous trails, many of them pre-Columbian with hand-laid
stonework, and meet primitive Indians, some of them famous as great
runners." The trip starts by train or bus from El Paso or Presidio to
Mexican villages and the canyon trailhead. A rugged and spectacular
9-day or 2-week trek for 4-16 packers. Rate for all trips: $65/day. (See
also *Canoeing, River Running*.)

VERMONT **VERMONT HIKING HOLIDAYS,** P.O. Box 845, Waitsfield, VT
05673. Att.: Michael & Clare Fishbach. (802) 496-2219.
Scenic hikes by day, country inns by night—what a delightful way
to see the mountains, lakes, valleys, and rivers from south-central
Vermont to the Northeast Kingdom. Each day combines 5 to 7 miles of
hiking with a trail lunch (bread, cheese, veggies, fruit, juice), a swim,
berry picking, mushroom gathering, and panoramic views of the
Green and White Mountains and the Adirondacks. Experienced guides
lead the way, and vans provide transport from trails to historic village
inns with delicious meals and evening slide shows, yoga, or just
relaxing. Up to 16 hikers per group; 2-day trips, $155; 3 days, $225; 5
days, $350; May-Oct. Also a maple-sugar-hike/ski trip on March
weekends; and several high-peaks trips for good hikers or enthusiastic
beginners. "My husband, son, and I thoroughly enjoyed our 3-day
trip," writes a vacationer from Stamford, CT. "Very well organized,
yet flexible. Hope to make another trip next summer."

WASHINGTON **LIBERTY BELL ALPINE TOURS,** Mazama, WA 98833. Att.: Eric
Sanford. (509) 996-2250.
One of Liberty Bell's most popular trips is a 50-mile trek from the
edge of the vast Pasayten Wilderness Area along high ridges of the
Cascade Crest Trail—the most spectacular scenery of the North
Cascades. You go from towering snow-capped peaks to the Pacific
Crest Trail, through majestic cedar forests and along tumbling streams

Eyeing snow-covered
Mt. Rainier—*Eric
Sanford, Jr. for Liberty
Bell Alpine Tours, WA.*

to Stehekin, ending with a scenic boat ride down Lake Chelan ($295).
On a 40-mile route through the Pasayten Wilderness—director Eric
Sanford calls it "a perfect family getaway among mountain lakes and
lots of wildflowers"—you hike for five days high up on Harts Pass and
follow the Pacific Crest Trail, then head south along Devils Ridge
($275). Another Liberty Bell trek on the Pacific Crest Trail involves
llamas to carry the gear on a 30-mile hike ($385). All trips start Sun.
evening, end Sat. morning; Jul.-Sep. (See also *Mountaineering,
Cycling, Kayaking, River Running, Ski Touring.*)

WYOMING

WILD HORIZONS EXPEDITIONS, Box 2348-A, Jackson, WY 83001.
Att.: Howie Wolke. (307) 733-5343.

If you backpack with a question mark—what's that? why? how?—a
trip with Wild Horizons will satiate your outdoor curiosity. Howie
Wolke is a well-known naturalist/conservationist. He and his

professional guides willingly pause to interpret the awesome flora, fauna, and geology of northwest Wyoming, and the southwest deserts and canyons of Arizona and Utah, and the northern Rockies of Idaho and Montana. Emphasis is on safe, low-impact hiking and camping techniques. Groups limited to 8. You carry 30-40 pounds about 6-7 miles per day through some of the wildest and most beautiful country in America, including Yellowstone, the Tetons, Gros Ventre, Wind River, and Absaroka ranges, the Escalante Canyon, and Organ Pipe Cactus National Monument. Rates for scheduled trips, 5-7 days, are $335-$450 per person. Custom trips, $85-$95/day/person for 2-4.

ALBERTA

SKOKI LODGE, P.O. Box 5, Lake Louise, Alta., Canada T0L 1E0. Att.: John M. Worall. (403) 522-3555.

From Temple Lodge in the Lake Louise Ski Area an alpine trail leads to Boulder Pass and Ptarmigan Lake, over Deception Pass, then into the valley and Skoki Lodge. It's an alpine hike of 2 to 3 hours, and those who have followed the foot trail through this unbelievable beautiful area consider themselves a part of the Skoki Legend. The lodge is the perfect base for a great variety of day trips and overnight hikes, and it's an ideal base for climbers who seek the challenges of the Canadian Rockies. The lodge accommodates up to 22 guests for overnight or prolonged stays. "The scenery of high alpine meadows is some of the most spectacular I have seen anywhere in Banff National Park or anywhere in the Canadian Rockies for that matter," reminisces one Skoki Lodge visitor. (See also *Ski Touring*.)

ONTARIO

WILLARD'S ADVENTURE EXPEDITIONS, Box 10, Barrie, Ont., Canada L4M 4S9. Att.: Willard Kinzie. (705) 737-1881 or 728-4787.

Willard Kinzie personally leads each of his 8- to 10-day backpacking expeditions along the north and south rims of the Grand Canyon in spring, a hut-to-hut hike through New Hampshire's White Mountains in July, Wyoming's Grand Tetons and Colorado's San Juan National Forest in August, the Great Smokies of North Carolina in the fall, and through the rugged Canadian Rockies July to August. In addition, Willard is offering a backpack trip to the Lost City of the Incas in Peru in September. "These trips are for the adventuresome," says Willard. "They are coed, and special attention is given to organization, details, and safety instruction." On one Canadian Rockies trip you set up base camps for day hikes. On others, you backpack exciting backcountry trail systems following the Great Divide in Banff and Jasper national parks. "You'll see the best of the Canadian Rockies," Willard promises. Rates: around $450 (Canadian funds) for 7 days, including meals and local transportation.

BRITISH
COLUMBIA

KOOTENAI WILDERNESS RECREATION, Argenta, B.C., Canada V0G 1B0. Att.: Zan Mautner. (604) 366-4480, 4287.

Tucked away among trees and lakes in the West Kootenay Mountains, KWR offers "opportunities for both novice and experienced backpackers to discover beautiful and varied terrain," according to director Zan Mautner. Take a day hike to a 9,000-foot peak and back, or spend 2 to 5 days exploring glaciers, waterfalls, alpine meadows, hot springs, alpine caves, and lush river valleys. At

A wondrous waterfall
beckons hikers—*Zan
Mautner for Kootenai
Wilderness Recreation,
B.C., Canada.*

the base camp you'll enjoy other activities: swimming, outdoor
cooking, fishing, and campfire get-togethers. Rates for 5-day sessions:
$275 (Canadian dollars). Bring packs and sleeping gear. Jun.-Oct.
Because groups are limited to 8 at a time, the atmosphere is flexible
and informal. Arrival: by air to Castlegar, bus to Nelson, B.C. (See
also *Mountaineering, Youth Adventures*.)

HIKING WITH PACKSTOCK

"Packstock" means a friendly, maybe amusing, sometimes ornery, four-legged pack animal, be it horse, mule, borro, llama, or dog. These trailmates tote the gear while you tote yourself and perhaps little more than a daypack. This makes it a great excursion for families with young children if it is planned for not-too-difficult terrain and manageable distances.

As with pack trips on horseback, outfitters for these hiking expeditions offer *moving* or *progressive trips* (on to a new camp each day) as well as *base camp trips* (staying put at one camp and circling the area on daily hikes). The latter is the more relaxed choice to wilderness living, since it's your choice whether you join the hikers each day, spend hours fishing, or just goof off and read a book in the shade of rustling pines. *Custom trips*—planned especially for you—are offered by all the outfitters, and some also schedule group departure dates for outings you can join.

The outfitters listed here offer a splendid selection of trips for hikers. Would you like to trek through the wildflower-blanketed valleys and alpine lakes in the Sierra or coastal ranges? Or perhaps you'd prefer the scenic backcountry of the Rockies or the rugged Copper Canyon in Mexico? There's still more to choose—the raw Canadian wilderness, ancient Indian grounds and volcanic craters of the Cascades, and the depths of Hells Canyon. Many of the trips let you combine hiking with other activities, like a float trip or a leisurely canoe trip, and of course, swimming, fishing, and climbing.

You'll find that the outfitters are experienced and extremely capable. They handle all the logistics, and provide the pack animals and camping equipment. Their guides are experts in camping know-how and culinary arts—cooking up breakfasts of buttermilk pancakes or dinners with sizzling rainbow trout caught that very day. It's a tremendous way to see, experience, and truly taste the wilderness.

Reminders—
Will the animals carry all the gear, or is some to be carried on your back? Is there a weight limit for personal gear? What do rates cover? Is there a transportation charge? How many miles a day will you cover, over what type of terrain? Do you need a fishing license? Where will you meet—at the ranch, road's end, or trailhead? Is this a scheduled departure or is it a custom trip for your group alone?

CALIFORNIA **ROCK CREEK PACK STATION,** Box 248, Bishop, CA 93514. Att.: Herb & Craig London & Dave Dohnel. (619) 935-4493. [Oct.-Jun.: (619) 872-8331.]

Countless lakes, streams, and meadows, major Sierra passes, and peaks up to 13,000 feet are features of the region where Rock Creek guides college groups and others into the John Muir Wilderness and Yosemite, Sequoia, and Kings Canyon national parks. Trek through wildflower-blanketed valleys, alpine lakes, and forested canyons. Add to the campfire cookouts with your catch of Golden, Rainbow,

CALIFORNIA

and Brown trout. Trips arranged for 6-25 hikers in excellent physical condition, 5 days or longer. Group rates. Bring sleeping and fishing gear. Jun.-Sep. Arrival: Bishop. (See also *Cattle/Horse Drives, Pack Trips*.)

SHASTA LLAMAS, P.O. Box 1137-AT, Mt. Shasta, CA 96067. Att.: Stephen Biggs (916) 926-3959.

Wilderness hiking and camping with llamas carrying the gear is Stephen's specialty. He raises and trains these gentle animals. A strong bond develops between hikers and the lovable, woolly llamas they lead. The animals are intelligent, curious, easily managed, and ideal for packing into the mountains. Their mountaineering heritage dates back to the Inca civilization. In small groups, hikers follow trails into the beautiful backcountry of Mt. Shasta, the Marble Mountains, and the Trinity Alps—some of the most spectacular mountains, lakes, and streams in California. Planned for the average hiker 5 to 10 miles a day with occasional layover days in camp for fishing or relaxing. Among the culinary delights at camp: buttermilk pancakes, seafood crepes, fine wines, green salads, and fresh fruits. Professionally guided fly fishing trips for the serious fisherman or for beginners. Trips from 3-5 days, Jun.-Sep., around $80/day, 10% less for children. Also group rates. Sleeping gear extra. To top off your holiday, Shasta Llamas arranges rafting trips on the nearby Salmon, Rogue or Klamath River as well as a Shakespeare performance and lodging in Ashland. Please write for a free brochure.

COLORADO

HOME RANCH LLAMA TREKS, Box 822A, Clark, CO 80428. Att.: Peter W. Nichols. (303) 879-1780.

Gentle, alert, with heads held high, Peter's lovable llamas carry the gear for trekking into "some of the most beautiful country in the world," according to one trekker. "We camped on a lake full of trout about 1,000' below the Continental Divide." Others praise the sensational food, first rate equipment, and the mix of good food and good friends around the campfire. For four years Peter has guided hikers to his base camp "with gourmet comforts" at 10,300' in the Mt. Zirkel Wilderness of northwestern Colorado. As a fish and wildlife biologist he gives interpretive insight on the wildlife and wildflowers. Each day's activities are geared to what the group wants to do—a long hike to a 12,000' peak, a short hike to another trout-filled lake, or a relaxing day in the sun with a good book. It's a delightful way to camp out in the Rockies for 3 to 6 days. Rates from $350/3 days to $480/6 days all inclusive. Jul.-Sep. Meeting point: Steamboat Springs motel.

MONTANA

DOUBLE ARROW OUTFITTERS (AG), Box 495, Seeley Lake, MT 59868. Att.: Jack Rich. (406) 677-2411, or 2317.

Double Arrow provides pyramid tents that accommodate 2 to 3 people and a 20-by-20-foot kitchen fly on their moving and base camp trips into the million-acre Bob Marshall Wilderness. They also take an extra saddle horse or two in case of any emergency—or sore feet. If hikers bring their own gear, the charge is only for each day the pack service is required. And if they have their own floating equipment, they can be dropped off on the South Fork of the Flathead River for a rafting trip, and picked up where they come out. Per person rates are $45/day, including food and cook (less with your own supplies.) Jul.-Sep. Arrival: Missoula, MT.(See also *Pack Trips, River Running, Youth Adventures.*)

Ready to hit the wilderness trail—*Wilderness Freighters, OR.*

OREGON

CAL HENRY, Box 26-A, Joseph, OR 97846. Att.: Cal Henry. (502) 432-9171.

On Cal Henry's trips you visit Hells Canyon, the deepest gorge in North America, or the alpine peaks of the Eagle Cap Wilderness. On travel days, hikes cover 6 to 10 miles, and on layover days there's time for fishing and "learning nature's secrets firsthand." Our goal is to travel through the countryside leaving behind no sign of our presence, so others can enjoy wilderness after us," as Cal explains it. Moving and base camp trips; rates on request. Bring sleeping gear. May-Sep. Arrival: Enterprise, OR (See also *Pack Trips.*)

HURRICANE CREEK LLAMAS, Rt. 1, Box 123-AT, Enterprise, OR 97828. Att.: Stanlynn Daugherty. (503) 432-4455.

When you trek into the Wallowa Mountains of northeast Oregon with Stanlynn Daugherty and her llamas, you can be sure of several things: you'll learn a lot about the local history, plants, and wildlife; you'll find much beauty in the stream-filled canyons, glacial-carved valleys, and high basin lakes of the Eagle Cap Wilderness; and you'll be intrigued by your curious, intelligent, wooly companions who safely transport the gear. It's a land of wildflowers, mountain goats, and bighorn sheep, and in the streams are rainbow, brook, and rare golden trout. Trips from 3 to 6 days for up to 10 participants are scheduled from June to mid-September. Stanlynn also plans custom wilderness journeys for families or groups, and "Llama Lunches" for a

OREGON   day's outing with a hearty luncheon banquet carried by a friendly llama. Rate: $75-$80 per day, 20% less for children. Bring sleeping bag. Trailheads near Enterprise and Joseph are the starting points.

WILDERNESS FREIGHTERS, 2166 S.E. 142nd Ave., Portland, OR 97233. Att.: John Simonson. (503) 761-7428.

Never backpacked? Not to worry. By the end of a week with John and his Alaskan malamutes—one specifically assigned to you—you'll

A well-deserved rest for two packers—*Wilderness Freighters, OR.*

be a pro. The only difficulty comes in parting with your four-legged trailmate at trip's end. John's six husky pack dogs bred for freighting are extremely friendly working companions. He provides gourmet trail meals and follows the wild flowers into infrequently trekked Indian Heaven—land of the Sasquatch ("Big Foot") at the base of Mt. Adams. Explore ancient Indian grounds, alpine meadows, huckleberry fields, volcanic craters. Flight over Mt. St. Helens optional. Trip concludes with meals, lodging, and a soak in the hot tub at the elegant Inn of the White Salmon. More strenuous hikes through Mt. Hood National Forest. Rates of $595/adult, less for children includes everything except personal gear. Arrival: Portland. (See also *Dog Sledding*.)

WYOMING

GAME HILL RANCH, Box A, Bondurant, WY 82922. Att.: Pete & Holly Cameron. (307) 733-4120.

Cattle rancher and mountain guide Pete Cameron teaches hikers about the flora, fauna, geography, and history of the Wyoming and Gros Ventre Ranges—a scenic backcountry of grassy meadows, acres of wildflowers, open slopes of sage, and cold mountain streams meandering through willow thickets and cascading into waterfalls. Each trip, for 2 to 6 hikers, is planned for weather and individual abilities, so the number of layover days varies. Hikers usually cover 5 to 10 miles a day and stay in comfortable but simple camps. The open-fire gourmet cooking is a plus. For moving and base camp trips: 3 days, $300; 5 days, $450; 7 days, $600; 10 days, $835. Arrival: Jackson, WY. (See also *Pack Trips, Ski Touring*.)

BRITISH
COLUMBIA

HEADWATERS OUTFITTING, LTD., P.O. Box 818, Valemount, B.C., Canada V0E 2Z0. Att.: Liz Norwell or Brian McKirdy. (604) 566-4718.

Hike with an experienced guide while horses or helicopters pack your gear through a Canadian wilderness. Most trips under 6 days go to Dave Henry Camp. Longer trips may include visits to Mount Robson Provincial Park, Jasper National Park, Valemount Area, or Willmore Wilderness Park. At Dave Henry Base Camp, you can relax, admire the view, paddle leisurely around the lake, or fish for rainbow trout. Trips arranged on a custom-basis only, for 2-12 hikers. Rates: $70-$100 (Canadian)/person/day, 4-day minimum. Price includes guide, cook, food, and tents. (See also *Pack Trips*.)

MEXICO

ULTIMATE ESCAPES, LTD., M-115 S. 25th St., Colorado Springs, CO 80904. (800) 992-4343 or (303) 578-8383.

From the very start, the Copper Canyon trip is an adventure. Board a train in Chihuahua for an 8-hour ride to Mexico's Sierra Madres and the brink of a canyon so extraordinary it seems like another world. Here you hike into the 4,000-foot-deep roadless gorge—a Mexican-style Grand Canyon, assisted with burros to carry the gear. On the unmarked canyon trails you see a prehistoric cliff dwelling, hike through stands of oak and mountain mahogany, and encounter the Tarahumara Indians, a proud and independent tribe known for their ultralong-distance competitive running—up to 200 miles! You camp at the canyon bottom, relaxing on a white sand beach and plunging into a clear green pool. Swim, climb, and explore for several days before the long climb back to the rim and the return ride by train. For 12 days, $595, Oct.-May. (See also *Pack Trips, River Running, Combos*.)

MOUNTAINEERING/ ROCK CLIMBING

It's so cold that your leader's beard is frosted with tiny icicles. The sunlight, bouncing back and forth between the vibrant blue sky and the glistening white snow, is the brightest you've ever seen. You take one more step and...you've reached the summit! Yes, it's been a long, hard climb—and you've loved every thrilling, agonizing, stimulating moment of it.

Why climb a mountain? If you need to ask, then this pursuit probably isn't for you. But, if Mt. Everest conqueror Sir Edmund Hillary's answer—"Because it's there"—rings true, then you may have found the challenge you've been looking for.

Mountaineering is, indeed, much more than scaling a mountain or a steep wall of rock. The spiritual and emotional rewards are widely known and well-documented; we'll leave that area to the poets. But the physical aspects of the activity include a vast range of arts—campcraft, map reading, orienteering, wilderness medicine, and survival techniques are just the beginning.

There are also the purely technical components, the specific skills of rope handling, rappeling, glissading, belaying, and the handling of pitons, nuts, and slings. Beyond that, there are the esoteric skills involved in alpine climbing: making steep ascents up snowy, ice-covered mountains that require intimate knowledge of an ice axe, rope, and crampons.

If you're a beginner, you can start small. There are half-day, daylong, and weekend introductions to climbing just about anywhere there's a mountain. As your level of expertise increases, so do the opportunities to learn; you can ascend to the highest levels of the sport. If you aim for the top, how about taking on North America's highest mountain, Alaska's Mt. McKinley—to its peak at 20,320 feet? There are experienced guides to lead the way.

If you're the sort of person who gets woozy peering down from, say, a fifth-story window, it's still possible for you to enjoy learning the techniques of climbing. There are teachers who offer mountaineering courses to confirmed flatlanders, with the assurance that your feet will never be more than 10 feet from the ground. There's no need to climb high; fun and satisfaction come from climbing well.

Mountaineering is a strenuous sport and can demand all the strength you possess. But to committed mountaineers, climbing provides one of life's peak experiences. These explorers endure freezing sleet, drenching rains, precarious footholds, and heart-stopping falls. But no matter, they say—the rewards are many. There's the joy of self-confidence, the thrill of achievement, the discovery of what you can do if you have to, and the indescribable exhilaration at the summit.

Why climb a mountain? Climbers reply: Why not?

Reminders
Become familiar with your equipment and get to know your instructor before you start the climb. Your instructor's abilities and judgment are invaluable. Be candid in describing your capabilities or limitations. What should you bring? What do rates cover? Are you arranging for a beginner, intermediate, or advanced excursion? How much weight will you be expected to carry? What preconditioning should your have? What are the

A technical climber reaching a high goal— *Yosemite Mountaineering School, CA.*

health requirements or age limits? Be clear on whether you are signing up for a course, an expedition, a trip from a base camp, rock climbing, glacier climbing, peak climbing, or whatever. Is the terrain rugged? What weather conditions are expected? Is the excursion for enjoyment, survival *training, or both? Are you joining a group or is this a custom trip? Is transportation to and from your meeting point supplied? What other activities are included? Who arranges pre- and post-trip lodging? (For excursions for teens, see the Youth Adventures chapter.)*

Tackling challenging peaks of the Alaska Range—*Gary Bocarde for Mountain Trip, AK.*

ALASKA

MOUNTAIN TRIP, Box 41161, Dept. AT, Anchorage, AK 99509. Att.: Gary Bocarde. (907) 345-6499.

"Alaska's mountains are serious, and to succeed one must know the environment," cautions Gary Bocarde. His climbs are for "a mentally ready and physically fit body" able to carry loads from 60-80 pounds and to travel long hours in bad weather. Established in 1973, Mountain Trip offers seminars and leads expeditions and technical climbs to Alaska's highest peaks—McKinley (20,320'), Foraker (17,400'), and Hunter (14,570'). The guides and trip organization are highly regarded by participants. A climber from Sheridan, WY, reports climbing Mt. McKinley "with storm days at 14,000', 16,200', and 17,200'." He proudly notes the moment they reached the summit—"7:10 p.m. on July 4th"—and tells of a lady from Chicago discovering that of all things, she had carried her American Express card to the top. Most of Gary's expeditions are for 4-6 climbers, from April-August, about 20 days, $1,990-$2,300; some from 10-12 days at $1,600. He encourages all-women seminars and in June schedules an all-women McKinley expedition. He also offers Yosemite climbs, and in January an Aconcagua expedition (22,835') in Argentina.

CALIFORNIA   **MOUNTAIN TRAVEL**, 1398-AG Solano Ave., Albany, CA 94706.
(800) 227-2384 or (415) 527-8100.
    With long-established mountaineering expertise, Mountain Travel
conducts seminars and leads climbs in the Alaska Range. Stamina,
endurance, and a full range of mountaineering skills are required for
an ascent of Mt. McKinley in Alaska's Denali National Park. At
20,320 feet it soars a dazzling 17,000 feet above the plains. (For a
22-day climb, $2,390.) A comprehensive course in climbing rock,
snow, and ice in the spectacular Kahiltna Glacier below Mt. McKinley
takes 14 days, $1,590. Or hone your mountaineering skills with climbs
up Mexico's highest peaks (including Orizaba at 18,851'), 14 days,
$890. Guides, 1 to every 4 climbers, are chosen for their ability to
assure safe and successful trips. (See also *Backpacking,
Canoeing—AK, River Running—AK, Wilderness Living—AK.*)

PALISADE SCHOOL OF MOUNTAINEERING, P.O. Box 694A,
Bishop, CA 93514. Att.: John Fischer. (619) 873-5037.
    The Palisades, most dramatic alpine region of California's Sierra
Nevada, stand 10,000' above the Owens Valley. The range contains
many precipitous summits over 14,000' and several active glaciers.
Since 1960 PSOM has earned a reputation for quality outfitting and
excellent leadership. John Fischer, PSOM director with 23 years of
climbing experience, has led hundreds of ascents here and abroad;
Gordon Wiltsie, chief guide, with 18 years experience, climbed
extensively in the Himalayas. With other PSOM professionals they
provide in-depth curriculum and guidance in winter ice climbing,
alpine trekking, basic and advanced alpine climbing, snow and ice
climbing, and a mountain photography workshop. Sample rates:
$145/2 days basic rock, $185/2 days ice climbing, $495/6 days basic
or $565/6 days advanced mountaineering. Mexican volcano climbs in
Oct. and Feb.: $885/14 days plus air.

YOSEMITE MOUNTAINEERING SCHOOL, Yosemite National
Park, CA 95389. Att.: Bruce Brossman. (209) 372-1335. [Sep.-Jun.:
(209) 372-1244.]
    YMS courses are designed to teach people the basics for climbing
safely, and include seminars in advanced free climbing, direct aid and
alpine climbing as well. During summer months, the school moves to
Tuolumne Meadows and offers basic and intermediate lessons, snow
and ice climbing, weeklong seminars, and guided climbs. Spring and
fall, classes are taught in Yosemite Valley. Students should be in
reasonable condition and 14 years old, minimum. Sample rates: Daily
classes, $30. Alpencraft Seminar, 5 days, starts on Mondays.
Advanced seminars, $50/day. Arrival; Fresno/Merced, CA. (See also
Ski Touring.)

COLORADO   **COLORADO MOUNTAIN SCHOOL**, Box 2106-A, Estes Park, CO
80517. Att: Mike Donahue. (303) 586-5758.
    "The best place to develop basic knowledge and learn skills is on
actual wilderness trips," claims Mike Donahue. "We use climbs and
trips as our classrooms." After a day or two participants are ready for
Mike's 7-day climbing camps in Rocky Mountain National Park. He

COLORADO

combines climbing and various mountain routes. The rate of $425 covers beginning rock camp. "Rock climbing is nothing more than a big pile of problems," Mike says. "It's solving these problems that makes climbing the tremendous joy that it is. Getting to the top isn't important. It's the overall experience that counts." With "winter as your playground," CMS conducts a climbing and ski mountaineering program, technical ice seminars, and scheduled expeditions to Alaska's Denali National Park and South America. Sample rates: beginning rock $40/day; snow school $60/day; ice climbing $80/day; group rates and private instruction. Open year round.

FANTASY RIDGE MOUNTAIN GUIDES, P.O. Box 1679, Telluride, CO 81435. Att.: Michael Covington. (303) 728-3546.
   "Since 1972, Fantasy Ridge has provided a full range of mountaineering and technical climbing programs to over 4,300

Braving nature's elements—*Fantasy Ridge Mountain Guides, CO.*

visitors," says director Michael Covington. From headquarters in Telluride, he offers year-round opportunities in the magnificent Uncompahgre and San Juan Mountains. Winter technical ice and alpine climbing from December to March include lodging and evening slide shows on technique in a 4-day program. Summer rock and mountaineering programs operate June to September, with daily and multi-day itineraries. Rates vary from $40/day for summer programs to $400 for 4-day winter climbing. For expanding interests and abilities Fantasy Ridge leads adventures worldwide, the most popular being expeditions on Mt. McKinley in Alaska from April to July, using various routes. "Step into a magical world," Covington urges. For 10- to 24-day expeditions the rate is $1,000 to $2,500. One participant from Boulder, CO, calls Covington "a virtuoso of the mountain and the soul. He knows how to play both to get the most out of his clients. Greatest experience of my life."

OUTDOOR LEADERSHIP TRAINING SEMINARS, P.O. Box 20281-A Denver, CO 80220. Att.: Rick Medrick. (303) 333-7831.

On 7- and 10-day mountaineering workshops you pack into a high alpine setting of the Sangre de Cristo Range, camp in tents, and bivouac in the open while learning the styles and techniques of general mountaineering (7 days, $375; 10 days, $545; all food and equipment included). OLTS rock climbing seminars offer intensive instruction in technique taught in small groups of 4 to 8 participants by professional climbers (5 days, $295). Comments one OLTS graduate: "Rick Medrick's insights into the human experience in the outdoors helped all of us get a better perspective on ourselves and others." Jun.-Sep. (See also *Backpacking, River Running, Ski Touring, Wilderness Living.*)

PARAGON GUIDES (The Mountaineering School at Vail), P.O. Box 3142-A, Vail, CO 81658. (303) 949-5682.

From a base camp at 11,000 feet, Paragon's instruction covers all phases of mountaineering with lectures, demonstrations, and practice in the magnificent alpine reaches of the Gore Range. You gradually tackle more difficult climbs while learning the basis of belaying, rock and snow climbing, rappeling, glissading, and other essential skills. "Expert, thorough instruction and excellent food," is one student's endorsement. Paragon offers a 6-day basic course for 4-8 climbers, 10-day advanced courses, and specially scheduled climbing trips. Rates from $60-$90/day include sleeping bags, tents, climbing equipment, and first night's lodging in Vail. Founded in 1970, the school operates under a National Forest permit. (See also *Backpacking, Ski Touring.*)

CONNECTICUT **OUTWARD BOUND, INC.,** 384 Field Point Rd., Greenwich, CT 06830. Att.: Pat Lyren. (800) 243-8520 or (203) 661-0797.

"The mental and emotional mountain climbing skills will be with me forever, and I will use them the rest of my life," is the quote of one satisfied Outward Bound participant. The 25-year-old adventure education organization offers mountaineering and rock climbing courses in nearly a dozen locations across the U.S. Among the areas: Colorado's raw white peaks, California's South Sierra Mountains and Yosemite National Park, Oregon's Central Cascades, southwestern Montana's Rockies, North Carolina's Blue Ridge Mountains and southern Appalachian Mountains, and the Canyonlands of southeastern Utah. You'll also learn the techniques of backpack travel, map and compass use, route finding, first aid, and search and rescue. Year round trips from 4-30 days, for $350-$1,600. (See also *Canoeing/Kayaking, Wilderness/Nature Expeditions, Youth Adventures.*)

MARYLAND **NORTH COUNTRY MOUNTAINEERING, INC.,** 1602 Shakespeare St., Historic Fells Point, MD 21231. Att.: Steve Schneider. (301) 563-4309.

Having introduced the 5.11 rock climbing standard to the Franconia Valley in New Hampshire, NCMI has a Washington, D.C. division offering top-notch instruction at Carderock and Great Falls in

Virginia. The basic 7-hour class, weekends in winter and spring, is
$30, all technical equipment included. The rest of the year NCMI's
mountaineering and rock climbing classes cover major faces and
summits in the East, including Cannon Cliff (NH), Shawangunk
Mountains (NY), and Seneca Rocks (WV). Open to all ages. Sample
rates: 7 days, $395; 15 days, $595; 29 days, $1,095. Instructor/student
ratio, 2:1. Also courses for new climbing instructors, custom
programs, and guided climbs. (See also *Youth Adventures—NH.*)

**NEW
HAMPSHIRE**

INTERNATIONAL MOUNTAIN CLIMBING SCHOOL, INC., P.O.
Box 239-A, Conway, NH 03818. Att.: Paul Ross. (603) 356-5287,
6317, or (603) 447-6700.

"All you need to do is bring a pair of boots; we supply everything
else," says director Paul Ross, a veteran of many first ascents both here
and abroad with over 20 years of rock climbing experience. Most
importantly, Ross supplies "responsible, experienced, and very
competent instructors—highly skilled climbers who keep abreast of
the latest developments in climbing and teaching techniques," he
assures. Practice climbs take place in the Presidential Range and the
White Mountains. Ross recommends the 2- or 4-day course for
beginners, but single-day bookings are also possible. Daily basic
classes limited to 3 students per instructor. Students are introduced to
rappeling, short rock climbs, knots, equipment, and belaying systems.
Daily class prices: $60/day for individual bookings, $50-$55/person
for 2-3 students, $75/person for private sessions. Also, a 4-day basic
course, $225; 3-day advanced, $175. Other offerings: specialized
instructor courses in general instruction and guiding techniques,
mountain safety/resuce and ice climbing, and mountaineering trips to
Britian in the spring. Ross is a member of the American Professional
Guides Assn.

NEW YORK

PEAK PERFORMANCE, Dept. A, 130 Mountain Rest Rd., New
Paltz, NY 12561. Att.: Russ Raffa or Lynn Hill. (914) 255-7017.

"There's nothing better than serious fun," claims Lynn Hill. This she
and Russ provide with instruction in safety, body mechanics, and
climbing techniques in the Shawangunk Mountains, about 1 1/2 hours
from New York City from April to November. "These people are true
professionals," raves a novice climber of Florham Park, NJ. "They
have a real knack for helping a student work through fear and
uncertainty with calm understanding and laughter."
Student/instructor ratio: 3 to 1. Daily rates: $100 for 1, $75 each for 2,
$60 for 3. Lynn and Russ also guide climbs in California, Colorado, or
Europe on a prearranged individual basis. In 1984 Lynn won the
American Alpine Club award for outstanding achievement in rock
climbing.

**NORTH
CAROLINA**

NANTAHALA OUTDOOR CENTER, US 19 West Box 41, Bryson
City, NC 28713. (704) 488-2175.

NOC assures rock climbers a safe indoctrination into the sport. The
novice spends weekend clinics learning knots, signals, holds, rope
handling, and other basic techniques for mastering the "vertical
environment," with practice climbing at Furnace Rocks in the

Nantahala Gorge and the Devil's Courthouse in Pisgah National
Forest. For meals Friday through Sunday night, equipment, and
instruction from "some of the best climbers in the South,"
$150/person. Apr.-Oct. Motel and hostel at the Center, campgrounds
nearby. Arrival: Asheville, NC or Chattanooga, TN. (See also
Backpacking, Cycling, Canoeing/Kayaking, River Running.)

OREGON

TIMBERLINE MOUNTAIN GUIDES, P.O. Box 464-C, Terrebonne,
OR 97760. Att.: Mike Volk. (503) 548-1888.

For a total range of mountaineering and rock courses, climbs,
seminars, and expeditions, consider the program offered by Mike Volk
of Timberline. He schedules hundreds of events in the mountains of
Oregon year round, and climbing Mexican volcanoes in winter. Rates
vary from $25 for a half-day rock course or $50 all day, to $260 or so
with 4 climbers for 2-day courses, and $445 for 5 days. Courses are for
1-4 participants, seminars for up to 10. "Our guides are ready to
equip, train, and guide you in a safe and enjoyable style," Mike
advises. For novice to advanced, it's a chance to improve skills to the
maximum along with the pure enjoyment of climbing. "Our guide
never made us feel like the novices we were," says a participant from
Pendleton, OR. "Reaching the summit of Mt. Hood was a high that
far exceeds its 11,235 feet!"

Discovering the impor-
tance of teamwork—
Outward Bound, Inc.,
CT.

WASHINGTON

AMERICAN ALPINE INSTITUTE, 1212 24th D, Bellingham, WA
98225. (206) 671-1505.

With professional climbers, skiers, and natural science educators
whose experience includes every major range in the world, this
Institute and School offer a staggeringly comprehensive program to

WASHINGTON climbers at all levels. Most instruction is in the North Cascades (WA); other courses and guided climbs from Alaska to Mexico. There are introductory programs in alpine mountaineering for 6-12 days, $360-$640; in rock climbing, 2-7 days, $100-$540. For more experienced climbers: ice climbing (6 days, $380), expedition training (10-12 days, WA or AK, $720-$1,190) and masters' rock (4 days, $320). On a Mt. McKinley expedition 6-8 climbers are lead by 2 guides to the summit of North America ($1,750); others attempt Mt. Foraker and Mt. Hunter. A Ruth Glacier mountaineering program combines some of the world's most spectacular ski touring with instruction in snow and ice climbing and several easy ascents (8 days, $740). In winter: high altitude climbing in Mexico (7-14 days, $460-$890).

Safely secured, a climber ponders her next step—*Susan Biddle for Outward Bound, Inc., CT.*

LIBERTY BELL ALPINE TOURS, Mazama, WA 98833. Att.: Eric Sanford. (509) 996-2250.

For those with little or no mountaineering experience, Liberty Bell's basic 5-day seminar includes equipment selection and use, knots and rope work, belaying, easy rock and snow climbing, ice ax use, route

finding, mountain safety, first aid and rescue, and rappeling and
descending techiques. It operates from a base camp in the Cascades,
and ends with an ascent of a major peak. For those wishing to
concentrate on rock climbing, a 5-day program includes face and
friction climbing, cracks and chimneys, and an ascent of Liberty Bell
Mountain. A 5-day snow and ice climbing seminar on the slopes of
10,700-foot Mt. Baker teaches ice axe and crampon use, rope handling,
crevasse rescue, glacier travel, and other techniques. Programs start
Sun., end Sat., Jun.-Aug., $345 up. Guides are members of the
American Professional Mountain Guides Assn. (See also
Backpacking, Cycling, Kayaking, River Running, Ski Touring.)

RAINIER MOUNTAINEERING, INC., Paradise, WA 98397. Att.:
Lou Whittaker & W. Gerald Lynch. (206) 569-2227. [Sep.-May: 201
St. Helens, Tacoma, WA 98402. (206) 627-6242.]

"RMI has the largest professional staff of trained snow, ice, and
rock climbing instructors in the U.S.," states Lou Whittaker. "We pride
ourselves on the comments made by thousands of novice climbers
whose experience with us was a highlight of their lives." Sample
courses and rates: 1-day introduction to ice and snow travel on Mt.
Rainier, $35; 2-day summit climb, $160; 5-day snow and ice seminar,
$355. Courses scheduled May through Sep. Bring or rent boots,
packs, crampons, ice axes.

WEST VIRGINIA **SENECA ROCKS CLIMBING SCHOOL INC.,** Box 53, Seneca Rocks,
WV 26884. Att.: John Markwell/Topper Wilson. (304) 567-2600.
[Evening: (703) 474-2335.]

"We are dedicated to teaching individuals of most any age to safely
enjoy the challenge and adventure offered by the vertical rock
environment," says director John Markwell. Most of the school's
classes are taught on the quartzite crags of Seneca Rocks which loom
900 feet over the beautiful North Fork River Valley. Courses include
basic and intermediate rock climbing, and mountain rescue. The basic
class lasts three days, is geared for people with little or no experience,
and limited to three students per instructor ($45/day), or private
instruction ($80/day). The intermediate course, for climbers who
want to start leading, lasts two to three days, $50/day in class of
three, $100/day private instruction. The school arranges mountain
rescue seminars for groups and individuals as requested. Students stay
at a local motel or camp out near the Rocks. Because of crowds,
weekday courses recommended. Minimum age: 12. No rentals.
May-Labor Day. Arrival: By air to Elkins, or by car to Seneca Rocks.

WYOMING **EXUM MOUNTAIN GUIDES,** Grand Teton National Park, P.O.
Box 56, Moose, WY 83012. Att.: Margo. Summer: (307) 733-2297.
Winter: (415) 922-0448.

An ascent of the Grand Teton, via the Exum Ridge, is a goal sought
by many. Take heart! It becomes attainable to anyone with the
desire—after qualifying in two days of climbing school, according to
Exum Guides. These mountain experts have operated in Grand Teton
National Park for 55 years. The staff includes well-known
mountaineers and guides, some of them with over 20 years experience.

WYOMING They offer a variety of fine routes on rock, snow, and ice for those wanting to expand their experience. For 1-day basic school, $38, intermediate, $48. For 2-day Grand Teton climb, $160. Rates include all climbing equipment and boat fare across Jenny Lake to climbing school area. Jun.-Sep. Arrival: Jackson, WY, or Idaho Falls, ID.

JACKSON HOLE MOUNTAIN GUIDES & CLIMBING SCHOOL, Box 547P, Teton Village, WY 83025. Att.: Andy Carson. (307) 733-4979.

"Our climbing school and guide service operate year round in the Grand Tetons, Wind Rivers, and Beartooths," states Director Andy Carson. "All ages and ability levels are welcome to join our personable, professional guides in our mountaineering way of life." Beginners learn technical skills and acclimatize for a guided ascent on the 4-day Grand Teton Climbing Course, with 3 nights at 11,000-foot High Camp ($375 with food and gear). Fun climbing classes on rock or snow: 1 day/$36-$46. Educational 8- to 12-day expeditions, $700-$850 with food and gear. Winter ice climbing, ski mountaineering, and ski touring, beginner to advanced, $50/day, to $695 for 7-day winter ascent of the Grand. Private guides for climbing or trekking, $75-$140/day. "We have an exceptional number of return clients and a low client-to-guide ratio," Carson comments. "We'll organize and guide trips to any range in the world."

SKINNER BROTHERS, Box 859, Dept. AG, Pinedale, WY 82941. Att.: Monte Skinner. (307) 367-2270.

"For the outdoor enthusiast, our month long 'Open Session' is the ultimate in mountaineering experiences," notes Monte Skinner. You spend 10 days at Burnt Lake at the foot of the Wind River Mountains learning mountaineering skills: search and rescue, emergency first aid and evacuation techniques, care and handling of ropes and other climbing gear, tent types and set-up procedures, high-altitude cooking, and basic rock climbing. Next you ride horses 12 miles into the wilderness to Leavell Lake to practice intensive rock climbing, then hike through alpine meadows to Mount Baldy where you become a competent snow climber. The remainder of the month is spent hiking to Titcomb Basin and climbing the surrounding peaks. Prerequisites: 16 or older, previous climbing experience. Begins Jul. 7 for 18 pupils, $1,575. (See also *Pack Trips, Ski Touring, Youth Adventures.*)

BRITISH **KOOTENAI WILDERNESS RECREATION,** Argenta, B.C., Canada COLUMBIA V0G 1B0. Att.: Zan Mautner. (604) 366-4480 or 4287.

On custom trips, Zan Mautner takes 1 to 4 participants on climbs that range from 1 to 7 days. You start from his base camp at 2,000 feet in the West Kootenays. There are many peaks over 10,000 feet in the adjacent Purcell and Selkirk Mountain Ranges. Glacier and ice climbing can be part of the experience, as well as rock climbing and wall climbing. Also a session for those interested in exploring a network of caves. "Participants should be in good physical condition and mentally ready to try as hard as they can to extend themselves," Zan advises. He plans each trip for the abilities of the group, and adjusts rates according to the activity desired. Bring your own boots,

A "thumbs-up" signals a successful climb—*Zan Mautner for Kootenai Wilderness Recreation, B.C., Canada.*

backpack, sleeping bag, crampons, and ice axe. Arrival: by air to Castlegar, bus to Nelson, B.C. (See also *Backpacking, Youth Adventures.*)

BY HORSE

CATTLE/HORSE DRIVES

Imagine the life of a cowboy in the saddle for hours, trailing hundreds of bawling cows and calves from the winter lowlands to summer pasture, chasing strays, averting stampedes, and yelling at the cows all day to keep them bunched together and moving ahead. Now imagine yourself as one of those cowboys, sitting high in the saddle and eating the dust of the slow moving herd.

For ten years or so a few of the old-time ranchers have let city dudes try their hand at trailing cattle over dirt roads, across meadows, down gullies, and along creek beds. The action doesn't end there. At cow camp you help with the branding, dehorning, castrating, vaccinating, and mothering up the calves who get separated along the way from their mothers.

Pack trip outfitters in the High Sierra offer a similar but less demanding experience to vacationers who want to tag along on a horse drive. In spring or early summer they move their horses and mules from winter pasture in the Owens Valley to their pack stations in the highcountry, and in the fall they drive them down again. It's several days of fast riding, spectacular scenery, hearty meals, and great fun.

Not only do the cattle ranchers get a fee for letting the dudes participate. They also expect a good day's work! But how else can a city slicker discover what cattle ranching is all about? For most who grew up on *The Lone Ranger* or *Spin and Marty* it's a dream come true.

A cattle drive can be hot, dusty work—or cold and wet under an all-day rain. "Believe me, it's a rough life," comments a Chicago businessman, a cattle drive participant for three years. "They earn their keep." A

banker from Switzerland remarked, "Don't let them change a thing!"

Your day begins at the crack of dawn. After a day in the saddle you devour the campfire cookout or chuckwagon fare (from good to delicious), spin yarns around the fire, and throw down your sleeping bag under the stars or in a tent. It's the real thing except for rigging a warm/hot shower at some camps for the dudes. A California "cowgirl" sums it up: "The endless space, endless food, and more jokes than I thought existed made for a fabulous two weeks. I felt frustrated at spending so much money when I was standing in cow patties in the rain; and frustrated that I couldn't stay there forever!"

So pull on your boots and jeans and checked shirt and western hat and get ready for a cowboy experience you'll never forget.

Over a decade ago this publication included the first chapter ever to appear in a travel guide about cattle and horse drives which would-be cowboys could join. The idea caught on, and ever since hundreds of city vacationers have been living the life of a cowboy for a week or so each spring, summer or fall.

This has become a specialty of the advisory and reservations activity at our office. For information please call (212) 355-6334—or call direct to any of the services listed here.

Reminders
Can you ride well enough? If not, are you choosing a ranch where you can learn? Are you to bring sleeping gear? Where will you meet? Will you need a fishing license, or overnight reservations before and after the trip? Are saddlebags provided, or should you bring a daypack for your camera and other essentials? The rancher will provide a list of what to bring.

Learning the art of branding the beef— *Buddy Mays for the TX Ranch, MT.*

CALIFORNIA   **MAMMOTH LAKES PACK OUTFIT,** P.O. Box 61, Mammoth Lakes, CA 93546. Att.: Lou Roeser. (619) 934-2434 or 6161.

"Head 'em up, move 'em out!" urges outfitter Lou Roeser. Each June he drives his herd of horses and mules from winter pasture in the Owens Valley to the pack station near Mammoth Lakes for his summer pack trips. He moves them back again in October for winter pasture. "These are old-time working trail drives," Lou warns. "There'll be long, strenuous hours in the saddle at a fast pace, covering about 20 miles each day for 3 to 4 days." A chuckwagon pulled by a four-up team of draft horses or mules accompanies the drive, and tired riders may hitch a lift. Camp on the trail at night with excellent food, and listen to guitars and fiddles and western ballads around the campfire. "You needn't be a cowboy," Lou says, but you're a working part of the crew and some basic riding experience is advisable. Bring sleeping bag. Rate in Jun.: $365/3 days, $420/4 days, $700/7 days. In Oct.: $500/5 days. Arrival: Mammoth Lakes or Bishop. (See also *Pack Trips*.)

MCGEE CREEK PACK STATION, Rt. 1, Box 162, Mammoth Lakes, CA 93546. Att.: The Ketchams. (619) 936-4324. [Nov.-May: Star Rt. 1, Box 100-AT, Independence, CA 93526. (619) 878-2207.]

Join the Ketchams in the fall (mid-Oct.) as they move their horses and mules from summer headquarters in McGee Canyon to their winter range near Independence. "You'll be riding with the herd for 75 miles," Jennifer Ketcham explains, "from the aspens and pine of the Sierra highcountry to the pinyon and sage of the Owens Valley pastures—some of the most spectacular country in the West." A rider from San Diego comments, "There are few things better for the soul than the beauty of the Sierras, great food, and companions (the Ketchams) who provoke great gales of laughter." Your horse, saddle, and food are provided. Bring a sleeping bag, and a tent if you wish, but most sleep under the stars! It's a 4-day trail ride that gives a flavor of the Old West. Rate: $250/person. (See also *Pack Trips*.)

ROCK CREEK PACK STATION, Box 248, Bishop, CA 93514. Att.: Herb & Craig London & Dave Dohnel. (619) 935-4493. [Oct.-Jun.: (619) 872-8331.]

This pack outfit gives you a chance to help herd horses and mules in Old West-style drives in June and October, and in April to drive cattle from Nevada to spring range in California. The purpose of the horse drives is to get saddle horses and pack animals from winter pasture in Owens Valley up to the packstation in the High Sierra for summer pack trips, then drive them back down in the fall. "We like to get an early start, ride in the cool of the day, and make camp early in the afternoon," Herb London explains. "The cook and crew set up a comfortable camp in advance with tents, but many prefer to sleep under the stars." There's hearty fare from the chuckwagon, swimming at every camp, and plenty of wrangling. (Up to 30 riders, 4 days, mid-Jun. and early Oct., $365/rider.) On the cattle drive in Apr. you start with orientation on cattle gathering, driving the cattle, and horseback conduct. Then it's 7 days of working with the cowboys to move 500 cows and calves from their winter range in Nevada up through pinyon forests where wild mustangs roam to spring range in the Sierra foothills. Overnights at cow camps, chuckwagon meals. Bring sleeping bag. Mid-Apr., 7 days, $700/rider. Arrival point for all drives: Bishop. (See also *Hiking with Packstock, Pack Trips*.)

ROCK CREEK COW CAMPS, Box 248, Bishop, CA 93514. Att.: Herb & Craig London & Dave Dohnel. (619) 935-4493. [Oct.-Jun.: (619) 872-8331.]

"Working the cattle" is a term you'll well understand after a week with Rock Creek at a cattle ranch in the Sierra. It's a chance to work with cowboys who go about their business the old-fashioned way--on horseback with a lariat in hand. You get the hang of the technique of gathering the cows and calves, branding the calves, vaccinating the herd, and driving them to high mountain pasture for summer foraging. Mothering-up the cows separated from their calves is a continuing part of the action. Tents and meals provided at cow camps. Bring your own sleeping bag. Early May, 4 days, $365/rider. Rock Creek also offers a nationally recognized wilderness course on packing, natural history, and veterinary medicine. Arrival: Bishop. (See also *Hiking with Packstock, Pack Trips*.)

COLORADO

FRENCHY'S MOUNTAIN, P.O. Box 646, Naturita, CO 81422. Att.: Bill & Carol Koon. (303) 728-3895.

If you'd like to get personally involved in oldtime ranch life—moving the cattle from pasture to pasture, branding, the calves, fixing fence—here it is in the scenic Rockies just southwest of Telluride. At cow camp, which is moved to higher country as the season progresses, you live in tents or in bunkhouses. No plumbing, radio, TV, or telephone. Spend days with the crew—maybe on a roundup or a trail drive or putting out salt and checking the cattle. "You should come for at least three days to get the feel of things," advises Bill Koon. "Staying five days to a week is better." A couple from New York writes, "We rode all day herding cattle and exploring 4,000 acres of breathtaking country with abundant wildlife. We feel extremely lucky to have happened upon Frenchy's Mountain." Pickup

A cow camp in the Colorado Rockies—*Frenchy's Mountain, CO.*

COLORADO

and return in Telluride ($40) or Grand Junction ($80). May-Sep., up to 8 guests, $85/day (no charge for 1st night). (See also *Pack Trips, Combos.*)

MW RANCH, 19451-195th Ave., Hudson, CO 80642. Att.: Bill Diekroeger. (303) 536-4206.

Trail Boss Bill Diekroeger drives cattle on the famed Tusas Trail across the CO/NM border in the authentic style of the 1870s and invites 20 drovers (that's you) to join him. You'll help push the herd over rolling prairie and high plains plateaus. Not a vehicle in sight—horse-drawn wagons haul the gear, and chuckwagon meals are cooked on wood fires. "You spend the first day getting into the swing of being an oldtime drover," Bill explains, "then you begin pushing the cattle cross country, never knowing what challenges the next canyon or ridge will offer." A mid-week shoot out, range rodeo, and evening campfire entertainment vary the pace, and by week's end each rider receives a handsome Drover's Belt Buckle, gets paid with "company script," and kicks up his/her heels at a last-night fandango celebration. Bring a sleeping bag, a sense of humor, and the curiosity to discover what the West was all about 100 year ago! Two drives in late Jun., Sun. to Sat., and two late Aug.; (not recommended for pre-teens); $700 per rider, $600 with you own horse. Arrival point: Alamosa, CO. (See also *Horse Trekking.*)

UTE TRAIL GUIDE SERVICE, 10615 County Road 150, Salida, CO 81201. Att.: Glenn & Jeanie Everett. (303) 539-4097.

From June through September the Everetts spend their time at cow camp, moving cattle from one pasture to another, gathering cattle to sell, packing salt to them, branding the calves, or just checking. They spend from half a day to 10 hours in the saddle. They're happy to have guests join them. "Cow camp" is located on a high mountain plateau at about 9,200' elevation. Herds of elk, deer, and antelope run the range. From their modern ranch house in Salida it takes an hour and a half to get to cow camp by four-wheel-drive vehicle up an old Ute trail. At camp there's a four-room log cabin with kitchen, dining room, a bunkroom for the Everetts and crew, and another for guests (coed). "Plumbing consists of an outhouse and a 'Saturday night' type bathtub," the Everetts explain. But they drive back to their ranch house every few days for hot showers. This is the authentic West at a ranch started by Glenn's grandfather in 1890. When you're not working the cattle you can ride to a ghost town, defunct gold and copper mines, and old granite quarries—all on the ranch—or fish for trout in the Arkansas River which flows through the property.

MONTANA

SCHIVELY RANCH 1062 Road 15, Lovell, WY 82431. Att.: Joe & Iris Bassett. (307) 548-6688.

In May and June when the snow has melted and grass has grown in the higher elevations, the Bassetts drive their cattle north from Wyoming's lowlands to graze for the summer in Montana's high country. In October they trail them back to winter pasture in Wyoming. It's an exciting and rugged trek for reasonably good riders who can stay in the saddle for hours at a time. Well-trained horses know how to do the work—chasing a stray, forcing a cow out of hiding in a brushy draw, averting a stampede, or trailing the herd to keep it moving. The Bassett family schedules drives for six consecutive weeks through May and early June, and again in October. A chuckwagon accompanies the drive for Western type meals you'll long remember. Bring a sleeping bag for sleeping in a trailer or under the stars. "The Bassetts are a very outgoing family," comments a guest. "They are interested in getting to know you and giving you a chance to understand all about cattle ranching. It's a rugged but thoroughly enjoyable experience." Dates: Sat.-to-Sat., May & early Jun. Rate: $485/person includes Billings (MT) pickup and return.

Driving cattle on the Montana range—
Buddy Mays for the TX Ranch, MT.

TX (TILLETT) RANCH, Box 453, Lovell, WY 82431. Att.: Abbie Tillett. (406) 484-2583.

At the TX Ranch on the Montana/Wyoming border vacationers arrive and depart Saturdays for a week or more of cowboying with the Tillett family. This is not something put on for the dudes. It's a genuine cattle operation in which guests may take part. After a week of branding, rounding up strays, cutting ornery cows from the herd, and trailing cattle to spring, summer, or fall range, you know you have experienced the real thing. From April through September you may share in this rough and ready life at cow camp. Good riders get into the action, but even for guests who are less proficient "it's fun and there's always an experienced cowpoke to lend a hand or provide a vehicle lift back to camp for the saddle-weary," Abbie Tillett reassures. They have gentle horses for those learning to ride. "Children thrive on this life," Abbie adds. She meets guests at the Billings, MT, airport Saturdays at 4 p.m. for the drive to cow camp. Return trips are made Saturdays in time for noon flights. At cow camp—hearty campfire meals, and sleeping under the stars or in tents. Rate $425/week. Bring sleeping gear.

HORSE TREKKING

Horse trekking is a popular sport in Europe for riders who do not camp at night but stay at delightful lodges in the countryside. They travel from one lodge to another, sometimes through villages, with luggage sent ahead by car and without the necessity of setting up camp at night.

The fact is in Europe there are no wilderness areas, and in our western wilderness there are no lodges.

But U.S. outfitters have come up with a solution for riders who want wilderness riding but do not want to pack their gear along or set up a camp each night. On these treks their luggage is transported by van, and they ride either to a lodge outside the wilderness or to pre-set camps that are unusually comfortable—"Cadillac camping pleasures," one outfitter calls it.

The result is western trekking through magnificent areas with knowledgeable guides who are historians as well—they'll fill you with plenty of awe-inspiring tales of cowboys and Indians, some true. And at night you bed down at as comfortable a camp as you'll find west of the Mississippi.

ARIZONA   **ADVENTURE TRAILS OF THE WEST,** Inc., P.O. Box 1494, Wickenburg, AZ 85358. Att.: Dana W. Burden. (602) 684-3106.

Dana combines trail rides with easy camping in a special variation of horse trekking. Ride through Arizona's spectacular wilderness by day for 10 to 15 miles. Emerge from the wilderness each night for a pre-arranged rendezvous with a truck carrying camping gear, food, and duffels. "Cadillac camping pleasures" Dana calls it. His scheduled treks are for 20 to 100 riders, many of whom bring their own horses. Custom trips for smaller groups. In Monument Valley you are guests of the Navajos and move camp only once on the 5-day ride, covering 10 miles of trail each day in the "majestic panoramic vastness," September 15-19. In Canyon de Chelly it's a "spectacular and intimate riding experience in a canyon paradise," June 16-20. Since men will be boys, Dana has reserved two trips just for the fellows—into the Superstition Mountains wilderness March 17-21; and from Wickenburg across desert terrain and up through chaparral at 7,000' to Prescott, October 19-23. Rates for all rides (including horse) are about $125/day. A special family ride along the Mogollon Rim out of Payson is scheduled for Jul. 7-11. (10% discount for 15 years and under.)

COLORADO   **MW RANCH,** 19451-195th Ave., Hudson, CO 80642. Att.: Bill Diekroeger. (303) 536-4206.

Lodges at the famous ski resorts of the Colorado Rockies are ideal stopovers for riders to explore the mountains on horseback in summer or fall. On this unusual horse trek you have an ultra-scenic 5 1/2-day ride from Silverthorne to Copper Mountain, Leadville, Fairplay, Brekenridge, Keystone and back to Silverthorne. Diekroeger schedules the trek for groups of six or more riders (maximum 12) Monday to Saturday during most weeks from early July to mid-September. He provides the horses and guides, and a pickup for transporting luggage. Riders make their own lodge reservations (a list is supplied) and arrange their own meals according to appetite and budget. (Diekroeger supplies box lunches on request.) The rate is $280 per rider in groups of 6 to 12, plus state tax & Forest Service fee. It's a great way to see the Rockies. For reservations contact the MW Ranch or the Adventure Guides office, (212) 355-6334. (See also *Cattle Drives.*)

WYOMING

JACKSON HOLE TRAIL RIDES, Box 110, Moran, WY 83013. Att.: Walt Korn. (307) 543-2407.

Bring your own horse or let the Box K supply one for five days of riding the scenic highcountry trails through the Teton Wilderness. You'll top out with a ride to the Continental Divide. Walt establishes a base camp near Togwotee Pass for participants, some of whom bring horse trailers and their own horses and tack. Spectacular daily rides skirt sparkling alpine lakes and cross lush green meadows. Riders return to camp at night for "the best cowboy chow" and sometimes a rousing hoe-down. The week ends with an "awards" barbecue. Sun.-Sat., airport transfers included: $506/rider, or $380 (including hay) if you furnish your own tack and horse. Arrival: Jackson Hole. (See also *Pack Trips*, Box K Ranch.)

L.D. FROME, OUTFITTER, Box G, Afton, WY 83110. (307) 886-5240.

L.D. Frome, an old hand at pack trips, adds a new twist with his horse trek. You ride each day through the backcountry of the Teton foothills just north of Jackson Hole from ranch to a mountain lodge. Back again after one or two layover days to ride and explore. Arrangements include lodging, dinner, and breakfast each day and a guide and trailside lunch for the day's ride. Daily trail rides cover about 8 miles up and over the mountains (15 miles at the most), and luggage is transported by car. All inclusive rates: $500 for 5 days, Jun.-Sep. Arrival: Jackson, WY. (See also *Pack Trips, Covered Wagons*—Wagons West.)

PACK TRIPS BY HORSE

You awake in your cozy sleeping bag to the clip-clop of horses' hooves. The smell of "cowboy coffee"—so-named because a horseshoe can supposedly float on its thickness—tickles your nose. A wrangler is rounding up the horses to saddle for a day of riding.

You think ahead to breakfast—perhaps two eggs fried over an open fire along with bacon, biscuits, flapjacks, and juice. The thought propels you out of your warm cocoon.

After breakfast you break camp—tents down, camping and personal gear packed in duffels, and all of it loaded and securely tied on the backs of pack animals. You leave the campsite looking as though no one has been there, and your pack string hits the trail—eight riders (maybe ten) plus wrangler, guide, and camp cook all on horseback, with nearly as many mules, horses, or burros packing the gear.

If you are tantalized by the idea of riding through a remote, spectacular, roadless wilderness, then a pack trip is for you. Apart from the romantic aspects of horseback adventuring—seeing the West in much the same way as the early settlers did—there are other, more prosaic advantages. With the gear carried by animals rather than on your own back, you can tote more equipment and a larger variety of food. And, not to be overlooked, the horse also carries you. Obviously you can cover more terrain with less effort on horseback than on foot.

To read a pack trip brochure you'll want some outfitter lingo. Originally the pack business was set up for hunters in the fall. To differentiate their summer trips for vacationers, outfitters introduced new terminology. They sometimes describe a summer pack trip as a sightseeing, scenic, custom, deluxe, or private excursion.

A *base camp trip* is one on which riders stay at a semi-permanent camp, circling the area each day from this wilderness base. A *moving,* or *progressive, pack trip* involves setting up a different camp each night—or taking a layover day before moving from one camp to the next. The moving trip, say aficionados, is the more rugged one and enables you to pack way into the wilderness, moving from one spectacular area to another. It also requires more pack animals and a larger pack crew to handle the gear—hence more expensive than the base camp trip.

A *spot* or *drop pack trip* is still another variation—an arrangement for packing into a base camp with an outfitter who then leaves you there for your own independent wilderness stay, returning to bring you out on an agreed upon day.

Some outfitters set dates for group trips which anyone may join; others handle custom arrangements for your own group of family or friends; or they offer both types of service.

Previous riding experience is not essential for many of these trips, but is a requisite for the more rugged ones. But if you are somewhat of a novice, it's well to find out about layover days. As one outfitter bluntly puts it, "It's hard on inexperienced riders to be on the trail every day. They get sore in the rear." So noted.

Happy trails!

Reminders
Outfitters will provide lists of what clothing to bring. Check whether their rates include accommodations before and after the trip, and where you will meet. Generally state taxes and a new 3% use tax imposed by the U.S. Forest Service are not included in trip rates. Are you going from

Trailblazing in the Utah wilderness—*Vinnie Fish for Piute Creek Outfitters, UT.*

near sea level to trails at high elevations? You might arrange several days at a ranch to get accustomed to the altitude—and the riding. Most outfitters can recommend specific ranches in the area. Doublecheck on who provides sleeping gear, and whether you need a fishing license. Let the outfitter know your level of riding ability so he can recommend the best trip for you.

ALASKA

KACHEMAK BAY HORSE TRIPS, P.O. Box 2004, Homer, AK 99603. Att.: Mairiis Davidson. (907) 235-7850.

"A very unusual and memorable trip," relates a guest. "The scenery was superb, and the opportunity to visit the homestead where Mairiis grew up and talk with her father was worth the whole trip." Her pack trip up the eastern shore of the Kenai Peninsula adds real adventure to an Alaskan itinerary. Starting near Homer (227 miles south of

Trailing the tides of Kachemak Bay—
Mairiis Davidson for Kachemak Bay Horse Trips, AK.

Anchorage), riders follow easy trails along Kachemak Bay's beaches timed to coordinate with the tides. Spectacular scenes hold their attention—bald eagles, glaciers, snow-capped peaks, many birds. Overnights are at historic homesteads where you may gather wild berries and edible sea greens, dig for clams, or catch a salmon for dinner. A cattle roundup, helping with the harvest, going to a local rodeo, or having a peek at the "Old Believers," a Russian settlement, gives one an insider's view of Alaskan life. "These are pleasant and gentle trips," Mairiis explains, though she arranges some for experienced riders only. She provides either English or Western riding on trips of 1-4 days, May-Sep., $55-$85/day, family and group rates. Custom trips combine riding and hiking. Also horse-drawn wagon trips along shore for families and groups. Arrival: Homer, AK.

ARIZONA

GRAPEVINE CANYON RANCH, P.O. Box 302, Pearce, AZ 85625. Att.: Gerry & Eve Searle. (602) 826-3185.

"We pride ourselves on our horses," observes Eve Searle. "No tired, lazy mounts. They are good looking, well fed, energetic, and extremely well behaved. They carry riders with safety and willingness all day long, day after day." The Searles arrange moving or base camp trips for two or three nights into the rugged Dragoon Mountains—"nearly as primitive and unexplored today as when Chief Cochise hid out from his government pursuers," Eve notes. Inexperienced riders get extra training from Gerry—trail boss, horseman, cowboy, rancher, a riding instructor for many years, and an expert on Western folklore and history. Rate for 3-day pack trip with night before and after at ranch, $335/rider. Year-round custom trips. Bring sleeping bag. Arrival: Tucson (airport pickup, $40).

HONEYMOON TRAIL CO., Box 4, Moccasin, AZ 86022. Att.: Mel Heaton. (602) 643-7292.

"For a taste of scenic horseback country, nothing quite compares with our 230-mile, 10-day custom-arranged trip," says Mel Heaton. "You're guided through a spell-binding wilderness, changing with every mile. From hidden red-rock canyons near Utah's Zion National Park to the painted sandstone spires of Bryce, you'll discover that the country has changed little since the early explorers traveled the course." Another trip route takes you through Canyon de Chelley, Monument Valley, Rainbow Bridge, and Navajoland backcountry, staying at some Navajo camps and absorbing the culture of these native Americans. Rides are easy to rugged and are designed for intermediate to experienced riders. Limit: 20 riders. May-Oct. $800. "It was a childhood dream come true," says one rider. "I had a honeycolored mustang who was unbelievably surefooted and never seemed to tire. There was lots of laughter and excellent camaraderie throughout." Arrival: St. George, UT. via Las Vegas, Salt Lake, or Phoenix. (See also *Covered Wagons*.)

CALIFORNIA

MAMMOTH LAKES PACK OUTFIT, P.O. Box 61, Mammoth Lakes, CA 93546. Att.: Lou Roeser. (619) 934-2434 or 6161.

Ride sure-footed mountain horses with pack mules carrying your gear through the spectacular John Muir Wilderness, Fish Creek Basin, and Silver Divide region of the High Sierra with its more than 100 lakes and streams. Throw your hook into an alpine lake or cascading stream, snap a picture of the alpenglow on the mountains, drink a cup of steaming cowboy coffee, sleep under the brilliant stars. Mammoth Lakes Pack Outfit, in the Sierra for more than 70 years, offers a variety of pack trips for individual parties and scheduled group trips focused on packing, horse management in the wilderness, fly fishing, watercolor workshop, or trail rides in the Sierra and Sweetwater Mountains and Mono Lake/Bodie country. "We take pride in offering the best of service, livestock, and personnel, and creating an unforgettable experience for our guests," says outfitter Lou Roeser. Trips from easy to difficult, 2-14 days, 2-25 riders, Jun.-Oct., $80/day up for partial outfitting, $110 up for full outfitting. Bring sleeping bag. Arrival: Mammoth Lakes. (See also *Horse Drives*.)

MCGEE CREEK PACK STATION, Rt. 1, Box 162-AT, Mammoth Lakes, CA 93546. Att.: The Ketchams. (619) 935-4324. [Nov.-May:

CALIFORNIA   Start Rt. 1, Box 100-AT, Independence CA 93526. (619) 878-2207.]
     Imagine yourself packing into McGee Canyon or Upper Fish Creek
in the John Muir Wilderness of the High Sierra—a land of wildflowers
and waterfalls, red slate and granite peaks, and 12- to 18-inch brook,
rainbow, golden and tiger trout. Packers load the mules and guide
riders on the Morgan horses which the Ketchams breed, raise, and
train. At 9,000- to 12,000-foot elevation, settle in at base camp. Take
riding lessons, and ride each day to a different alpine lake or trout
stream. Or the packers will pack up camp every day or so and move
on to new country. "We have mostly girl packers—they're good with
guests, handle the horses well, and are non-drinkers, a natural for
taking families into this spectacular wilderness." A Los Angeles guest
comments, "The Ketchams are knowledgeable, humorous,
easy-going, and capable. They let us enjoy the trip at our own pace."
Pack trip rate: $80/day/rider. They also offer several types of
fully catered, organized group trips, 4 days or more, 2-25 riders,
Jun.-Oct.; and spot pack and dunnage service. (See also *Cattle/Horse
Drives*.)

A serene saddle-ride
through Navajoland—
*Melinda Berge for
Honeymoon Trail Co.,
AZ.*

ROCK CREEK PACK STATION, Box 248, Bishop, CA 93514. Att.:
Herb & Craig London & Dave Dohnel. (619) 935-4493. [Oct.-Jun.:
(619) 872-8331.]
     "We've made a specialty of wilderness trail rides in the Sierra and
are pleased to share our experience with you," states Herb London,
who has operated Rock Creek since 1947. Mules carry your packs as
you ride horseback through varied terrain—an area with wildlife,
glaciers, and 13,000-foot peaks which John Muir considered his

favorite backcountry. Rock Creek schedules rides which all may join and handles custom trips, both base camp and moving pack trips, into the John Muir Wilderness, Inyo and Sierra national forests, and Sequoia, Kings, and Yosemite national parks. Jun.-Oct., 5-12 days, about $75/day. (See also *Hiking with Packstock, Cattle/Horse Drives.*)

ROCK CREEK WILD MUSTANG RIDES, Box 248, Bishop, CA 93514. Att.: Herb & Craig London & Dave Dohnel. (619) 935-4493. [Oct.-Jun.: (619) 872-8331.]

Wild mustangs have made the Pizona area of the Inyo National Forest their home. It is a region of pinyon forest, streams with Brown trout, hot springs, wildflowers, old Indian campsites where arrowheads and petroglyphs are found, and spectacular sunsets over the Sierra and White mountains. Ride to a central meadow camp and spend several days tracking the mustangs and exploring the area. Learn from experienced tracker-guides about the wild horses' social behavior and current struggle for survival. Bring sleeping bag. Late May, early June, 4 days, $325/rider. Arrival Bishop. (See also *Hiking with Packstock, Cattle/Horse Drives.*)

TRINITY TRAIL RIDES, Coffee Creek Ranch, Dept. AG, P.O. Star Route 2, Box 4940, Trinity Center, CA 96091. Att.: Mark & Ruth Hartman, (916) 266-3343.

"We set up camp next to a lake or running stream in the Salmon Mountains-Trinity Alps Primitive Area," the Hartmans tell us. "Fishing for brook trout and German browns is good in all backcountry lakes, and most areas have a gorgeous view of Mt. Shasta." Spend evening singing around the campfire, taking hayrides, or square dancing. Rates for moving and drop pack trips, Jun.-Oct.: saddle or pack stock, $25/day; packer, $75/day. On all-inclusive guided trips you bring only your sleeping gear: $100/day or $375 for special 5-day trips (up to 8 riders). The Hartmans say the trails are too rugged for children under 7, but novice adults do "just fine." Jul.-Sep. Arrival: Redding, CA. (See also *Ski Touring*—Coffee Creek Ranch.)

COLORADO   **C & R STABLES & OUTFITTERS,** P.O. Box 40221-AT, SilverCreek, CO 80446. Att.: Ray Miller. (800) 526-0590 or (303) 887-2131.

From the luxurious Inn at SilverCreek, ride into the Indian Peaks Wilderness in the Rockies or explore the Williams Fork of the Colorado River—for a few days or up to three weeks. "For your first adventure we recommend a 2-night, 3-day trip to our base camp," Ray advises, "with rides each day to explore the backcountry." On the longer "Packer" trips you'll follow trails high in the Rockies and move camp every day or so. Ray keeps his pack trips operating into October. "It's one of the best times to camp in the backcountry," he insists. "The elk are in their bugle and all the wild critters are getting ready for winter." Riders don't go hungry on these trips. Campfare is a specialty, with chops, roasts, steaks, and tantalizing desserts—almost nothing freeze dried. Rate: $70/day per rider. Bring sleeping bag. Also all-day rides (no camping out) in Indian Peaks Wilderness or along the Fraser River Ridge, $40/rider. Arrival: Granby (via Amtrak), or

COLORADO   Denver plus 2-hr. drive. (See also *River Running—*Silver Creek
                Expeditions.)

DELBY'S TRIANGLE 3 RANCH, Box 14, Steamboat Springs, CO
80477. Att.: Delbert Heid. (303) 879-1257.
      "Exhilarating, exhausting, exciting…three days and two nights of
the most incredible scenery," wrote one thoroughly satisfied traveler of
her pack trip into the Mt. Zirkel Wilderness Area. Del Heid likes to
take families into the 114-square-mile preserve with over 40 lakes,
streams, and miles of beautiful trails. His moving and base camp trips
feature "very good mountain horses, good equipment, good food, and
helpful, knowledgeable hands to assist you." Del has been guiding and
packing horses into this area for over 30 years and plans each trip
specifically for what your group wants—the amount of riding,
number of days, time to catch brookies, German browns, native
cutthroats, rainbow trout, or whatever. Rates for 3-10 days; from
$45/day if you bring your own food to $75/day for individuals.
Jul.-Oct. Group size: 5-10.(See also *Youth Adventures.*)

Riding through a Utah
canyon—*Honeymoon
Trail Co., AZ.*

FRENCHY'S MOUNTAIN, P.O. Box 646, Naturita, CO 81422. Att.:
Bill & Carol Koon. (303) 728-3895.
      You can plan anything from an overnight campout on horseback to
a weeklong pack trip with this outfitter in the scenic highcountry of

the Rockies near Telluride. But Bill Koon advises you to come for at least three days—and better yet, five days or a week if you can make it. "We like to feel that our guests will go away a little more aware of things that are happening in this part of the world," he says. "The decisions concerning wildlife and land use are important for all of us to understand." He suggests a fishing trip to Navajo Lake or Upper Bilk Creek, packing into the Wilson Mountains or Dunton Hot Srings, or in the fall riding in lower country to see the wild horses. Riders get thoroughly involved in these trips, and the campfare is "fantastic" according to one guest. For 2 to 6 riders, Jul.-Oct., $85/rider per day. (No charge for arrival night.) Pickup and return in Telluride ($40) or Grand Junction ($80). (See also *Cattle Drives, Combos.*)

SID SIMPSON GUIDE SERVICE, 1148-3950 Dr., Paonia, CO 81428. Att.: Sid Simpson. (303) 527-3486.

"I've been a guide and a packer for 37 years and think I'm mighty lucky to live and work in these awe-inspiring mountains," claims Sid when describing what it's like to pack into the Gunnison and West Elk Wilderness of the Rocky Mountains. "We plan each trip to suit your interests; you'll have a 6-day tailor-made trip." Riders stay at two base camps about a day apart, with a day ride out of each. Good lake and stream fishing, wildflowers, wildlife, and evidence of trails once used by Indian hunting parties, fur trappers, and miners. "Sid gave us the most memorable family vacation we've ever had," says one pack tripper. Mon.-Sat., Jun.-Sep;. 4 or more riders, $390 each. Arrival: Montrose, CO or drive in.

ULTIMATE ESCAPES, LTD., M-115 S. 25th St., Colorado Springs, CO 80904. (800) 992-4343 or (303) 578-8383.

Explore the wildest highcountry in the West over almost non-existent trails," urges Gary Ziegler of Ultimate Escapes. "We ride to hidden alpine valleys, across windswept ridges, and through silent pine forests." This "Ultimate Horsepacking" trip is for experienced riders only in the high mountain country of the Sangre de Cristo Range. You travel light with modern equipment and a minimum number of pack horses, ride over 12,000-foot passes, camp near secluded trout-filled streams, view wildlife such as deer, elk, or black bear, and have hearty ranch-style campfire meals. For 5 days, $525, Aug. & Sep. Other pack trips in the Sangre de Cristos are for riders of any experience: 3 days/$235, 5 days/$375, May-Oct., with departures every Mon. from Colorado Springs. (See also *Hiking with Packstock, River Running, Combos.*)

IDAHO   **HAPPY HOLLOW CAMPS,** Star Route Box 14-A, Salmon, ID 83467. Att.: Martin R. Capps, (208) 756-3954.

Martin Capps leads you over the skyline of the Salmon River Mountain Range to his comfortable base camp. Here you ride remote trails, fish for trout, photograph the surrounding wilderness, go for a swim, or just relax. "Martin lets you pick your own level of roughing it on these trips," comments a guest. "There's more food than you can eat, more breathtaking scenery than you can absorb, and more fun than you can keep track of." Base camp trips average $75/day for 1-10

IDAHO   days. Bring or rent sleeping gear. Also drop pack service, group and
children's rates. Minimum age, 6 years. May-Sep. (See also *River
Running*.)

PALISADES CREEK RANCH, P.O. Box 594-H, Palisades, ID 83437.
Att.: Elvin or Bret Hincks. (208) 483-2545.
    Elvin Hincks has guided hunters for years into the highcountry and
has taken out trail riders. Now he invites riders on pack trips in this
wilderness he knows so well. "There's outstanding fishing,
photographing, hiking, mountain climbing and wildflowers," Elvin
comments. Sometimes see a herd of 300 elk. "The best part is no
worries, no cares," writes one guest. "Just the great outdoors. The
second best part is Elvin. He was brought up in the mountains, and he
filled us with stories of their magic and lore. The most refreshing
vacation we've had." He offers moving, base camp, and drop pack
trips for 5-10 riders, 3-5 days. Pack trips: $75/day/rider ($50 with
your own food). Bring sleeping gear. May-Sep. Arrival: Idaho Falls.

Time-out to take in the
scenery—*Grapevine
Canyon Ranch, AZ.*

SALMON RIVER LODGE, P.O. Box 348, Jerome, ID 83338. Att.:
Dave Giles. (208) 324-3553.
    Just getting to Salmon River Lodge is a wilderness experience! Drive
from Salmon to the Corn Creek campground, crank the old telephone
at the side of the road to call the lodge, and they'll cross the river
(Main Salmon) by jet boat to pick you up. You pack into the remote,
seldom-visited Salmon River Breaks Area of the Salmon National
Forest on moving trips. Ride amid snow-capped mountains, through
timbered valleys, across flower-filled meadows. Swim and fish in
crystal-clear mountain lakes and enjoy your catch for dinner. See elk,
deer, bighorn sheep. Finish by jet boating upriver to the lodge. Dave
Giles welcomes riders of all levels. "Our horses know the trail and the
beginning rider does just fine," he says. Rates: $110-$130/day; 5-11

days; up to 15 riders. Jul.-Sep. Bring or rent sleeping bag. Arrival: Boise or Missoula, air charter to Salmon, drive or arrange pickup to river. (See also *Jet Boating, River Running*.)

MONTANA

BOB MARSHALL WILDERNESS RANCH, Seeley Lake, MT 59868. Att.: Barbara Burns. (406) 754-2285.

Ecology-minded Virgil Burns, an expert packer, specializes in custom trips for families and groups into the Bob Marshall Wilderness. "Can't say enough about our great fishing in pristine mountain lakes, streams and rivers," Virgil says, speaking of Cutthroat, Rainbow, Dolly Varden, and a fly fisherman's paradise. He refers to the Bob Marshall as "an awesome sweep of peaks, tier upon tier—a world of eagles and mountain goats." He and Barb are considered "tops." Moving and base camp trips, 5-10 days, up to 15 riders, Jul.-Sep; $85-$100/day. Bring sleeping gear. Rates include lodging and meals at ranch the night before and after trip and transport to and from Missoula, the arrival point.

CIRCLE 8 RANCH, Box 729, Chateau, MT 59422. Att.: Al & Sally Haas. (406) 466-5564.

You cover a wide variety of terrain from river bottoms and meadows, to prairie flats and Jack Pine forests, to the foothills of the Rockies during 10-day pack trips for 4-8 riders. It's good country for photography, birdwatching, fishing, and of course, riding your fine mount—a Quarter Horse, Morgan, and Tennessee Walker breeding. The riding is easy—perfect for beginners and children young as 8 years. Be forwarned: you may put on a few pounds, eating plenty of fresh foods at your campsite and ranch-style dishes (complete with homemade breads) back at the Circle 8, south of Glacier National Park. Tents are provided on the pack trip, but bring your own sleeping bag. Jun.-Sep. Arrival: Great Falls or Chateau, MT.

DOUBLE ARROW OUTFITTERS, (AG), Box 495, Seeley Lake, MT 59868. Att.: Jack Rich (406) 677-2411 or 2317.

"We pack in the vast Bob Marshall Wilderness, where man is a visitor, warmth and fellowship are the rule, and western history overshadows everything you do," writes Jack Rich. "Following trails through wild valleys, we explore the Chinese Wall of the Continental Divide, the Flathead Alps and Bullet Nose Mountain with its ice caves. Kids from 5 to 80 find enjoyment, and the fishing is exceptional." Trips for 4-15 riders, 3 or more days, Jul.-Sep. Rates of $65-$95/day (depending on size of group and length of trip) cover all but sleeping gear. Arrival: Missoula, MT.(See also *Hiking with Packstock, River Running, Youth Adventures*.)

EAGLE MOUNTAIN OUTFITTERS, P.O. Box 1, Ovando, MT 59854. Att.: Larry and Rebecca Larson. (406) 793-5618.

"You will travel by horse and your gear by mule string through some of the most beautiful country in the world," says Larry Larson of his trips through Montana's Bob Marshall, Scapegoat, and Great Bear wilderness areas. He refers to 3-day trips as "A Touch of Wilderness"—opening the door to a glimpse of nature's treasures. His

MONTANA

7- and 12-day trips, "A Look Beyond," take you to the Chinese Wall where you follow the Continental Divide, see elk and deer, explore ice caves, and hunt for geodes on Bullet Nose Mountain. Larry's Pack trips have appeal for people of all ages. A horseman from Milton Mills, NH, tells of taking both his grandsons on trips and writes, "I'm waiting for another grandson to get old enough for his trip. He's two." Rates are approximately $85/day; Jun.-Aug.; up to 8 riders with 4 crew. Minimum age 10 (or 6 on custom trips). Arrival: Great Falls or Missoula, MT.

GARY DUFFY, Box 863, Corwin Springs, MT 59021. (406) 848-7287.

"We usually take people on progressive pack trips to remote regions of this scenic wilderness," Duffy explains, "but we are happy to arrange a base camp trip for families who want to stay at one camp and ride out from there each day." For 15 years he has packed into the 920,000-acre Absaroka/Beartooth Wilderness, the wild north country of Yellowstone, and the Gallatin National Forest. "The mountain flowers and alpine scenery are breathtaking, and the fishing is of a quality few people ever experience," he says. Evenings, riders relax around the campfire in the luxury of canvas lounging chairs. Trips from 5-14 days, for 4-10 riders. Rate: $100/day, less for children. Bring or rent sleeping gear. Jun.-Sep. Arrival: Bozeman, MT.

GLACIER OUTFITTERS, East Glacier, MT 59434. Att.: Gary Abbey. (406) 226-4442. Jun.-Aug. [Sep.-May: Rt. 2, Box 108 Ronan, MT 59864. (406) 675-2142.]

"Most of our trips take in the remote country around the Middle Fork of the Flathead River in the Bob Marshall Wilderness," explains Gary Abbey. "It would be difficult to find a concentration of rugged mountain splendor in an equal area of as many acres." His trips are personally tailored for no more than 6 guests, and run from 8 to 14 days to allow camping at several sites. On layover days you'll fish for black-spotted cutthroat and take side trips to scenic spots. Daily rates of $95/person cover everything but sleeping bags. "An excellent guide who knows the region well," writes one vacationer who has taken 6 trips with Gary. "The food will fatten up even the most diet-conscious dude." Jun. & Aug. Arrival: Kalispell, MT.

JJJ WILDERNESS RANCH, P.O. Box 310-A, Augusta, MT 59410. Att.: Max & Ann Barker. (406) 562-3653.

Horseback camping in the Bob Marshall Wilderness nearly a million acres of roadless virgin land—is an experience of a lifetime, the Barkers promise. (The area is featured in the May '85 *National Geographic*.) Terrain varies from rugged ridge tops to flower-blanketed alpine meadows and forested river bottoms. At the Chinese Wall—a 15-mile-long, 1,000-foot-high spectacular Cambrian limestone reef—you see mountain goats and discover fossils a billion years old. Other activities: hook and cook a trout, dismount and hike, photograph wildlife, pick wild berries, savor the solitude. Moving and base camp trips, 4-10 riders, 7-10 days, $95/adult, $85/under 16 years. Jun.-Sep. Rate includes lodging and dinner at ranch before and after trip. Also drop pack trips. Bring sleeping gear. Arrival Great Falls.

JAKE'S HORSES, Box 191, Canyon Route, Gallatin Gateway, MT 59730. Att.: Kate & Jake Grimm. (406) 995-4630.

"This trip is the perfect way to get a taste of Montana's Big Sky country," raves a rider from Ohio. "We simply don't have moose, elk, mountains, and meadows back home." The Grimms pack you into their basecamp in the backcountry at the northwest boundary of Yellowstone National Park. Besides moose and elk, the area supports bighorn sheep, mule deer, bear, grouse, eagles, coyotes, squirrels "and a lot of other little critters," reports Jake Grimm, "and fishing for brook or cutthroat trout normally ends up with a good batch for chow if anyone has a knack for the sport." He suggests at least a 3-day trip for enough time to enjoy camp. With more days he takes you further into the wilderness, setting up additional camps. Jake promises "more good food than the average man can eat and good, sound mountain horses accustomed to the ups and downs of the scenic mountain trails." The Grimms plan custom trips to fit your requirements, and pick you up at the Bozeman airport. Jun.-Sep.; Rate: $75/day per rider, 3-day minimum.

KLICK'S K BAR L RANCH, Augusta, MT 59410. Att.: Nancy Klick. (406) 467-2271. [Winter & spring: (406) 264-5806.]

From Great Falls or Augusta you drive up the Sun River Canyon to Gibson Lake, then proceed by jet boat to the K Bar L—or in fall ride in by saddle horse and pack mule. The ranch is "beyond all roads and within a stone's throw of the Bob Marshall Wilderness," Nancy explains. Mountains and rivers are at your door, and pack trippers choose from trails leading in every direction—some to the Chinese Wall and White River and along the Continental Divide. Nancy mentions wildflowers and birds you can't believe, and promises that on layover days your catch of wild rainbow trout will vary from 12" to 20". Most of these custom trips range from 4 to 7 days, never cross the same trails, and take in 60 to 75 miles "on the best mountain horses in the west." Gear is packed on mules. Rate: $100/day for up to 6 riders. Jul.-Aug. Arrival: Great Falls.

LONE MOUNTAIN RANCH, Box 69, Big Sky, MT 59716. Att.: Bob & Viv Schaap. (406) 995-4644.

Bob Schaap describes his pack trips as "specifically designed to meet the interests of our riders: wildlife observation, photography, backcountry thermal areas, trout fishing, wildflower identification, high alpine lake scenery, Indian trails—and just plain riding, camping, and sightseeing. Because the Spanish peaks and Yellowstone areas are so varied, it's often possible to cover many interests in one trip." Your wrangler guide puts up camp, cooks the meals, and shares his knowledge of the highcountry. The Schaap's historic ranch, homesteaded in 1915, is the heart of the gorgeous Gallatin Valley. Moving and base camp trips (3-14 days) for 3-6 riders; $115/day, including pickup at Bozeman, MT, airport. Minimum age: 10 years. Also drop pack service. (See also *Ski Touring*.)

SEVEN LAZY P GUEST RANCH, Box 178-A, Choteau, MT 59422. Att.: Chuck Blixrud. (406) 466-2044.

MONTANA   "The grandeur of the Chinese Wall at sunrise, the beargrass
blossoms in the high alpine basins, high passes with mountain goats
scampering on the ledges above, the solitude of the tall spruce, pine,
and fir trees—there's so much to be gained from this experience,"
Chuck Blixrud feels. All his leisurely trips (5-14 days, 4-15 riders) into
the spectacular Bob Marshall and Great Bear Wilderness Areas feature
fishing, swimming, and watching wildlife (sometimes even a grizzly or
two). "The trips are professionally run, with excellent stock, a
friendly, congenial staff, first rate food and equipment," writes a
frequent guest from Hamden, CT. Cabins at ranch before and after
trip. Moving and base camp trips: 10 days, $950/rider. Also drop
pack trips. Jun.-Sep. Bring sleeping gear. Some riding experience
needed. Great Falls, Mt. (Pickup extra.)

SIXTY-THREE RANCH, Box 979-AT, Livingston, MT 59047. Att.:
Mrs. Paul E. Christensen & Mrs. Sandra Cahill. (406) 222-0570.

A proud angler displays
the day's catch—*Cahill
Photo for Sixty-Three
Ranch, MT.*

"We take you into some of Montana's most spectacular country," says Jinnie Christensen, "up wooded canyons to rushing waterfalls and trout-filled lakes in the 900,000-acre Absaroka-Beartooth Wilderness." Moving and base camp trips run from 3-10 days and are planned to fit average family needs, with special emphasis on scenic beauty and good fishing. The quality trips feature good horses and equipment, hearty food, and guides who love their work. Rates: $100/rider/day, all-inclusive. Before and after your trip, you can stay at the ranch. Jun.-Sep.; Arrival: Bozeman, MT.

TRIPLE TREE RANCH, 5520 Sourdough Rd., Bozeman, MT 59715. Att.: Bill Myers. (406) 587-4821 or 8513.
"The way to see Yellowstone National Park is on a pack trip of five or more days," Bill Myers advises. "You'll see geysers, mud pots, and hot springs as well as the deer, elk, bear, buffalo, moose, and antelope who live there; and the fishing is great!" An outfitter since 1963, and his father since the 40's, the Myers specialize in the "smaller, more service-oriented trips," with routes tailored to your interests. On a mid-September ride they'll show you "wild elk in full rut-bugling and all." Up to 10 riders, 5 or more days, $90-$95/day, Jul.-Sep.; Arrival: Bozeman.

WILD COUNTRY OUTFITTERS (A), 713 Poplar, Helena, MT 59601. Att.: Don & Meg Merritt. (406) 442-7127.
Don Merritt describes his moving and base camp trips as high-quality, scenic wilderness adventures. "We catch cutthroat trout, look for wildlife, explore wilderness, and interpret nature. Our rides over skyline trails in the Bob Marshall and Scapegoat Wilderness areas are for everyone age 8 and up. We show beginners how to take the 'bumps' out of trail riding so they can enjoy it." The pleasures of wilderness living are enhanced by delicious campstove meals and fireside yarn swapping. There are layover days to enjoy the beautiful scenery, swim, fish, and relax. For 6-11 riders; 7- to 12-day trips, $85/day, including transport between trailhead and Helena. Family and group rates. Bring sleeping gear. Jun.-Sep. Arrival: Helena, MT.

WILDERNESS OUTFITTERS, 3800-A Rattlesnake Dr., Missoula, MT 59802. Att.: Smoke and Thelma Elser. (406) 549-2820.
"The wilderness is our way of life, and we've learned to love, respect, and cherish it," the Elsers tell us. They run a small, exclusive outfitting business packing small groups (6-12 riders) into the Bob Marshall Wilderness. You ride gentle mountainwise horses through virgin forests and flower-studded alpine meadows, drink from pure mountain streams, pull 10"-12" trout (cutthroat, rainbow, and Dolly Varden) out of fast-water rivers, camp on the site of an old Indian battleground, wake each morning to the aroma of frying bacon and coffee, and enjoy evening conversation around a crackling campfire. The ringing of bells on the horses grazing near camp provides a musical background. Moving and base camp trips. For 6-12 riders, $100/day, all inclusive; children 20% less. Private trips: 2 riders, $175/day; 3-5, $125/day. Jun.-Sep. Arrival: Missoula.

NEW YORK   **COLD RIVER TRAIL RIDES, INC.**, Coreys, Tupper Lake, NY 12986.
                  Att.: John Fontana. (518) 359-7559.
                       "Pack trips into the Adirondack Wilderness were our hobby—now
                  they're our specialty," notes John Fontana. Leave from their cozy
                  ranch house each morning. When you return in the evening, Marie
                  has a hearty hot meal ready. "If you like pure water, fresh air, and
                  trout fishing—this is for you," they say. A 1-day trip with lunch is $47,
                  2- to 3-day trips with meals and lodging—including the night before
                  the ride—are $170-$240, Maximum: 9 guests. Also custom overnight
                  pack trips. May-Oct. Arrival: Saranac Lake, NY. (See also *Ski
                  Touring*.)

NORTH   **CATALOOCHEE RANCH,** Rt. 1, Box 500-G, Maggie Valley, NC
CAROLINA   28751. Att.: Alice & Tom Aumen. (704) 926-1401.
                       Riders follow trails directly from the ranch into the Great Smokey
                  Mountains National Park. Open range riding alternates with forested
                  land at 5,000 and above you'll not forget the panoramic views of the
                  Blue Ridge and Great Smokies. Start with day rides and overnights at
                  the ranch—then it's up Pine Tree Gap, across Cataloochee Divide,
                  down Rough Fork, and through beautiful Cataloochee Valley to set up
                  camp for 4 nights in Pretty Hollow Creek. Ride 12 to 16 miles each
                  day—cross virgin forests, ford streams—then back to the ranch.
                  May-Sep., for 8-15 riders, minimum age 12, 8 days (7 nights), about
                  $600. Overnight pack trips, 2-4 riders, $140-$150. Bring or rent
                  sleeping bag. In mid-September a special 8-day ride is scheduled for 16
                  riders with moderate to extensive experience. Arrival: Asheville, NC
                  ($18 round trip pickup charge).

OREGON   **CAL HENRY,** Box 26-A, Joseph, OR 97846. Att.: Cal Henry. (503)
                  432-9171.

Riding along the Snake
River—*Cal Henry, OR.*

Cal Henry's trips take you into the alpine splendor of the Eagle Cap Wilderness and awesome Hells Canyon of the Snake—areas rich in wildflowers and animals where you can fish crystal-clear lakes and streams and forget everything but the pleasures of living outdoors. Moving pack trips are $86/day for groups of 4 to 10 riders. May-Sep. Bring sleeping gear. Cal can arrange almost any type of horseback excursion, including drop pack trips and pack/float combo trips on the Snake River. He also has a remote guest ranch with log cabins and home cooking, accessible only by horse or plane. Arrival: Pendleton, LaGrande, or Joseph, OR. (See also *Hiking with Packstock*.)

LUTE JERSTAD ADVENTURES, LJA, INC., P.O. Box 19537, Portland, OR 97219. (503) 244-4364.

Lute Jerstad Adventures offers adventuresome 3- and 5-day horsepack trips into the beautiful Eagle Cap Wilderness of the Wallowa Mountains—"some of the most beautiful natural wilderness remaining in the nation." Start at rustic lodges/ranches (delicious family-style meals) where your horses await for your climb into the mountains. Travel over an 8,600' pass and through forests of fir, spruce, and pine. Camp by serene mountain lakes, fish in crystal clear waters ("superb trout fishing"), and live as the Indian once did. There are hunderds of elk and mule deer, bighorn sheep, and bear, and scores of wolves, cougar, and bobcat. Count on memorable sights and possibly a climb up one of the peaks. Jerstad, who has climbed Mt. Everest and led a remarkable career as expedition leader, filmmaker, and educator, promises that LJA's trips "will continue to be the best!" Can be combined with an exciting whitewater trip on the Snake River. Jul.-Sep. Rate: $95/day. (See also *River Running*.)

UTAH

PIUTE CREEK OUTFITTERS, Rt. 1-A, Kamas, UT 84036. Att.: Barbara & Arch Arnold. (801) 783-4317 or 486-2607.

Piute's base camp in the Wasatch National Forest—a wild country of uncharted trails, canyons, and peaks—is only an hour from Salt Lake City Airport. Guests can be in camp beside a mountain lake the day they arrive, surrounded by scenery familiar to Piute hunters centuries ago. Riders praise Arch's "great team of wranglers, cook, and helpers...the gentle horses and excellent equipment...and the magical world of aspens and wildflowers and wilderness lakes"—and they return for more of the same. Moving and base camp trips for 5-10 riders, 4-10 days, $80-90/day, including sleeping gear. Jun.-Sep. Also overnight trips, group and family rates. Arrival: Salt Lake City. (See also *Ski Touring*.)

WYOMING

BOX K RANCH, Moran, WY 83013. Att.: Walt Korn. (307) 543-2407.

"This northwest corner of Wyoming boasts 6,600 square miles of isolated country—the same now as when Lewis and Clark saw it," writes Walt Korn. "We pack into the Tetons and Yellowstone, and get way back to see more wildlife." There's breathtaking scenery—mountains, lakes, wildflowers, streams. "If you've never ridden a horse, we teach you, and we travel at a pace you'll enjoy," Walt adds. He advises hunting with a camera ("you can even capture the appealing beauty of a skunk"), and says you'd think he was

WYOMING

spinning a yarn if he told you how good the fishing is. Trips Sat. to Sat., up to 8 riders, Jul. & Aug.: airport pickup, Sat. night at ranch, Sun.-Fri. Moving pack trip to Continental Divide, return to ranch & airport Sat.; $760/rider. Arrival: Jackson Hole. (See also *Horse Trekking*, Jackson Hole Trail Rides.)

CABIN CREEK OUTFITTERS, 1313 Lane 10, Rt. 1, Dept. AG, Powell, WY 82435. Att.: Duane & Betsy Wiltse. (307) 754-9279.

At Cabin Creek's base camps in the Absoraka Wilderness, large herds of elk, moose, deer and big horn sheep create "truly a photographer's paradise." Buffalo Bill once hunted here. The Wiltses specialize in family trips—one group included 8 children under age 11. A satisfied parent of Salt Lake City writes, "The children were thrilled at having their own horses for the 11-mile trip into camp...and the outfitter had the foresight to bring a college girl along to keep an eye on the younger ones. An unexpected luxury." Three base camps with wall tents, Indian tepees, showers, latrines, wood stoves; riding and fishing; hearty meals in dining tent. Trips Mon.-Fri. for 6-12 riders. Jul.-Aug., $495/adult, $395/child under l5. Arrival: Cody, WY.

GAME HILL RANCH, Box A, Bondurant, WY 82922. Att.: Pete & Holly Cameron. (307) 733-4120.

Game Hill Ranch borders the National Forest, and wild country is just across the fence. The Camerons usually pack right from the ranch. Ride a short distance and you'll spot game and enjoy the wilds of nature. "Our horses are at home on the mountain trails." Pete says, "and provide gentle, dependable transportation over sometimes rugged terrain. After riding many miles, a true camaraderie develops between horse and rider." A leisurely pace allows for side excursions and exploring. Lakes, streams, and beaver ponds offer a variety of fishing. Rates: 3 days, $300: 5 days, $450; 7 days, $600; 10 days, $835. Arrival: Jackson, WY. (See also *Hiking with Packstock, Ski Touring*.)

Packing it up for the trail—*Jack Hollingsworth Productions for Rimrock Dude Ranch, WY.*

GRIZZLY RANCH, North Fork Rt. A, Cody, WY 82414. Att.: Rick Felts. (307) 587-3966.

"We pack into the unspoiled high country of Yellowstone National Park and the wilderness area of the Teton and Shoshone National Forests," comments Rick Felts. "Our moving pack trips are for the adventurous; they recapture the spirit of yesteryear." Trips are usually 5-10 days and for up to 8 riders, with time for fishing in high country lakes and streams. A side trip to Cody can be arranged so you can give your saddle-sore muscles a rest and take in some shopping and sightseeing. Rates: $100/day, including sleeping gear. Writes one rider: "The beauty and solitude were magnificent. Jun.-Sep. These trips have given our children some of the most memorable experiences of their lives and drawn us closer as a family." Pack Trips may be combined with a stay at the ranch. The ranch is 26 miles west of Yellowstone. Arrival: Cody, WY, or Billings, MT.

HEART SIX RANCH, Moran P.O. Box 70-AT, Jackson Hole, WY 83013. Att.: Cameron & Billie Garnick. (307) 543-2477 or 733-6994.

"Our trails through the Teton Wilderness and Yellowstone Park take you so high you feel like you're a part of the sky," says outfitter Cameron Garnick. "You ride through, feel, and smell the same unspoiled wilderness that John Colter walked nearly 200 years ago. It is virtually unchanged. These are custom trips for families or small groups, arranged for packing into a wilderness base camp, or for moving on to different camps. Trips from 3- to 10-days. Travel over rugged trails, mostly walking. For 4-15 riders, 3-10 days. Rates: $100-$140/day. All gear including sleeping bags, cots, and tents provided; lodging at the ranch arranged. Jun.-Sep. Arrival: Jackson, WY. (See also *River Running*—Snake River.)

L.D. FROME, OUTFITTER, Box G, Afton, WY 83110. (307) 886-5240.

On L.D.'s individually tailored pack trips for families and small groups you begin by riding to a base camp. From there: follow trails into wilderness areas—Teton, Washakie, Gros Ventre, and Yellowstone Park—where you fly fish the streams for cutthroat trout, hike or ride across the Continental Divide, and enjoy mouth-watering fresh food cooked along the trail. With portable equipment and deluxe tents, you move camp one day and layover the next. For added adventure L.D. takes you on rides into rugged country away from the trails. An excellent family trip according to a packtripper from Palo Alto, CA: "Our twin boys first went when they were only four. When they were ready to nap the outriders carried them in their arms on horseback!" Rates are $105/day (minimum 4 days) for all but sleeping gear, Jun.-Sep. Arrival: Jackson, WY. (See also *Horse Treking, Covered Wagons*—Wagons West.)

MONK'S SUMMER CAMP, Box 12 R.F.D., Lovell, WY 82431. Att.: Charles N. Monk. (307) 548-6686.

Charles Monk maintains his camp on top of the Big Horn Mountains between Lovell and Sheridan, a short distance from the mysterious Medicine Wheel, center of the religious life of the Indians.

WYOMING   During July and August you ride from here into the Big Horn National
                 Forest on base camp or moving pack trips. It's an area where you can
                 catch trout in crystal clear streams, ride forest trails through
                 backcountry full of wildflowers, wildlife and majestic mountain
                 scenes. His 6-day base camp ($350, up to 12 riders) provides sleeping
                 tents, cook tent, and horses for fishing trips and trail rides. His
                 moving pack trips ($85/day up to 6 riders, 5 days or more) start and
                 end at the base camp. Bring sleeping bag and fishing gear. Plan an
                 extra day or so to explore the Pryor Mountain Mustang Range, Big
                 Horn Canyon National Recreation Area, and Yellowstone National
                 Park. Arrival: Lovell or Cody.

Coffee and conversa-   **RIMROCK DUDE RANCH,** Box FS, 2728 Northfork Rt., Cody, WY
tion around the camp-   82414. Att.: Glenn Fales. (307) 587-3970.
fire—*Jack*
Hollingsworth Produc-   "Our 1-week progressive pack trip with a choice of two itineraries is
tions for Rimrock Dude   best for most families, "Glenn Fales advises. "Both routes offer good
Ranch, WY.   fishing and unforgettable mountain scenery in the backcountry of
                           Yellowstone Park and the Teton and Shoshone national
                           forests—country tourists never see." Ride a trusty saddlehorse; mules
                           carry the gear. A Rimrock trip allows for cowboy fantasies. "Parisian
                           Jacques Martin-Kavel, who had long dreamed of being a cowboy,
                           worked hard to act the part of John Wayne," writes a pack tripper
                           from Saddle River, NJ. "One night when the tables were set, a buffalo
                           charged through camp taking the food with him on his horns. It was
                           Jacques, holding an expensive French wine, who never spilled a drop!"
                           Trips for 3-10 riders, 5-21 days, Jul.-Aug. Extra days arranged at
                           ranch, 26 miles east of Yellowstone. Pack rate: $95/day. Jun.-Sep.
                           Arrival: Cody, WY.

SKINNER BROTHERS, Box 859, AG, Pinedale, WY 82941. Att.: Robert Skinner, (307) 367-4675.

The Skinner Brothers promise "excellent fishing in over 100 beautiful alpine lakes and unsurpassed photographic opportunities of mountains and wildlife" on their summer and fall pack trips in the Bridger Wilderness of the Wind River Range. The outdoor cooking is really excellent—top grade. Rates begin at $75/day for 3 or more days. Monte, Robert, Courtney, and Ole Skinner have spent their lives in the outfitting and guiding business, continuing the service their parents started in 1920. Arrival: Pinedale, WY. (See also *Mountaineering, Ski Touring, Youth Adventures.*)

THOROFARE OUTFITTING, Red Pole Ranch, Wapiti, WY 82450. Att.: Donald C. Schmalz. (307) 587-5929.

Chief Arapooish once said, "There is no country like the Crow Country...The Great Spirit has put it exactly in the right place." Don Schmalz has chosen this area—Yellowstone backcountry and the Absaroka, Teton and Washakie wilderness areas—for pack trips ranging from 5-10 days with as many as four camps. "Our expeditions offer something new each day, the world's best fishing, and the finest mule string in the Rocky Mountains," Schmalz claims. A frequent guest from Eureka Springs, AR, writes, "There has never been a road built or a tree cut since the good Lord made it. That's what I escape to. Last year I caught dozens of trout, never under 17" long. Jun.-Aug.; 2-12 riders of any level. Approximately $100/day. Arrival: Cody, WY.

TOGWOTEE MOUNTAIN LODGE, Box 91-D, Moran, WY 83013. Att.: Dave & Judie Helgeson. (307) 543-2847.

Just 30 minutes from Yellowstone participants gather for the "Togwotee Packer"—a 6-day/5-night horsepack wilderness adventure. Riders explore the headwaters of the Yellowstone, the Teton Wilderness, and the Bridger-Teton National Forest. Daily itineraries are based on guests' interests: fishing, rockhounding, photography, scenic rides, and hiking. The 7-day package includes pre- and post-trip lodge stays with full-menu and gourmet specials, access to all lodge facilities—sauna/whirlpool spa, Red Fox Saloon, game room, TV lounge, and fireside activities. Rates: $690/person. Packages for 3 days and longer—tailored to your desires. Jun.-Sep. Shorter, longer, or drop pack trips possible. Bring sleeping bag. Arrival: Jackson, WY. (See also *Ski Touring.*)

TWO BAR SPEAR RANCH, Box 251, Pinedale, WY 82941. Att.: Grant & Abigail Beck. (307) 367-4637. [Nov.-May: Box 86, Florence, MO 65329. (816) 368-2801.]

"The best thing for the inside of a person, is the outside of a horse," claims Grant Beck who has been leading pack trips into the Jim Bridger Wilderness of the Wind River Mountains for 35 years. The first day's ride is only 2 1/2 miles, from the ranch's pack-in corral to the Trapper Lake campsite at 8,500'. You move to a new camp (a 3-hour ride) every other day or so. It's a relaxed tempo to fish, hike, explore, spot elk, moose, deer, bighorn sheep—or just lay back. Routes arranged for special interests. A rider from Pembroke, KY, reports: "My grandson had such an exciting time on our trip that he has gone back six times." A Wyoming attorney writes: "The horses are strong, spirited, but gentle. Food is unbelievably good and the whole crew fun, accommodating, and reliable," Average trip: 8 days, $90/day, $45 under 10 years. Jun.-Sep; Bring sleeping bag. Pickup in Jackson or Rock Springs, $50.

ALBERTA

AMETHYST LAKES PACK TRIPS LTD., Box 508, Jasper, Alta., Canada T0E 1E0. Att.: Wald & Lavone Olson. (403) 866-3980. [Oct.-May: Brule, Alta., Canada T0E 0C0. (403) 865-4417.]

Within Jasper National Park in the Canadian Rockies is the Tonquin Valley—an area of vivid greengrass, brilliant masses of wildflowers, and dark velvety pines against black, jagged peaks known as the Ramparts. Here, on Amethyst Lakes, is a cabin camp—reached only by riding or hiking—where you may ride, hike, fish, go boating, or just relax. At the Mount Edith Cavell trailhead, a short drive from Jasper, the Olsons meet you with saddle and pack horses for your ride in. "Perfect for the whole family," reports a guest from Cape Elizabeth, ME. "Even our six-year-old was enthralled with the 6-hour ride into camp." Rate (Canadian): $280 per rider, 3 days, 2 nights, including cabin and family-style meals, all inclusive; $75 each additional day. For hikers, it's $65/day in camp with cabin and meals. Jun.-Sep. Arrival: Jasper, Alta.

Packing into the Canadian Rockies—*Ron Warner for Holiday on Horseback, Atla., Canada.*

HOLIDAY ON HORSEBACK, The Trail Rider Store, Box 2280, Banff, Alta., Canada T0L 0C0. Att.: Warner & MacKenzie Guiding & Outfitting Ltd. (800) 661-8352 or (403) 762-4551.

"The best things on our trips are free, and everything else is a bargain," claims Ron Warner. We tend to agree. At present exchange rates riders pay $56 per day for W & M pack trips into the majestic beauty of Banff National Park in the Canadian Rockies. You view picturesque lakes and valleys against a backdrop of high peaks, snowcapped even in summer. W & M can arrange whatever you want from an overnight to 6-day trip. Their 6-day "Full-Circle Rides" with three layover days depart from Banff each Sat., Mon., and Wed. by van to the trailhead corral, then it's on by horseback to the headwaters of Stoney Creek, Flint's Park, and the beautiful Mystic Valley before circling back to the trailhead. A variety of trips are scheduled May-Sep. Arrival: Banff or Calgary (80 miles away).

Fording a stream in Banff National Park— *Trail Riders of the Canadian Rockies, Alta., Canada.*

MCKENZIE'S TRAILS WEST, Box 971, Rocky Mountain House, Alta., Canada T0M 1T0. Att.: Mildred McKenzie. (403) 845-6708.

"Our 3-, 6-, and 12-day pack trips offer spectacular beauty and adventure in Alberta's magnificent Rockies," writes the McKenzies. "We believe we have one of the most beautiful unspoiled areas anywhere in Canada. On the longer trips we travel over 100 miles in the Job Valley and Brazeau River area outside Jasper National Park." The terrain is rugged, but the experienced horses know their way—as do the McKenzies. "This is no 'pork-and-beans' trip," comments one packtripper. "Meals are first class: fresh salads and hot menus and lots of it! With the McKenzies, customers come as guests and leave as friends." Rates: 3 days, $350; 6 days, $695; 12 days, $1,200 (Rates in Canadian dollars.) Group rates; custom trips. Bring sleeping gear. Jun.-Sep. The McKenzies meet you at the Calgary, Alta., airport.

TRAIL RIDERS OF THE CANADIAN ROCKIES, Box 6742, Station D, Calgary, Alta., Canada T2P 2E6. (403) 263-6963.

For 63 years, members of this nonprofit organization have explored the varied wilderness areas of Banff National Park. Base camps rotate around the park each 5 years, allowing riders to become acquainted with most areas. Each day's ride about 12 miles. "We offer nine trips in July and August, including one Family discount ride," Secretary Marlene Lea tells us. "Interested people should write me for trip details and what to bring." Transportation to the trailhead from Banff or Calgary can be arranged in advance through TRCR office. Cost: $540/rider in Canadian funds (less in U.S. $) for 6-day trips starting Sundays. Arrival: Calgary (bus service to Banff).

BRITISH
COLUMBIA

HEADWATERS OUTFITTING LTD., P.O. Box 818, Valemount, B.C., Canada V0E 2Z0. Att.: Liz Norwell or Brian McKirdy. (604) 566-4718.

Beginners and experienced riders travel over rugged and easy trails, mostly walking. Headwaters prepares custom trips only, keeping parties small and personal, with base camp trips for 1-8 riders, moving trips for 2-6 riders. Trail rides into Jasper National Park, Mount Robson Provincial Park, Willmore Wilderness, or British Columbia Crown Land. Help as much or as little as you like with camp chores. Layover days are planned for good fishing and highcountry exploration. "At our Dave Henry Creek base camp many folks are content to relax and admire the view," Brian writes. "Admittedly, it's hard to stay relaxed when a big rainbow grabs your hook!" Rate: $80-$100/person/day (Canadian). Rates include meals, cook, guides, tent, foam mattress, and horses. Bring personal gear and sleeping bag. Minimum 3 days. Jun.-Oct. (See also *Hiking with Packstock*.)

3 ON WHEELS

COVERED WAGONS

A long time has passed since the early pioneers first crossed the vast open plains, pushing their way westward and carving their way into the wilderness and into history. But the ruts are still visible in many parts of the country—deep, grass covered furrows etched by iron-rimmed, wooden wheels, the labored autograph of covered wagon trains that lumbered across the plains more than 100 years ago. In Wyoming, there are hewed markings on trees and rocks—work done to accommodate the cumbersome wagons through the rugged canyons.

In several western states, you can join a covered wagon train and relive the old-time journeys over prairie sod or mountain trails.

"Wagons ho!" cries the wagonmaster as he whips his hat in the air. Your wagon lurches forward as your team of horses (and sometimes mules) tug hard at their harnesses. It doesn't take long to get used to the rhythmic rocking motion and the thunder of the wheels on the hard, dry ground.

The pace of the wagon train is slow by today's travel standards—about 16 miles per hour—but it's enough to tire you out and build up a hefty appetite. You dine at dusk on grilled steaks, potatoes and ranchstyle beans, filling your plate not once but twice, and washing your meal down with some steamin' joe. You lean back against a rock and warm your toes with the heat from a crackling campfire. Your cowboy companions tell a few tall tales and play some homespun songs on their guitars. Well before midnight you climb into your bedroll, quite ready to do nothing more than count the skyful of stars.

Reminders

Shifting your personal gear from a bulky suitcase to a duffel or lightweight bag is more convenient for this form of travel. Double-check what to bring, your rendezvous point, how to arrange overnight accommodations before and after the trip, what the rates include, if there's a tax, and whether sleeping gear is provided. Where will you park your car and extra luggage? Will you have a chance to fish? What about a license? Happy pioneering!

ARIZONA
HONEYMOON TRAIL INC., Box A, Moccasin, AZ 86022. Att.: Mel Heaton, (602) 643-7292.

"For 5 wonderful days, you can live the life of a pioneer as you travel by covered wagon through what was once the most difficult and spectacular route to Arizona from the north," says Mel Heaton, who has 10 years experience organizing covered wagon trips. You meet your wagon, trail boss, wranglers and fellow trippers, in Kanab, UT, at a cowboy-style campfire dinner. Roll 13 to 15 miles each day, over trails through scenic country—giant vermilion cliffs, endless sagebrush plains, canyons, and deserts. Sit in the wagon, walk alongside, or trade off with others to ride a horse. Meet villagers along the way. Visits to the Grand Canyon and Bryce Canyon are part of your fare! Sleep under the stars in a sleeping bag, a tent, or the wagon. "Nothing can replace the solitude and peace of the wide-open spaces.

Traveling the prairie, pioneer-style—*Honey- moon Trail, Inc., AZ.*

The food was delicious, and the group lots of fun," are one vacationer's words of praise. Rate: $375/adult, $250/child. (See also *Pack Trips*.)

KANSAS

FLINT HILLS OVERLAND WAGON TRIPS, INC., Box 1076, El Dorado, KS 67042. Att.: Ervin E. Grant. (316) 321-6300.

Spend Saturday night in a covered wagon in the Flint Hills near Rosalia? Where's Rosalia? Today's "pioneers" are detouring to this town, just 14 miles east of Interstate 35 (about 34 miles east of Wichita, 14 miles east of El Dorado) to join the locals (a lawyer, doctor, teacher, and others) for a day of rolling over prairie land into the scenic Flint Hills. Trekkers meet on Saturday morning at the Rosalia High School and drive to the trail. Then it's on across the prairie in a wagon train—authentic mule- and horse-drawn wagons and stagecoach. Sleep overnight beside a stream "out in the middle of God's creation." (Amenities: portable restrooms, no shower.) A chuckwagon provides a hefty trail lunch, and a hearty pioneer-style dinner is cooked over an open fire—followed by tall tales and strumming guitars. Bring a sleeping bag and bunk down in (or under) the wagon or on open ground. After a stick-to-the-ribs breakfast, roll on to the end of the trail, back in Rosalia by noon. Participants write lyrically of soft breezes, meadowlarks, earth smells, the wide horizon, an incomparable sunset, and a star-studded sky. Jun.-Oct. Adult, $85; 17 and under, $50; family and group rates.

NEBRASKA

OREGON TRAIL WAGON TRAIN, Rt. 2, Bayard, NE 69334. Att.: Gordon Howard. (308) 586-1850.

"Take a wagon—and a little imagination—and discover life as it was on the Oregon Trail," says Gordon Howard. His trips begin with an afternoon of pioneer living at base camp, then 2 or 3 days rolling through tall prairie grass from towering Chimney Rock past the Wildcat hills in a great loop, following original pioneer wagon ruts. Nightly chuckwagon cookouts (with hoecakes, sourdough bread, vinegar pie, and cowboy coffee), square dancing, an "Indian raid," and encounters with pony express are part of the fun. The prairie schooners are the real thing, old wagons with wooden wheels. Horses and mules do the pulling. You can ride alongside on a saddle horse. Cost: 3 days/$225, 4 days/$315; children 20% less. Also daily treks, chuckwagon cookouts, trail rides, and canoe rentals on the North Platte River. Jun.-Sep.

WYOMING

BAR-T-FIVE OUTFITTERS, P.O. Box 2140S, Jackson, WY 83001. Att.: Bill Thomas. (307) 733-5386.

In 1889 "Uncle Nick" Wilson drove the first covered wagons over Teton Pass into Jackson Hole. Today his great-grandson Bill Thomas recaptures the experience with covered wagon treks along the backroads of the Targhee National Forest, between Yellowstone and Grand Teton National parks. Wagons move to a new camp each day—two of them on the shores of high mountain lakes. Horseback rides, chuckwagon style meals, campfire singing and old-fashioned hoedown square dances round out the day's fun. Group size: 20-50 people. For 4 days & 3 nights, $380/adult and $325/child 4-14 years. Airport pickup and return included, can arrange lodging night before trip, sleeping gear. Group and youth discounts. Jun.-Sep. Arrival: Jackson, WY.

WAGONS WEST, L.D. FROME, OUTFITTER, Box G, Afton, WY 83110. (307) 886-5240.

There's a lapse of either an hour or a century, depending on how you look at it, from your Jackson Hole motel to a Conestoga wagon at Sagebrush Flat or Skull Creek Meadows. It's modernized with rubber tires and foam-padded seats that convert to deluxe bunks, but it looks like the real thing. Horses or mules pull wagons and chuckwagon over trails and remote backroads in the Grand Teton area. Dutch oven cooking, cowboy songs, fishing, riding, and spotting wildlife are part of a day's trek. Jun.-Sep. Rates: 2 days, $190, 4 days, $350; 6 days, $480; everything but sleeping bag included. (See also *Horse Trekking, Pack Trips*—L.D. Frome.)

CYCLING

You're astride a streamlined 10-speed, following a winding road wherever it will take you. The fragrance of ripe MacIntosh apples hangs heavy in the air. The endless miles of maple trees are taking on their fall colors; you're dazzled by the fiery oranges, reds, yellows, and rusts. Soon you'll stop for lunch, and already you anticipate the crisp snap of fresh-pressed cider.

Just a glimpse into the world of bike touring makes you realize it is one of the great ways to travel. You move forward at an easy and peaceful pace, and can savor every experience the journey offers. As one novice cyclist observes, "We were able to see more—the architecture of the quaint houses, the wildflowers, and the faces of the people." There's more to see than you realize.

You won't have any problem finding cycling trips. In fact, the difficulty comes in trying to choose one from the endless variety offered. They take you through ideal cycling country with winding roads, easy grades, few cars, small towns, and camping spots, hostels, or "bike inns"—a chain of which has been established on the TransAmerica Trail.

You may pedal through California's lush Napa Valley or wondrous spots such as Crater Lake or Carmel. In the Pacific Northwest you can tour the San Juan Islands or the Canadian Rockies further north, and in Virginia the Tidewater region. In rural New England make your way from one quaint county to the next, and in Hawaii cycle past fields of pineapple and sugar cane, with time off to dive into the Pacific.

Once you've chosen your destination, there are even more options. Most services offer a variety of cycling routes within each trip so that your journey can be as relaxing, or as physically demanding, as you want.

Sometimes a van follows to cart your gear from place to place. If your energy flags, it will tote your bike—and you, too. This rescuer of weary cyclists is known as the "sagwagon."

If you don't have a bike, or would rather not tote your own, no problem. Many operators supply top-notch cycles. The only thing you need to bring along is your enthusiasm. And while it helps to be in reasonably decent shape, many planners offer routes that can be tackled by the greenest of beginners.

You might consider weekend touring before setting forth on an extended cycling journey. It gives you a chance to test both your stamina and your equipment—the basic personal gear to take and the bags to pack it in; and the maps, tools, bike accessories (fenders, lights, carriers), and other essentials you'll need.

The start of a two-wheel adventure can be the classified section of the telephone book, where bike dealers and rental services, usually familiar with local routes, are listed. Another source is *Bicycling* magazine, c/o Rodale Press, 33 Minor St., Emmaus, PA 18049 (subscription, $15.97). Bicycle USA, a national bicycling organization, also lists more than 150 tour sponsors throughout the U.S. in its *Tour Finder* publication, available by sending $2 for postage and handling to Suite 209, 6707 Whitestone Rd., Baltimore, MD 21207. But right in these pages you'll find excellent services for dozens of wonderful tours.

A final plus of cycling tours: they are inexpensive vacations. You'll get a close up look at the area, enjoy exquisite cuisine, meet wonderful people, and get in shape—all without putting a serious dent in your wal-

Engulfed in the glorious foliage of autumn— *Vermont Country Cyclers, VT.*

let. And you'll come back looking better than ever. What more could you ask from a vacation?

Reminders

How many miles a day can you cycle? Since trips vary in distance and speed, check with the touring service for specifics. Do they provide a sagwagon (a station wagon or van assigned to pick up sagging riders and carry luggage)? Is there an extra charge for it? Do rates include meals and overnights? Bikes and insurance? Is the route level or hilly? What's the best time of year to enjoy the scenery? Are you apt to have headwinds? Can you extend the trip a day or two if you choose? Make sure you know where the trip begins and ends.

CALIFORNIA

ALL-OUTDOORS ADVENTURE TRIPS, 2151 San Miguel Dr., Walnut Creek, CA 94596. Att.: George Armstrong. (415) 932-8993.

Cycling through fields of sugar cane and pineapple, sunning on sandy beaches, and snorkeling in exotic coral reefs...these are only a few of one's vivid memories after a Hawaiian cycling tour on Kauai (the Garden Isle), Maui (the Valley Isle), and/or Hawaii (the Big Isle). Ample time for scenic stops and island frolicking. 7-day segments on each of the islands. (Jan.-Feb. 7-days, $395 plus air.) "For an adventure in California's Sierra, with more downs than ups, cycle the most pleasurable biking miles from Carson Pass to Yosemite," George urges, "and travel the others in our van." Jul.-Aug., 4 days, $145.) A sagwagon accompanies trips "to assist when fatigue surpasses pleasure." Participants receive instruction in cycling technique, maintenance, repair, and conditioning. (See also *Backpacking, River Running.*)

Spinning wheels on the North Rim of the Grand Canyon—Backroads Bicycle Touring, CA.

BACKROADS BICYCLE TOURING, P.O. Box 1626-M48, San Leandro, CA 94577. Att.: Tom Hale. (415) 895-1783.

"We're proud to provide the most professional, personalized service

possible," states Tom Hale of BBT. Their western bicycle vacations are scheduled on the California Coast, in Wine Country, Sierra Foothills, Canadian and Colorado Rockies, Yellowstone, Puget Sound, Oregon Coast, Bryce, Zion, and the Grand Canyon. They run winter cycling adventures in Hawaii, Baja, and New Zealand. BBT specializes in catered bicycle-camping tours or bicycle-inn tours that feature historic hotels and two/room privacy. "Top-notch leaders, professionally outfitted support vehicles, trailers, and lightweight 18-speed bike rentals help you get the most out of your bicycling vacation," Hale adds. Ride only as far or as fast as you like. The tours involve fine dining, gourmet picnics, down-home hospitality, and incomparable scenery and are for couples, singles, and families of all abilities. Year round. Rates range about $100/day, more or less, for trips from weekenders to 7 days, or 10 days in Hawaii. Bike rentals and van transfer available.

ON THE LOOSE, 1400 Shattuck Ave., Space 7, Box 55, Berkeley, CA 94709. Att.: Ed Tilley. (415) 527-4005.
San Francisco and Oakland are the getaway points for "scenic and exciting places that can best be explored by bicycle," Ed claims. Napa Valley, Lake Tahoe, Crater Lake, Carmel, and the Big Sur are among the wondrous locations on his 2- to 9-day itineraries. Some tours feature camping, others comfortable hotel overnights, or both. Riders cover 20-70 miles a day, and some prefer a bit of beachcombing, shopping, swimming or waterfall-watching along the way. Optional loops vary the distance for each rider, and a van supports all trips. Year- round trips for 8-20/group, all ages. All-inclusive rates from $135 for 2 days to $775 for 11 days. 10-day tours in Hawaii, winter, $825.

DISTRICT OF   **AMERICAN YOUTH HOSTELS, INC.,** Travel Dept. P.O. Box 37613,
COLUMBIA   Washington, DC 20013-7613. (202) 783-6161.
Pedal through the seaside trails of Cape Cod and Martha's Vineyard for 2 weeks. On a 3-week tour cycle along the sunny coast of California, or over the backroads of New England and Canada. Your travel budget need be no more than about $195/week including overnight accommodations, food, tips, taxes, transfers while on trip, entrance fees, and guide. The highly respected and oldest bike touring operator in the U.S., AYH offers dozens of tours in North America from 9 to 70 days for youths and adults. Budget-saving features—hostels, campgrounds, and tourist motels—keep the tour prices amazingly reasonable. A qualified leader for each tour concerns himself with the safety of the group and sees to it that the tour brings fun and adventure to each participant. It's one of the great ways to see America. For information on more than 50 bicycle tours contact AYH. (See also *Youth Adventures.*)

MARYLAND   **CHESAPEAKE BICYCLE TOURS,** Box 345-T, Westminster, MD
21157. Att.: James Hiatt. (301) 876-2721.
Sniff the salt air, watch the sails catch a breeze, and follow the graceful flight of shore birds as you cycle along the magnificent Eastern Shore of Maryland's Tidewater Region, steeped in history. Ride about 25 miles a day and then reward yourself with a night at a

historic inn and a delicious Eastern Shore dinner. A couple from Creve
Coeur, MO, tells of visiting Washington, D.C., for five days, and then
driving through Virginia and Maryland to meet "our superb host," Jim
Hiatt. "Riding more slowly than we were accustomed, we were able to
see more—the architecture of the quaint houses, the wildflowers, and
the faces of the people. Wonderful to combine an active two days with
sightseeing in Washington." Some weekend tours include a 6-hour
skipjack sail on the Tred Avon River and into the vast Choptank.
Trips fully guided; bike and helmet rentals; 4-28 cyclists. All inclusive
rates: 2 days, $85; 3 days, $150-$180.

MONTANA

BIKECENTENNIAL, P.O. Box 8308-A3, Missoula, MT 59807. (406)
721-1776.

Discover America on two wheels! Bikecentennial routes you all the
way from coast to coast, or looping around a single region. They offer
three styles of tours. *Light touring*: 5 and 6 days, where you carry
your own personal gear and have the benefit of one or two leaders and
a comfortable inn for overnights and meals; *van-supported touring*, 5-
or 6-day mountain bike tours with leaders, overnights and gourmet
meals at nice lodges, and a van to transport your personal items; and
self-contained touring, for cyclists 18 years or older, 12 to 90 days,
with a trip leader, mostly campsites for overnights, sharing the
cooking and cleanup chores, and carrying some of your personal gear.
Your route choice varies from 4,400-mile TransAmerica Trails (90
days, $1,680), to a 3,200-mile Missoula-to-Anchorage ride (68 days,
$1,495), to two or three weeks circling parks in the U.S. and Canadian
Rockies, the Northwest Coast, or following a New England trail, or a
Virginia-to-Florida route. Six-day trips loop into Big Sky Country
from Missoula, or from Seattle to countryside trails on the San Juan
Islands. "An outstanding organization with accomplished guides,"
recommends an ophthalmologist from Washington.

NEW YORK

COUNTRY CYCLING TOURS, 140 W. 83rd St., New York, NY
10024. Att.: Peter Goldstein & Gerry Brooks. (212) 874-5151.

"We often find ourselves browsing in antique shops, stopping at
roadside fruit stands, and rumbling over the floorboards of covered
bridges," reports Peter Goldstein. He offers 14 different 1-day
excursions for adults and families within easy driving distance of New
York City ($19-$33/per person). Weekend tours, 3-day holidays, and
5- and 7-day inn-to-inn tours in NY State, MA, VT, NH, RI, PA and
MD, $109 to $649 with all lodging (at comfortable country inns),
breakfasts, dinners, some lunches, professionally trained leaders,
maps, and route directions. For a small fee, you can book round-trip
CCT van transportation from Manhattan for you and your bike on all
tours. The days are leisurely; you cycle at your own pace in groups or
alone. Bailen bicycle helmets and lightweight 12-speed Nishiki
bicycles, specially outfitted for touring, can be rented. Apr.-Nov.

NORTH
CAROLINA

NANTAHALA OUTDOOR CENTER, US 19 West Box 41, Bryson
City, NC 28713. (704) 488-2175.

With the theory that bike touring is the ideal way to see the country,
meet people, and get a feel for history. NOC launches cyclists on fall
foliage and spring wildlfower tours in the Blue Ridge Mountains of the

Carolinas, on the Old Natchez Trace (Mississippi, Alabama, and
Tennessee) and in the Tennessee Smokies. Most trips gather Sunday
evenings for dinner and a session on bicycle-touring techniques. Then
it's off in the van to the starting point for 4 or 5 days of pedaling 30 to
40 miles a day along ridge tops, through forests, fields, and farmlands,
past waterfalls and bubbling streams. Rates of $45 to $60/day include
guide, meals, first night's motel. Bring tent and sleeping gear for
campouts. The van does the hauling. New this year—biking weekends
around the Great Smokies and Joyce Kilmer National Forest, with
lodging, a van, and a more relaxed pace. (See also *Backpacking,
Mountaineering, Canoeing, River Running.*)

An afternoon feast for
hearty appetites—*Tom
Hale for Backroads
Bicycle Touring, CA.*

VERMONT   **BIKE VERMONT,** P.O. Box 207A, Woodstock, VT 05091. Att.: Bob
McElwain. (802) 457-3553.
   "TV and film producer Norman Lear once said 'Vermont is what I
wish the real world were.' After five days of bicycling through this
beautiful state, I think I agree," wrote cyclist Judy Ross. With its many
trips, Bike Vermont helps you discover the state. Easy to moderate
cycling is the order of the day, with enough flexibility for the
advanced cyclist. A limit of 15 to 20 pedalers to a group allows a
personal approach. Among the wide variety of tours is one to appeal

VERMONT   to nearly every level of biker. Some tours, called First Stagers, are
               designed for newcomers and dawdlers who follow their own leisurely
               pace on a 10- or 15-mile basic route. Weekend tours with Friday
               dinner and two nights at a charming Vermont inn are $160/adult,
               $145/child. On 5-day midweek trips ($425/adult, $390/child), pedal
               from inn to inn on quiet backroads past farmlands, covered bridges,
               and picture-book villages. Rates include lodging, guides, van
               transport for luggage, hearty breakfasts, and excellent dinners.
               May-Oct. Bring or rent bikes.

               VERMONT BICYCLE TOURING, Box 711-BV, Bristol, VT 05443.
               Att.: John S. Freidin. (802) 453-4811.
                   "Vermont Bicycle Touring is America's original country inn
               bicycling vacation, and is designed for adults and families with a spirit
               of adventure and a taste for country hospitality," explains John

Cycling past silos in the
quiet countryside—
*Bruce Burgess for
Vermont Bicycle
Touring, VT.*

Freidin, VBT director and author of *25 Bicycle Tours in Vermont.* "We
spend evenings at country inns, where the tone is informal and meals
are home-cooked. Each day you have a choice of routes to fit the
distance you want to ride." Rates include lodging, breakfast, dinner,
taxes, gratuities, tour guides, and other services. Having pioneered
inn-to-inn cycling through Vermont in 1972, VBT offers a variety of
trips: 12-75 miles/day for novices to advanced cyclists. Also: rentals,
a bike repair clinic, private trip planning. SuperSaver rates in May,
Jun., and late Oct.

VERMONT COUNTRY CYCLERS, P.O. Box 145696, Waterbury Center, VT 05677. Att.: Bob & Cindy Maynard. (802) 244-5215.

Vermont Country Cyclers offers deluxe bicycle tours for adults and families in Vermont, Maine and Ireland. Tours last 2-, 3-, 5- and 12-days. Nights are spent at deluxe country inns. Tours are van-supported and accompanied by 2 experienced leaders. VCC offers tours in May-Oct. Costs range from $159-$459 and include breakfast, dinner, lodging, and much more.

VIRGINIA

BIKE VIRGINIA, INC., P.O. Box 203, Williamsburg, VA 23187-0203. Att.: Allen A. Turnbull. (804) 253-2985.

Begin each morning with an orientation session and receive a detailed map and route directions. Then set out at your own pace, adding extra miles as you wish. (Daily routes range from 10 to 50 miles.) Cycle past broad rivers, flowering dogwood, manicured vineyards, and explore Civil War battlefields and 18th century colonial villages. Stay at inns, from historic to rustic, with old-fashioned home cooking to nouvelle cuisine. Virginia's moderate temperatures are ideal for cycling 12 months a year and riders from 7 to 75 enjoy Allen's fully-guided trips. A support van follows the 5-day inn-to-inn tours, through Virginia and Maryland—the Tidewater Region, Virginia hunt country, the Shenandoah Valley, and Colonial Williamsburg. Departures year round, 10-20 cyclists, 3-5 days, 10-45 (plus) miles/day. Rates: weekend, $189; 5 days, $485-$525; lunch extra. Also custom trips, rentals.

OPEN ROAD BICYCLE TOURS, LTD., 1601-AG Summit Dr., Haymarket, VA 22069. Att.: Bud Reed. (703) 754-4152.

"Stop whenever you want, take time to explore, and enjoy yourself," Bud advises. With professional guides and a selection of routes, cyclists have their choice of as little as 8 miles or as much as 20 on shorter rides, and from 40 to 70 miles on more challenging tours. Test your mettle on a weekend trip, looping back to the same inn each night. Pedal through Colonial Williamsburg, Maryland's Eastern Shore, Pennsylvania Dutch Country, Shenandoah Valley, or the hills near Berkeley Springs, West Virginia. Then graduate to 4- and 5-day inn-to-inn trips or a magnificent 10-day cycle through Nova Scotia. Here you'll see the great tidal bore, the jagged coastline, picturesque fishing villages, and quaint lighthouses. On all trips, stay at quiet antique-filled country inns and enjoy three hearty meals. There's always a support van that carries all luggage and "sweeps" your route, so even if you get tired and decide to snooze along the way, you'll be picked up. Year-round departures; also custom trips; 6-21 riders; rentals. All-inclusive rates: 2-5 days, $172-$469; 10 days in Nova Scotia, Jul.-Aug., $659.

WASHINGTON

BICYCLE ADVENTURES, INC., P.O. Box 7537, Dept. A, Olympia, WA 98507. Att.: Bob Clark. (206) 786-0989.

"A wonderful trip! Food was good, people were great, scenery gorgeous. I came back in better shape than when I left," remarks a San Diego cyclist about her Puget Sound tour. Bicycle Adventure offers weekend and 1- and 2-week fully supported bicycle vacations in the

WASHINGTON   state of Washington. Tour the San Juan Islands, Olympic Peninsula,
Cascade Mountains, wine country. Experience fantastic scenery, quiet
country backroads, evergreen forests. "Enjoy first-class lodging
(two-per-room privacy), great food, a support van to carry your
luggage, professional tour guides, superior bicycle rentals, and new
friends," Bob Clark urges. "The camaraderie of interesting adults
sharing an exciting adventure together is only one of the special
rewards."

LIBERTY BELL ALPINE TOURS, Mazama, WA 98833. Att.: Eric
Sanford. (509) 966-2250.
    Roll your bike onto the ferry from Seattle to Friday Harbor on the
San Juan Islands for 5 days of cycling and camping on winding roads
cooled by sea breezes ($345). Or cycle the backroads of the Methow
Valley. It's a fun and relaxing trip, with 3 nights at the Mazama
Country Inn, then on to Lake Chelan for 2 more days along the lake
($325). A 40-mile Cascade Mountain camping tour is what mountain
bikes were made for. Easy riding over old mining roads, through ghost
towns, and up to Harts Pass, with time to hike and fish along the way
($275). Or experience the good life on a wineries tour, pedaling
winding roads through lush country with nights at country inns, and
great eating ($475). Rates include meals, 18-speed touring bike,
transport, and lodging, Sun. p.m. to Sat. a.m., Jul.-Sep. (See also
*Backpacking, Mountaineering, Kayaking, River Running, Ski
Touring.*)

NORTHWEST BICYCLE TOURING SOCIETY, 6166 92nd Ave. S.E.,
Mercer Island, WA 98040. Att.: Lloyd Jones. (206) 232-2694.
    With 12 years of touring experience, NBTS guides you through
some of the most scenic areas of Oregon, Washington, and British
Columbia on its 2- to 9-day cycling tours. Whether you're a beginner
or an experienced cyclist, there is a trip for you. Select an easy
120-mile weekend tour from Seattle to Port Townsend, $33. Or
explore Washington & British Columbia—9-days, 450 miles, from
Seattle, $85. Also: a 125-mile trip from Orting to Millersylvania State
Park and back ($30/adult, $18/child 12 and under), a century or
half-century in Mount Vernon, a scenic 50-mile loop in the
Skagit-Samish Flats area, and overnight Mount Rainier tours. Rates
include accommodations (campground, cabin, or resort), breakfast,
supper, sagwagon, tour guide, and maps. Groups range from 70-140.
May-Oct. "It's the best biking and camping and fun to be had
anywhere—an adventure worth taking," writes a cyclist from
Michigan.

TOURING EXCHANGE, P.O. Box 265A, Port Townsend, WA 98368.
Att.: Bonnie Wong. (206) 385-0667.
    Touring Exchange offers bikepacking, mountain biking, or
bed-and-breakfast biking in Mexico the Pacific Northwest, and New
Zealand. "Traveling with Bonnie Wong is always a pleasure—each
tour is well organized with good directions,' report a California couple
who have taken several of her trips. In Baja you cycle well-paved or
dirt roads well off the beaten track on mountain bikes. A unique way

A cyclist's serenade by the Baja seashore— *Bonnie Wong for Touring Exchange, WA.*

to see exciting country at only $26-$33/day. Basic riding skills, good conditioning, and willingness for no frills camping are recommended. In California's Sacramento River Valley, join the annual spring ride—2 or 3 days, $40 or $50 including catered meals, ride choices of 30-80 miles a day. In Washington's Puget Sound region, the San Juan Islands, and North Cascades, choose bed-and-breakfast tours. Fees from $65-$75/day include transport in and out of Seattle. These B&B's focus on a music festival, a 5,000-ft. downhill ride, a lake cruise in the mountains, or other special features. Tours are for 8-12 cyclists, 5 days to 4 weeks. Rentals available.

ALBERTA

ROCKY MOUNTAIN CYCLE TOURS, Box 895-A, Banff, Alta., Canada T0L 0C0. Att.: Mary Jane & Larry Barnes. (403) 678-6770.

"If you really want to experience the Canadian Rockies," say the Barneses, "why not do it on a bicycle?" Their mountain resort tour combines 5 days of cycling with 6 nights at handsome, rustic inns and lodges (including a night in Banff at the beginning and end of your tour). You'll pedal about 20 miles daily through spectacular highcountry with a day for hiking, horseback riding, canoeing, or relaxing. Another tour, from Banff to Jasper in 5 days, combines camping and lodge nights and averages 40 miles a day over mountainous terrain. The rewards are many: mighty waterfalls and deep blue lakes, glimpsing a bear or moose, visiting the Columbia Icefield and Kananaskis Park (site of the 1988 winter Olympics). Hearty campfire meals. Rates except for bikes and sleeping bags: 5 days, camping/lodge tour, $390; 6 days, mountain resort tour, $625. Bike rental, $45/week. Self-guided tour booklet with maps, $7.95 postpaid. Rates in U.S. dollars. Spring tours in San Juan Islands; fall tours in France.

JEEPING

"The only difference between a horse and a jeep is that the jeep doesn't stop for a drink when you cross a creek," says a onetime passenger for the benefit of those who might think this is a tenderfoot trek. In fact, a wilderness jeep trip can combine first, second, and reverse with the stomach-churning buckboard bounce of a horse and carriage at full gallop. Still, if you can stand a sore bottom and hair-raising curves, it's an excellent way for the entire family to trail blaze together.

Jeeping services offer just about everything and will take you just about anywhere. You travel on roads so remote they're often only accessible by four-wheel drive vehicle. There are old railroad grades, pioneer trails, and stagecoach routes to explore. You can enjoy day trips to ghost towns and abandoned gold mines, breakfast cookouts in the backcountry, weeklong excursions with chuckwagon trailers and deluxe camping gear. And not to be forgotten is the scenery:

12,000-foot high mountain passes, deep river canyons, crystal clear streams.

Jeep services are always willing to plan customized trips, whether you prefer trout fishing, fossil and rock hunting, or geology. Or, if you prefer, they'll help you combine your jeeping with a totally separate activity such as rafting or skiing. Whatever destination or activity you choose, you'll find your guides to be invaluable resources, filling you with information about the area's history, wildlife, and plant life.

Reminders
Does the trip provide for camping out or sleeping at a lodge or ranch? Do rates include overnights? Are sleeping bags provided? Is any recreational equipment provided (fishing poles, ice coolers, etc.)? Will the outfitter arrange lodging before and after the trip? What weather will you encounter? If altitude affects you, find out what elevations you'll experience. Clarify whether you would like to join other travelers, or whether you want a custom trip. Check rendezvous points.

COLORADO

THE MOUNTAIN MEN, 11100 East Dartmouth 219, Denver, CO 80014. Att.: Burt Green. (303) 750-0090.

This long-established service (19 years with a perfect safety record) takes you over rough jeep trails to remote super-spectacular Rocky Mountain scenery on 1-day and longer excursions. These outings are scheduled from July to September, though easier half-day and 1-day trips are arranged year round. "Our guide was not only sensitive to the needs of our 98-year-old father, but he was a boon companion who demonstrated his knowledge and driving skills through the absolute delights of Phantom Canyon and the oh-my-god road," remarks a New Jersey participant. Another specialty is jeeping to remote areas for trout fishing, including guides, meals, horses, or inexpensive drop camps, as needed. In winter MM provides four-wheel-drive ski area shuttle from Denver's Stapleton Airport.

RIVER RUNNERS LTD., 11150 Highway 50, Salida, CO 81201. Att.
Ghost Town Jeep Tours. (800) 525-2081 natl. or (800) 332-9100 in CO.
   Visit famous—and infamous—Old West "ghost towns" by jeep
following the old stage coach routes and Indian trails. Learn about the
"boom days" and why the ghost towns were abandoned. At one
well-known town many buildings still survive, including the saloon
and jail. Explore a prospector's cabin; learn how to pan for gold and
try your luck. Visit old mines and get samples of ore and minerals:
gold, silver, iron, copper, mica. On one full-day tour, visit 11 ghost
towns—St. Elmo, Tincup, and others. Follow the abandoned narrow
gauge railroad and cross four mountain passes above 12,000 feet.
Twice you cross the Continental Divide. Plenty of picturesque vistas
and wildlife up here in these unusual, unique places only accessible by
four-wheel-drive vehicle. Half-day and 1-day tours, $19 and $34;
(children, $14 and $27). (See also *River Running*.)

UTAH

TAG-A-LONG TOURS, P.O. Box 1206, 452 N. Main St., Moab, UT
84532. Att.: Paul M. Niskanen. (800) 453-3292 or (801) 259-8946.
   "Most jeepers have no idea how exciting the trails can be," says Paul
Niskanen. "We operate dependable rigs up and down rocky ledges,

Van camping in Utah's
spectacular
Canyonlands—*Tag-A-
Long Tours, UT.*

UTAH

small cliffs, and sloping rock walls, but keep driving time short so guests have opportunities for hiking, taking pictures, and examining Indian ruins." On these trips you explore some of the Southwest's most beautiful regions—seen by few people—and love every thrill-filled minute. Niskanen's 4-day jeep expedition into Canyonlands National Park can be combined with rafting Cataract Canyon. And a 1-day excursion winds north through the "Island in the Sky"—a high mesa offering panoramic views—or south to Angel Arch, "one of the largest and most beautiful in the world." Custom expeditions booked for 3 or more. Year round, but main season is Apr.-Oct.; 1-7 days. Fine food cooked over an open fire. Sleeping bag rental. Arrival: Moab, UT. (See also *River Running, Van Camping*.)

LIN OTTINGER TOURS, 137-A, North Main St., Moab, UT 84532. Att.: Lin Ottinger. (801) 259-7312.

Lin Ottinger describes Canyonlands National Park as a vast area of astonishing beauty with deep canyons, towering cliffs, buttes, pinnacles, balanced rocks, and natural stone arches—all spectacularly carved by wind, rain, and the Colorado and Green Rivers. It's an area he knows well, having guided tours here since 1960. Lin is a photographer, geologist, and naturalist. "They even named a dinosaur after me," he says. He offers a free sterographic map of the Canyonlands to anyone who writes for it. All-day and half-day tours begin at his rock shop in Moab. Custom tours specialize in geology, fossil and rock hunting, or discovering unnamed arches and formations in seldom-seen areas. Also backpacking treks from 1-8 days, and combined rafting and jeep trips. "Lin's enthusiasm and depth of feeling for the land is without comparison," comments a tripper. Rates: $30/day; child and group discounts. Apr.-Nov.

VAN CAMPING

Van camping may very well be the modern-day substitute for the family vacation of yesteryear. Instead of the family station wagon, you travel in a spacious van, with your newly adopted family—about a dozen traveling companions. To a large extent, it is these people who make van camping a particularly enjoyable way to see the country. "Within a day we were coming up with nicknames for each other," said one vacationer. "I've never been on a vacation where I became so close to so many people and had so many laughs." It is the scenery that is the next best part of van camping. "We went on a hike and saw caribou less than 100 yards away, arctic flowers, and the mountains in the distance," reminisced a visitor to Alaska.

Van camping trips are designed to be small and personal. Your group learns to travel as a team. Together you shop for food, cook, set up camp, plan your menus, and make destination decisions. Sometimes you camp under the stars in the midst of the wilderness, other times you stay in top hotels.

Your itinerary is meant to be flexible and relaxing. There's always free time to hike, swim, cycle, or canoe. Some services plan trips around one particular activity like photography.

The guides, you'll find, are experienced, knowlegeable, and extremely likeable. They'll not only drive you confidently on course, they'll lead you to some of the most historic, scenic spots in the United States. "I smile remembering how much fun I had," said one van camper.

Reminders
Check on your rendezvous point. Find out how many nights will be spent camping and how many in hotels. Is the cost of food included in the price? Are meals in restaurants included? How about gas? Do you need to bring your sleeping bag? How many miles should you expect to cover each day on the road? How many people will be traveling in the vehicle? Will there be children on the trip?

ALASKA   **CAMP/ALASKA TOURS,** P.O. Box 872247, Suite 4, Wasilla, AK 99687. Att.: Tim Adams. (907) 376-9438.

If seeing Alaska is your dream, CampAlaska is ready to turn it into reality. By day, explore the rugged natural beauty of this vast land in a 15-seat van. As night falls, cook a meal over the campfire and sleep under the stars at one of the state's magnificent natural parks. CampAlaska offers 6 different van tours that combine the "coach and hotel" idea with the spirit and excitement of wilderness backpacking. A knowledgeable tour leader takes you to the most interesting historic and scenic spots, but the relaxed schedule offers plenty of time for hiking, canoeing, bicycling, or just plain loafing. New this season is a 14-day trip including 2 days of white water on the Chickaloon River and a 3-day canoe expedition from Dawson City to Eagle. The trips are designed for young adults 18-40 (most of them single). May-Sep., from 6-26 days, for up to 12 participants. Rates: $334-$1,124

including food kitty for camp fare, but not restaurant meals. Shared
accommodations at departure hotels. Bring sleeping bag. Depart
Anchorage or Seattle.

ARIZONA

WILD & SCENIC, INC., P.O. Box 460, Dept. AT, Flagstaff, AZ 86002
Att.: Patrick & Susan Conley. (602) 774-7343.

Longtime residents of the Southwest, the Conleys have selected
some of its outstanding scenic areas for 8-day photography
workshops. Departing from the traditional fixed-base seminar, they
travel in specially equipped vans with deluxe camping equipment.
Experienced backcountry guides lead the small groups to remote
canyons, arches, Indian ruins, slickrock, and high mountain
meadows. World-traveled photojournalists teach the techniques of
filming the colorful panoramas in ever-changing light and shadow. In
the amazing beauty of the Arches and Canyonlands national parks,
participants work out of each camp 2 days capturing the remarkable
scenes. In Navajolands, they photograph seldom visited parts of
Monument Valley, Canyon de Chelly, and Hovenweep. Their photos
in Escalante Canyon and Capitol Reef National Park feature a
petrified forest, silty clays of vivid hues, a tableland of white rim
sandstone, an unearthly jagged skyline. On Lake Powell with its
tapestried cliffs and vermilion rock spires, the base of operations is a
houseboat, with powerboat transport to Rainbow Bridge and other
unbelievable photogenic settings. Fares for each 8-day workshop,
May-October, on which non-photographers also are welcome, begin
at $895/person. In the northern Rockies, another workshop features
the high peaks, wildlife, and rushing rivers and waterfalls of
Yellowstone and Grand Teton national parks. (See also *River
Running.*)

CALIFORNIA

TREK AMERICA, P.O. Box 1338, Gardena, CA 90249. Att.: Mark
Sheehan. (800) 221-0596.

"Our key words are fun, freedom, and flexibility," says Mark
Sheehan of Trek America. He offers 2- to 9-week adventure camping
holidays throughout the U.S., Alaska, and Canada for adults (ages
18-35). "This is a great opportunity to discover North America with
fellow passengers from all points of the compass, at the same time
rubbing elbows with the locals," notes Mark. The trips are geared for
small groups, with 13 passengers and a professional leader per van.
Accommodations range from top hotels to wilderness campsites. You
spend some overnights in places such as Las Vegas, New Orleans,
Quebec City, and Anchorage; and others at the Grand Canyon, Lake
Powell, Yellowstone National Park, the Florida Keys, and the Rocky
Mountains and other scenic spots. On a 3-week "Canyon Trail" trip,
for example, activities include horseback riding, a ranch visit,
whitewater rafting, waterskiing, a desert jeep ride, a flight over the
Grand Canyon, a steam train ride, a national park hike, and seeing
Disneyland and the sights of Los Angeles—all for $628. The 13 other
itineraries, each led by a well-trained guide, range from 11 days for
$345 to 9 weeks for $1,950. Bring a sleeping bag and a sense of
adventure. Year-round departures. (See also *Youth Adventures.*)

UTAH **TAG-A-LONG TOURS,** P.O. Box 1206, 452 N. Main St., Moab, UT 84532. Att.: Paul M. Niskanen. (800) 453-3292 or (801) 259-8946.

This 5-day van-camping tour takes you through some of the most spectacular country of the entire West, departing from Las Vegas and ending at the Grand Canyon (or in reverse). You explore both ancient and modern Indian cultures, visit several national parks, camp in scenic places, and travel in rugged 4-wheel-drive vehicles to gain access to remote spots most people never see. Visit Zion, Bryce, and Capitol Reefs national parks and swim in the blue waters of Lake Powell. Explore Monument Valley, home of the Navajos, and Canyon de Chelly with its ancient Anasazi cliff dwellings. See the pueblo-type structures of the Hopi Indians, their beautiful jewelry, and possibly a colorful tribal dance. Then on to the Grand Canyon and its unbelievable beauty. Expert, fully informed guides provide background details. Rate: 5 days, Mar.-Nov., $650. (See also *Jeeping, River Running.*)

4 BY BOAT

BOATS / CRUISES

You're stretched out on the deck of a 40-foot sailing yacht, gazing up at the clean, white sails filled by the tradewinds that are gently propelling your boat to its next idyllic anchorage. You glance sideways at the sparkling turquoise of the Caribbean Sea. You're sailing on your own chartered yacht, and should you stop to think about it, you realize that you just can't imagine anything better than this.

Sailing cruises can be enjoyed by everyone, from landlubber to old salt, since it is possible to charter a sailing or a powered yacht complete with captain and crew. Or, if you are a skipper yourself, you can take matters into your own hands with a "bareboat" charter (without crew).

On a crewed charter everything is supplied—all provisions, whatever sports equipment you request, gourmet meals, and a captain and crew who pamper you like royalty. On a bareboat charter you may request different degrees of bareness—with or without food and beverages. Bareboating, the less expensive arrangement of the two, is a way to be a part-time yachtsman without the responsibility of yacht ownership. There are sailing schools (please see page 107) which specialize in transforming landlubbers into qualified bareboat skippers.

Either way, crewed or bareboat, chartering a boat is the open sesame to delightul vacations and an exhilarating sense of freedom. In the Caribbean you can anchor in a sheltered cove and discover your own private reef for snorkeling, or join a flotilla—sailing separately by day but anchoring with the other boats at the same harbor for socializing at night. Cruising off Maine's rugged coast can be combined with putting in at colorful ports or having your own clambakes or lobsterbakes on a remote beach. On the west coast you can sail among the migrating grey whales off Baja California, or north in the San Juan Islands, or up the Inside Passage to Alaska in some of the world's most spectacular scenery.

If these visions are among your daydreams, read the pages that follow. They can transform fantasy into reality.

ALASKA **FRONTIER ADVENTURES ALASKA YACHT EXCURSIONS,** 7850 Old Glacier Hwy., Juneau, AK 99801. Att.: Charles Kelly. (907) 789-0539.

"Your only worry is whether to wrestle with a mighty King Salmon, tackle a monsterous halibut, or just sit back and enjoy some of the world's most spectacular scenery and wildlife," says Capt. Kelly of his yachting cruises aboard the Frontier Queen. "Our excursions are limited to 6 guests at one time, so you'll enjoy first-rate, personalized service. The majority of the areas we visit are accessible only by smaller vessels such as the *Frontier Queen*. Cruise from the San Juan Island (north of Seattle) up the fabled Inside Passage along the British Columbia shore to southeast Alaska. Rates are $1,200/week/person, including airport/hotel transport, yacht facilities, fishing gear, and gourmet meals. Capt. Kelly also offers cruises from 3-21 days through

Cruising amidst some of the world's most spectacular scenery— *Frontier Adventures Alaska Yacht Excursions, AK.*

Boaters eye a magnifi-
cent catch—*Frontier
Adventures Alaska
Yacht Excursions, AK.*

ALASKA

Alaska's Marine National Wilderness, Admiralty Island National
Wilderness, and Glacier Fjords (Apr.-Oct.) Reports one recent guest
"the scenery was magnificent, the accommodations were great, and
Charlie and Cameron Kelly were super hosts. I would recommend
cruising with them to anyone who wants to experience Alaska's
hospitality and beauty."

M/V HYAK, Box 2071, Wrangell, AK 99901. Att.: Gary
McWilliams. (907) 874-3084.
   The *M/V Hyak* is a 52-foot wooden boat of classic design. She
comfortably accommodates four guests (five on special arrangement).
"We specialize in 7- to 14-day natural history tours of coastal Alaska,
sailing out of Ketchikan," says Captain Gary McWilliams. We observe
Alaska's sealife, geology, and glacialogy, its flora and fauna, and have
specific expertise to share in the areas of ornithology, wild edibles, and
mineral collecting (crystals and fossils)." The *Hyak* features gourmet
preparation of freshly acquired seafood and a canopy-covered aft
deck for all weather nature observation and photography. She is
equipped with a motorized skiff, canoe, kayak, binoculars, fishing
gear, and tools for collecting mineral specimens. "One of the great
ventures in our family life," comments a passenger from WI.
All-inclusive rate for 4 or less, $600/day; $100/day extra for 5th
person.(See also *Canoeing/Kayaking*.)

OUTDOOR ALASKA, Box 7814-AG, Ketchikan, AK 99901. Att.: Dale Pihlman. (907) 225- 6044 or 3498.

From a height of up to 8,000 feet, southeast Alaska's jagged mountains drop sharply into the rivers and fjords of the 2.1 million-acre Misty Fjords Wilderness. "It's a young and spectacular land, still being shaped by ice and water—a geological drama," director Dale Pihlman notes. He and his guides—all lifetime residents—lead a personalized excursion through this majestic, primeval wilderness. "For a period of each cruise we turn off our engines so you can 'hear' the overwhelming silence," Dale points out. "The greatest disturbance may be the splashing of a salmon or the cry of an eagle." Raves one passenger, "I recommend Outdoor Alaska to anyone who wants to see the beautiful scenery, and be treated with warm Alaskan hospitality." The highly personalized journeys are for no more than 32 passengers, for 1-4 days. Rates: 12-hour trip, $120; 8-hour cruise/fly, $159; 3 days of kayaking, $160.

CALIFORNIA

OCEAN VOYAGES, 1709 Bridgeway, Sausalito, CA 94965. Att.: Mary Crowley. (415) 332-4681.

With a fine network of easily accessible sailing programs throughout the North American home waters, and the Caribbean, these voyages are for both novice and expert sailors. From Alaska to Baja California, and down the Eastern Seaboard into the Caribbean, typical sailing includes whale-watching among the San Juan Islands (off WA), learning to sail on a classic 44' Alden yawl among the California Channel Islands (CA) and in Hawaii. OV's director, Mary Crowley, has sailed over 50,000 miles and has selected personally the boats and skippers used in these programs. It's a chance for small groups (4-12 participants) to learn maritime lore, marine biology, and other specialties on an adventurous voyage. Rates from $575/week all-inclusive. (See also *Windjammers*.)

FLORIDA

ADVENTURE SAILING ESCAPE, P.O. Box 06079, Ft. Myers, FL 33906. Att.: Ron Drake. (813) 489-0344.

Sailors alert! Board a sailing yacht and join a flotilla fleet which docks each night at one of the barrier islands. Dine at such luxury resorts as the Sonesta Sanibel Harbour in Punta Rassa, the South Seas Plantation on Captiva, or Tween-Waters Inn, the Cabbage Key Hide-A-Way, or Useppa Island Club. It's a luxurious life—dining and dancing at night and by day sailing in the warm sun and light breeze where the dolphins play. These cruises attract families, couples, and singles who have the expertise to skipper without on-board supervision and to respond to radioed instructions by the Fleetmaster from his lead yacht. Should this not be part of your expertise, fret not. There is a 2-day optional Skipper School which fits the novice for docking under power, basic sailing techniques, chart reading, and radio operation. Each crew chooses from among 27' to 41' yachts. With only five boats sailing in any one flotilla, a camaraderie develops when they anchor at the same harbor after a day of charting their own courses. Flotilla cruise: 4 days, $425/person; 7 days, $690-$920; all inclusive; children's rates less. Year round. Arrival: Ft. Myers. (See also *Sailing Schools*.)

Sailing up fjords of the
fabled Inside Passage—
*Bluewater Adventures,
B.C., Canada.*

FLORIDA

THE MOORINGS, LTD., 1305 U.S. 19 South, Suite 402-AT,
Clearwater, FL 33546. (800) 535-7289 or (813) 535-1446.

"Our high standards for yacht design, preparation, and service are
maintained by a year round staff," says Marketing Director Simon
Scott. "This results in consistent high-quality service winter and
summer." Summer, according to Scott is one of the best times to enjoy
yachting. The winds are gentler and dependable every day, and the
harbors aren't crowded with noisy weekenders. He recommends
group charters for clubs, families, and racing rivals as the way to go,
with rates significantly lower on multi-boat charters. You travel in
style on the Moorings' luxury yachts as you cruise any number of
exotic destinations—Tortola in the British Virgins, for example, or
Marigot Bay, a beautiful harbor on St.Lucia's protected western side
and a water sports wonderland. Besides daysailing and short cruises (3
nights in combo packages with 4 nights at the resort), there are sunfish
and sailboards (with instruction available), paddleboats, swimming,
and a diving program for all levels of experience. "Whether you go
bareboat or with skipper or full crew, you'll be chartering one of the
best-maintained sailing yachts in the islands," Scott assures. Other
services: cruising course, scuba instruction, food provisioning.

NEW YORK

MID-LAKES NAVIGATION CO., LTD., 11 Jordon St., P.O. Box
61-AT, Skaneateles, NY 13152. (315) 685-5722.

"A canal cruise on New York's waterways beckons the adventurous
vacationer or anyone who wants to just lean back and relax," says
Capt. Peter Wiles. "This is a chance to see New York in a way few ever
experience." The canal system would long since have become a thing

of the past had not Capt. Wiles and others with pride in their state's history persuaded the Legislature to provide funds to teach and pass down the skills of operating the complex canals. The 10-year effort resulted in preserving the state's historic water heritage. Horses still pull the canal boats on one section of the original Erie Canal. With five boats, Mid-Lakes offers cruises on many waterways—the Erie, Champlain, Cayuaga-Seneca, Oswego, and Oneida Lakes and the Finger Lakes. Each 2-, 3-, or 4-day cruise includes all meals, land transportation, lodging, admission to side trips, and return to point of embarkation. Along the towpaths you can visit Albany's tulip festival, Lockport's canal festival, the historic Schuyler Museum, the National Wildlife Refuge in Montezuma. Rates: 2 days, $220-$368; 4 days, $420-$468; for 1-3 per room. All cruises depart at 9 a.m., return late in afternoon or early evening of the last day. Jun.-Oct. Also dinner and luncheon cruises on Skaneateles Lake. Some boats available for charter.

WASHINGTON   **NORTHWEST MARINE CHARTERS, INC.**, 2400 Westlake Ave. N., Suites 1 & 2, Seattle, WA 98109. Att.: Robey Banks (206) 283-3040.
    "The Pacific Northwest has the finest protected cruising water anywhere," Robey Banks maintains. "There are driftwood and fossils on the island beaches; clams, crabs, wild oysters onshore; whales and porpoises offshore; Coho, silver, and king salmon fishing for the 'pro' and flounder and cod for the 'meat' fisherman; tea and crumpets in Victoria—and unbelievable beauty everywhere!" NMC offers a choice of over 100 boats 28 to 125 feet, each completely equipped for extended cruising (6-day minimum). Sample rates: $930/week for 34-foot U-Drive cruiser (sleeps 6); $1,050-$1,510/week for 37- to 41-foot diesel trawlers (sleep 6); $700/day for 60-foot skippered and crewed luxury yacht for 4-6 passengers. Also houseboats and U-sail sailboats. To avoid disappointment and have best selection, Robey suggests reserving 3 to 6 months in advance.

PACIFIC CLIPPER CRUISES, P.O. Box 243, Port Townsend, WA 98368. Att.: Bill & Helen Curry. (206) 385-5885.
    Sail aboard a classic wooden schooner through the inland waters of The Pacific Northwest," urge the Currys. The *Red Jacket* departs weekly from historic Fort Townsend for the San Juan Islands and Victoria. Special cruises include Expo '86, an expedition to Desolation Sound, Canada, schooner races at the Classic Boat Show and Wooden Boat Festival, and a photography workshop. Individual fares: $485/saloon berth, $610/private cabin. Charter rates for 6 days, 5 nights: $3,050 for 1-4 persons to $3,293 for 5, and $3,535 for 6, fares all inclusive. Season: May-Oct. "Cruising is a perfect way to spend your vacation," says one California resident. "The quietness and tranquility is a unique pleasure. Bill's exceptional seamanship and Helen's gourmet cooking were wonders to behold. This was the greatest experience of a long, long life."

CARIBBEAN   **NICHOLSON YACHT CHARTERS**, 9 Chauncy St., Cambridge, MA 02138. Att.: Julie P. Nicholson. (617) 661-8174.
    "Yacht cruising with us is the smell of coffee brewing as one takes a

CARIBBEAN

Anchored ever so close
to paradise—*Kimberly
Cruises, Virgin Islands.*

pre-breakfast swim," enthuses Julie. "It is bustling markets, long sandy
beaches, pearly pink dawns, and exhilarating sailing." The oldest
established yacht charter broker in the world, Nicholson has upwards
of 300 beautiful yachts—sail and motor, bareboat and
crewed—available between St. Maarten and Grenada, and the Virgin
Islands. Also the Mediterranean and New England in summer.
Accommodations are for 2-18 guests; snorkel and fishing equipment is
always carried on board. Most have wind surfer boards and some
have scuba gear. All-inclusive rates average $100/person/day.

STEVENS YACHTS, INC., 183 Madison Ave., Suite 1106, New York,
NY 10016. (800) 638-7044 or (212) 686-3822.
    It's a delightful life—relaxed sailing, superb snorkeling, a barbecue
a secluded beach, a shore excursion, an evening at a "jump up" party
at an island hotel, and sailing to another beautiful anchorage each
day. In the Caribbean, St. Lucia, Tortola, and Granada are bases for
Stevens Yachts. For Sea of Cortez cruising, the base is La Paz, Baja
California. Stevens is the only charter company permitted by Mexico
to charter-cruise these magnificent and unspoiled waters. From 30 to
56 feet, the yachts are chartered with crew of two, or without crew
(bareboat charters) if you have extensive offshore sailing experience.
They also offer a 7-day sailing course in the Windward Islands to
qualify you for bareboat chartering. Charters are tailored to each
group's requirements. The rate, for example, for the Stevens Custom

56 with crew and 4 guests is $4,900/week. For the SC50 ketch, crewed, it's $3,920. Rates quoted for Dec. 15-Apr. 14. Bareboat rates range from $1,995/week for a SC39 to $2,940 for a SC47, Aug.1-Oct.31. Complete or partial provisioning for bareboats is another service.

TRIMARINE BOAT CO. LTD., Homeport, St. Thomas, V.I. 00801. Att.: Duncan & Annie Muirhead. (809) 494-2490.

For luxurious sailing and diving in Caribbean waters, it's difficult to beat the 56-foot *Misty Law* and 95-foot *Lammer Law*. The two trimarans have 4 and 9 cabins respectively, private baths, excel in spaciousness and stability, and carry a full range of diving equipment, tenders for water skiing or going ashore, aquaplanes, windsurfer, music library, stereo, and (on the *Lammer Law*, "largest trimaran in the world") projection equipment and seating for up to 30. Excellent American/English fare with special touches is one specialty, and diving instruction—plus scenic dives through wrecks, caves, and exotic reefs—is another. No spear fishing. For non-divers it can be as leisurely and lazy as desired. Both boats may be booked on individual or whole boat basis. Per person rates with crew, meals, drinks, all sports, instruction: *Misty Law*—$120/night, year round, 7-14 days; *Lammer Law*—$140/night, year round, 7, 10, or 15 days. (See also *Scuba Diving*.)

HOUSEBOATING

So you've always wanted to skipper your own ship. Well, matey, slip into your deck shoes, plot your course, and lift anchor. You're at the helm of an 18-foot, multi-ton houseboat, making your way slowly across a placid lake or down a winding river.

Houseboating is perhaps one of the most relaxing forms of vacationing. You drift at 10 m.p.h. past colorful canyon walls or scenic shorelines, explore hidden coves, anchor whenever you want to frolic on a beach or do some fishing, or go ashore at river towns or waterside resorts. At night you head for a marina, anchor in a shallow bay, or tie up to an island.

If this leisurely life seems almost too leisurely, you can tow a powerboat along. Anchor your houseboat at some ideal spot and take off for an hour's, or a day's, excursion. This adds to the cost of your vacation, but also to the exploratory possibilities.

Basic houseboat rentals can be as low as $10 to $15 per day per person if there are ten of you sharing the cost of a boat that sleeps your whole group. Besides, it provides transport, sundecks, and equipment items such as pots and pans and lifejackets. Houseboats are generally designed with compact beds and convertible couches, a marine toilet, a galley with a 3- or 4-burner range, and a shower stall. (It may have to be a short wet-down if your supply of fresh water is limited.)

One of the best things about houseboating is that you don't have to be a skilled sailor to handle the craft. Almost any landlubber can master it with little more than an hour at the wheel. Rental operators claim that "if you can drive a car, you can drive a houseboat." For some cruising areas, however, operators require previous boating experience. If you are playing skipper for the trip, it's helpful to study the route in advance, and to try cruising around a day or so before taking a more ambitious trip.

In general food is not provided. You can bring supplies from home and replenish perishables at stores near the marina. Before setting out, make certain you receive a list of what the operator will provide. Are bedding and linens included? (You may want to bring sleeping bags anyway so you can sleep on deck under the stars.)

You may want to ask about the size of the refrigerator, the amount of stow-away space, if there are guard rails, where to get maps, whether fishing licenses are required, and what recreational equipment is on board.

Other useful items you won't want to be without are two pairs of tennis shoes (one pair is usually wet), suntan lotion, sunscreen, sunglasses, a portable radio for news from civilization, a lantern, flashlight, and sports gear.

So—park your car, board your floating home, stow your provisions, check your fuel level, fill the ice chest, and figure out the bow from the stern. Anchors aweigh!

Reminders
Check the extent and arrangement of the sleeping quarters beforehand. Make sure your maps detail the location of channels, harbors, anchorages, and marinas. Be sure to find out what safety euqipment is on board and if there is an auxiliary generator. Ask about the cost of fuel, how much you'll need for the cruise you plan, and where it's available. You should find out if rentals apply toward purchase—just in case you decide you want to own a dream houseboat of your own.

ARIZONA

LAKE POWELL RESORTS & MARINAS, DEL E. WEBB RECREATIONAL PROPERTIES, P.O. Box 29040, Phoenix, AZ 85038. (800) 528-6154; in AZ, (602) 278-8888.

Lake Powell, formed by damming the Colorado River, stretches from northern Arizona well into southern Utah, and lies at the center of the highest concentration of national parks, national monuments, landmarks, and historic sites in the U.S. Often described as a "Grand Canyon with water," this 186-mile-long reservoir boasts 96 major side canyons and 1,960 miles of shoreline, At its land-accessible marinas on Lake Powell—Wahweap, Bullfrog, Hall's Crossing, and Hite—houseboats (36' to 50') may be rented for cruising on the unbelievably beautiful Lake Powell. They come completely equipped with cooking utensils, dishes, and instruction is included. The marinas offer full-service facilities, lodging, optional boat tours, rentals, and powerboats which can be towed behind houseboats. Guide service makes for excellent striper, largemouth bass, walleye, and crappie fishing. You can cruise to Rainbow Bridge National Monument, the world' tallest natural bridge and Lake Powells' biggest attraction. Seasonal discounts 25% to 40% apply Oct.-May (dates vary at each marina). (See also *River Running*—Del E. Webb Wilderness River Adventures, AZ.)

ARIZONA
NEVADA

PLAYMATE RESORT MARINAS, 730 S. Cypress St., La Habra, CA 90631. (800) 752-9669 in CA only, or (213) 691-2235.

Two truly beautiful and unique lakes created by dams on the Colorado River, Mohave and Mead, are best explored from the deck of a houseboat with all the comforts of home. Mohave Lake, above Davis Dam, offers 237 miles of everchanging shoreline. Cruise the waters at your leisure—pause at sandy beaches and view sheet rock cliffs "that vault hundreds of feet piercing the blue sky." When you tire of cruising, use the houseboat as a home base for waterskiing, swimming, or fishing. Lake Mead above Hoover Dam on the Arizona/Nevada border, half an hour from Las Vegas, is another vacationer's delight with its 550 miles of shoreline. Anglers come here for striped bass. You can water ski or fish between the rock walls of the Grand Canyon by day, and settle down in the comfort of your houseboat by night. Weekly rates in 6- and 10-sleepers from $585-$1,550/week depending upon the season. Year round activities.

CALIFORNIA

HERMAN & HELEN'S MARINA, Venice Island Ferry-A, Stockton, CA 95209. (209) 951-4634.

With 71% of their business from previous customers or referrals, it's obvious that this marina provides a service people like. The staff gives personal attention to each one, helping them choose the route they want in the thousand-mile network of beautiful waterways of the Delta which irrigate the San Joaquin Valley. The centrally located marina is one of the oldest and largest, dating back to 1935 when "river rat" shorty Davis established it as a fishing resort. You can rent pontoon houseboats ranging from 26 feet (which sleep 4) to 42 feet (sleep 10) for summer rates from $565 to $1,025 per week. Spring, fall, and winter rates are less. The boats are designed for convenience, comfort, and safety, with roomy interiors and the entire roof a deck

CALIFORNIA   for sunbathing. It's about a 2-hour drive from the Bay Area to this dreamy holiday of exploring hidden coves and mysterious bayous or just plain loafing.

PLAYMATE RESORT MARINAS, 730 So. Cypress St., La Habra, CA 90631. (800) 752-9669 in CA only, or (213) 691-2235.   In a fully equipped houseboat supplied by PlayMate, you can explore Lake Shasta in northern California, the state's largest lake, or the California Delta, a 1,000-mile network of rivers, tributaries, and channels two hours from San Francisco. At Shasta, you float along some of the 370 miles of shoreline past abandoned mines and wooded shores. Or take out your tackle and catch some of 17 varieties of game fish. In the Delta you'll find waters with an "unusual charm," say these houseboat specialists. "It seems not to have been sullied yet by the trappings of civilization." The Delta waterways also are inhabited by a variety of fish—catfish, striped bass, sturgeon—and you'll find fine restaurants and historic river towns. "Bring food and friends and you're on your way." Year round boating. May-Sep. rates in 6- and 10-sleepers from $545-$1,550/week.

FLORIDA   **SUNSHINE LINE INC.,** Dept. A.T., P.O. Box 3558, Deland, FL 32723. Att.: T.W. Adolph. (904) 736-9422.
        Bring binoculars and a camera. You'll glimpse blue herons among the water hyacinths, startle a sunbathing turtle, follow the flight of egrets, or spot a shy manatee. Bright butterflies, exotic wildflowers, and iridescent dragonflies flitting over mirror-smooth backwaters highlight the scene as you drift past cypress groves veiled with Spanish moss. In this nature world on the St. Johns River you tie up at friendly fish camps, swim or skindive in crystal-clear springs, do some water skiing, or try your luck at angling—it's called the "Bass Capitol of the World." The lazy cruise houseboats are equipped with heat, air conditioning, hot water, linens, cooking utensils, gas range, refrigerator, deck barbecue, dinghy, swimming ladder, and rooftop sundeck. Weekly rates: $727-$971 for 5, $1,081-$1,444 for 10, Mar.-Oct.; also daily, midweek, and low-season rates.

NEW YORK   **REMAR RENTALS, INC.,** 510 Theresa St. Clayton, NY 13624. Att.: Robert V. Lashomb. (315) 686-3579.
        Gather friends and family and board your very own boat—the *River Queen, Sea Going,* or *Stardust*—for a cruise of "America's Scenic Playland," the Thousand Islands. With access to over 1,800 islands, you can drop anchor to frolic on bathing beaches, enjoy water (or land) sports, go berrypicking in the woods, and visit the area's numerous historic sites. Or drop a hook and fish for bass, pike, pickerel, muskie, and perch. Cruise the St. Lawrence Seaway or traverse the Rideau Canal to the Ottawa River. All boats are fully equipped with linen, utensils, TV, electric heater. Weekly rate for 38- to 55-foot houseboats: $800 to $1,250 weekly; weekend, $400-$625; mid-week, $475-$675. Jun.-Sep. Also powerboat rentals. Rates: for 18-foot supersports with 70 horsepower motors: $70/day, $420/week. Off-service discounts. "For the third year in a row, we rented a houseboat from Remar. We can't say enough about the owners. They

and their staff have been most accommodating, reports one couple from New York.

TENNESSEE   **DALE HOLLOW MARINA,** Rt. 1, Box 94, Celina, TN 38551. Att.: Jan Chapin, (615) 243-2211.

Dale Hollow Lake spills into both Tennessee and Kentucky, creating a perfect houseboating getaway for those who like to fish, swim, and cruise a scenic shoreline. In summer the water is 80 degrees, and fishermen hook largemouth and smallmouth bass, lake and rainbow trout, muskie, walleye, and catfish. Jan Chapin recommends "spring for the best fishing, summer for recreation and family fun, and fall for breathtakingly beautiful scenery." The 48' *Voyageur* accommodates 10 and comes equipped with everything but towels. Rates $795/week Memorial Day-Labor Day; $495 off season. DHM orients new skippers to their craft and maintains a "ship's store" for groceries, camping supplies, and boating needs. Mar.-Nov.

JET BOATING

Gentle spray tingles your face. The breeze blows your hair. The sun's warming rays keep you from shivering as you glide smoothly over riffles in the sparkling water or sway sharply as your jetboat hits the big rapids.

You are heading back upriver after several days of rafting, kayaking, or canoeing downstream. Or perhaps your destination is a river lodge accessible only by water or charter flights to an airstrip. Or you're simply on a day's outing to see and enjoy a strikingly beautiful canyon.

Jetting up as well as down the Rogue and Main Salmon rivers and through Hells Canyon of the Snake gives you an exhilarating, scenic, enjoyable, exciting, and leisurely ride. In an hour you can cover a distance that could take you all day to run on a raft. If you're jetting to a river lodge or fishing camp, you gain vacation time at your destination through the jet vs. rafting approach.

The outfitters listed below are expert in navigating the wild white water. Whether for just a day or longer, they will give you a great wilderness experience.

Reminders

Some trips are scheduled on a daily basis; others (custom trips) may be planned especially for your family or group. Outfitters can arrange overnights at river lodges (which in some cases are their own), and can handle logistics for overnight campouts.

IDAHO

HELD'S CANYON TOURS, P.O. Box 1961, Lewiston, ID 83501. Att.: Gary Watson. (208) 743-0890.

Many years of experience on the Snake through Hells Canyon have made it more fascinating than ever for Gary Watson. He loves to tell people about the old timers who once lived at a particular spot, and chances are you'll climb up the bank to check on an old foundation or some remnant of early ranching in the canyon. You see the place Chief Joseph led the Nez Perce Indians across the river—the braves on horseback and women and children floating over on rafts made of horsehide. You learn about the early miners. But most of all you feel the depth of the canyon—the world's deepest river gorge with walls up to 7,900 feet. Gary provides snacks along the way and a delicious picnic lunch his wife prepared that morning. "This was our 7th trip west," writes a New Jersey couple, "and our trip with Gary was the highlight of them all." Rates: $80/adult, $40/10 yrs. or under.

SALMON RIVER LODGE, P.O. Box 348, Jerome, ID 83338. Att.: Dave Giles. (208) 324-3553.

In the spring, when the big game animals are still down along the Main Salmon River and the wildflowers are out, Dave takes jet boaters on scenic trips. They camp on the riverbank, stop at old ranches in the roadless wilderness, and visit with the people. You see

Indian paintings on the rocks, hike in to old mining cabins, and bathe in hot springs. In both spring and fall, (Feb./Mar., Oct./Nov.) jet boating and camping along the Salmon is a favorite pasttime among steelhead fishermen. The fish run from 6 to 20 pounds. To get there, drive from the town of Salmon along the river to Corn Creek campground, and crank the roadside phone for jet boat pickup. (See also *Pack Trips, River Running*.)

OREGON

HELLS CANYON ADVENTURES, P.O. Box 159, Oxbrow, OR 97840. Att.: Gary Armacost. (800) HCA-FLOT or (503) 785-3352 (in OR).

"Sign up only if you're ready for action," warns Gary Armacost of his jet boating excursions. He offers 2-hour or all-day jet boat scenic tours. You visit the "awesome" Hells Canyon from the comfort of a covered power boat. The 2-hour trip is for anyone—from infants to grandmothers. During the tour, you see an ancient Indian village, learn about the geology of the area, and look into the deepest part of the canyon to Pittsburgh Landing, negotiating 4-plus rapids. See ancient Indian writings and early-day homesteads. At Kirkwood, enjoy the Living History Museum. Accessible for the camper and fisherman. Daylong and overnight charters. Lodge accommodation and fishing on the Snake and Salmon rivers. Prices, lodging, and transportation information on request. (See also *Combo Trips*.)

Jet boating, a favorite sport on the Rogue— *Court's Rogue River Trips, OR.*

JERRY'S ROGUE RIVER JET BOATS & WHITE WATER TRIPS, Box 1011, Gold Beach, OR 97444. Att.: Bill McNair (503) 247-7601 or 247-4571.

You'll grope for your sunglasses just minutes after leaving Gold Beach fog as your jet boat whips upriver into the Rogue's rigged backcountry loved by Herbert Hoover and made famous by Zane Grey. Occasionally guides neutralize the engines so you can observe sea lions, deer, bears, eagles, and ospreys in quietude; spot landmarks of 1850's Indian conflicts; or be regaled with tales of early miners and other river folk. On the 64-mile round trip you lunch at a river lodge in Agness. Trip rate: $22.50/adult, $10/child 4-11. Smaller boats churn 20 miles further along upriver through masses of white water: 104 miles round trip, $45/adult, $20/child. May-Oct. Group rates.

SAILING SCHOOLS

You're captain of a 25-foot sailboat. You're at the tiller, keeping the boat headed for a marker on a distant shore before tacking in another direction. Your crew is capably handling the mainsail and jib. The sun is bright, the wind is strong, and best of all, you're right on course.

It's hard to believe that until a few days ago your closest approach to sailboats was the America's Cup Race on your TV screen. What swiftly turned you from spectator to seafarer was a stint at a sailing school where the emphasis is on learning by doing.

There are many choices. If there's a decent-sized body of water somewhere near you, most likely there's a sailing school. If you've never sailed and want to learn, or if you've mastered the basics and are ready for more sophisticated seamanship, there are schools on both east and west coasts that teach everything from tacking to celestial navigation and competitive racing.

Most courses combine classroom sessions with firsthand, on-the-water experience and can be scheduled to suit your needs—over a period of several weekends or in one intensive week. For the old salt, there are refresher courses and specialized clinics. Most of the services we've listed here give courses that qualify you for bareboat chartering. However, teaching landlubbers the techniques is the prime concern.

It's surprising how quickly you can pick up the fundamentals. At first the endless list of nautical terms can be daunting, but after a few days of instruction, you'll be slinging the lingo like an oldtimer.

Once you have mastered the basics, you're ready to go cruising. How about a two-day introductory course, followed by a five-day cruise through the Caribbean's British Virgin Islands? Or a week weaving your way through California's Channel Islands? Or learning to handle a yacht on the pristine waters of Maine's Penobscot Bay? These are only a few of the opportunities available.

While the emphasis is always on learning to sail, other pleasures are not ignored. In some courses you do all your cooking on board over an alcohol stove. In others, you stop each night at a luxurious resort where you'll savor the efforts of a European-trained chef. And don't forget the swimming, snorkeling, hiking, bird watching, and just plain reveling in the joy of being away from the mundane concerns of daily life.

Little preparation is necessary for a stint at a sailing school, since the school takes care of everything. Just bring casual clothing and a positive attitude. If you're heading for a warm-weather destination, you'll probably spend most of your on-board time in a bathing suit and, of course, layers of sunblock. In cooler climates, jeans and a sweater or sweatshirt will do the trick.

One necessity is a pair of non-slip deck shoes. You'll be clambering up and down ladders, over railings, and across the sometimes precariously-tilted decks. Like a set of functional snow tires, deck shoes give you the traction you need regardless of how wet the surface is. And speaking of wetness, take along raingear.

Once you've gotten a taste of the salt air, you might well be hooked on the lures of sailing. It's a sport that will take you as far as you want to go. You can master the historic art of chart reading. You can learn to steer by the stars. Ask any yachtsman and he'll agree: There's no end to the possibilities.

A week at a sailing school, and, who knows? It just might change your life.

A billowing "class-room" for seagoing students—*California Sailing Academy, CA*.

CALIFORNIA   **CALIFORNIA SAILING ACADEMY,** 14025 Panay Way, Marina Del
Rey, CA 90291. Att.: Paul J. Miller, (213) 821-3433.
    For year-round, 7-days-a-week sailing instruction, call CSA's
comprehensive sailing center and club. Their curriculum covers basic
to advanced sailing, racing, coastal piloting, celestial navigation,
seminars and clinics on selected topics, and 2- to 10-day cruising
courses in California's Channel Islands, the Baja Peninsula, Mexico's
offshore islands, and Hawaii. Their impressive fleet of 16- and 40-foot
sailing yachts are "classrooms" for instruction or may be chartered for
bareboat or skippered cruises. "We teach in all weathers—private or
group lessons, some of them college-accredited," says Director and
former Annapolis sailing coach Paul Miller. "Video replays are part of
the program so that students can actually see why they won or lost a
game." A 14-hour beginner, cruising, or racing course is $199.
American Sailing Assn. accreditation available to students.

FLORIDA   **ADVENTURE SAILING ESCAPE,** P.O. Box 06079, Ft. Myers, FL
33906. Att.: Ron Drake. (813) 489-0344.
    So you dream of sailing southern seas but haven't yet mastered such
terms as jib, sheet, stay, tiller, tack, or coming about? No need to join
the Navy. Get your instruction with a week of hands-on,
learning-by-doing, flotilla sailing which includes such delights as
docking each night at world-famous luxury resorts on barrier
islands—Sanibel, Captiva, Gasparilla, Estero, and Useppa. Your
classroom is the table at breakfast and dinner, your boat anchored at
the dock, and at sea during follow-up radio—never far from the
ocean-blue eyes and Dutch-accented radio commands of your
ever-attentive Fleetmaster, Jacques Rollfs. You learn basic sailing
techniques, docking under power, chart reading, and radio operation,
how to navigate between channel markers, determine the direction of
currents, hoist sails, and other seaworthy skills. As you progress, you
have plenty of time for free sailing. Diplomas are granted in Basic
Sailing and Basic Coastal Cruising in an optional certification
program. Rates: 4 days, $425; 7 days, $690-$920. Year round. Arrival:
Ft. Myers. (See also *Boat Charters*.)

MAINE   **MAINE WATERWAYS CAMPS,** Deer Isle Sailing Center, Box 62,
Deer Isle, ME 04627. Att.: Carl W. Selin. (207) 348-2339. [Winter:
(305) 743-4676.]
    Capt. Selin's trips around Penobscot Bay (2 weeks coastal
cruising/camping or 3 weeks advanced sailing) cover all aspects of
sailing in a setting of deep green forests, craggy shorelines, and
countless bays and inlets. Rate: Jul.-Aug., $595 for 2 weeks. Charter
boats include day sailers from 12 feet to cruising vessels 26 feet and
up. MWC also offers a 2-week day-sailing program and a special
racing season. In winter Capt. Selin's instruction moves to the Florida
Keys with Learn-to-Sail weeks for adults. (See also *Canoeing*—Maine
Wilderness Canoe Basin, & *Youth Adventures*.)

MARYLAND   **ANNAPOLIS SAILING SCHOOL,** P.O. Box 3334-ATG, Annapolis,
MD 21403. (800) 638-9192 or (301) 267-7205.
    Sailors please note: Whether you live near the home base for this
sailing school or far away, you'll find an Annapolis Sailing School in

superb sailing waters close by. They are located in San Diego (CA), St. Petersburg and the Keys (FL), Charleston (SC), Galveston Bay (TX), Lake Geneva (WI), Lake of the Ozarks (MO), and St. Croix (VI). The school has taught more than 70,000 people how to sail, cruise, and qualify for bareboat charters since 1959 when it became America's first sailing school. With 22 sailing vacation courses at various levels, it's beginning courses get any landlubber off to a good start. For example: Become a Sailor in One Weekend ($150), and a 5-day New Sailor's Vacation Course ($300). For a sailing-minded family, the Weekend Introduction to Cruising ($295 for 5) may be followed by 5-, 9-, and 10-day cruises. Some packages include accommodations in St. Petersburg, San Diego, Virgin Islands, or Annapolis. Advanced courses include piloting, coastal and celestial navigations, handling a cruising auxiliary, a 5-day preparation for bareboat chartering, MORC and one-design racing, offshore cruising. Whichever your choice, it's a delightful way to learn to sail.

Would-be skippers learning the ropes—
Offshore Sailing School, Ltd., NY.

NEW YORK   **OFFSHORE SAILING SCHOOL, LTD.**, Dept. AT, East Schofield St., City Island, NY 10464. (800) 221-4326 or (212) 885-3200.
      Vacationer alert: You need not be a resident of New York City to take advantage of Offshore's sailing instruction. These experts, who started their service in 1964, now operate branches in some of your

NEW YORK   favorite vacation spots—Newport (RI), Bar Harbor (ME), Captiva
                        Island and Bay Point (FL) Tortola (BVI), and City Island (NY). What a
                        way to take a holiday—learning sailing techniques (basic to advanced)
                        while enjoying the attractions of resort life. "OSS takes hard-core
                        urbanites and transforms them into skippers in less than a week," says
                        New York Magazine. The smooth incorporation of thorough
                        instruction with a weeklong vacation is their specialty." Rates
                        $395-$525; (tuition only; packages including accommodations
                        available). For its graduates OSS organizes bareboat and crewed
                        charters in New England, the Caribbean, and Europe.

WINDJAMMERS

You're helping to cat the anchor—quicker to say than to do on a high-masted sailing ship. You sail from the harbor under power—then, with power off, all is quiet except for the lapping of waves in the spanking breeze. With a dozen (or so) other "sailors," you heave ho on the mainsheet to hoist the sail.

Later, under the captain's not-thoroughly-trusting eye, you'll take a trick at the wheel. But for the moment, it's a delicious feeling to lie back in the sun, throw your cares to the wind, and listen to the splash of the water as you sail effortlessly across the open sea. Today's destination: a quiet lagoon somewhere on a tropical island—it really doesn't matter which one.

Whether the lure is cruising the Caribbean from one tropical isle to another, sailing the New England coast and putting in at old whaling ports, plying the inland freshwaters of Lake Champlain, or exploring the fjords of the Inside Passage to Alaska, sailing in "tall ships" abounds with romance. Columbus you're not, but you can't resist imagining what it must have been like 500 years ago—sailing, for all you knew, to the edge of the world, but fortunately sighting a palm-fringed tropical island instead, much like the one you are heading for today. You think of buccaneers and buried treasure and of landings at Plymouth Rock.

Windjammers were the engineless sailing ships first built to haul cargo in the 1800s. Once hailed derisively by steamer crews, the stately two- or three-masted ships have been thoroughly refurbished since their freight carrying days, or newly built in the design of the originals. Today they are welcomed with cries of delight and have great appeal for seafaring vacations.

Today's windjammer provides passenger comforts such as cabins with two to four bunks and hot-and-cold running water, electric lights, hot showers and tiled heads. Well-equipped galleys turn out from good to gourmet meals for seagoing appetites. A sailing skiff provides extra activity at anchor, and a launch transports passengers ashore to visit villages or to sunbathe and swim at a sandy beach.

For the romance of reliving the sailor's life of yesteryear with the comforts of today, windjammers give you a get-a-way that can't be beat.

CALIFORNIA   **OCEAN VOYAGES, INC.,** 1709 Bridgeway, Sausalito, CA 94965. Att.: Mary Crowley. (415) 332-4681.

Ocean Voyages has a worldwide network of boats, skippers, and crews, including beautiful schooners, ketches, and square-riggers, for sailing the world's oceans. Captains who are experienced instructors are carefully chosen. "This is the element that turns our cruises into windjamming with a difference," says director Mary Crowley. You learn the finer points of marlinspike sailing on classic yachts. Seamanship, navigation, whale and porpoise behavior, marine biology, and scuba may all be part of a windjamming experience. "Sailing on a fine schooner or square-rigger is a handsome, incredible

adventure," Crowley adds. "It allows a type of exploration of beautiful oceanic areas that can be experienced no other way." (See also *Boat Charters*.)

NEW ENGLAND **COASTING SCHOONER HERITAGE,** Box 482-G, Rockland, ME 04841. Att.: Capts. Douglas K. & Linda J. Lee. (207) 594-8007.

You can just take it easy, or help raise and lower the sails, haul the anchor aboard, and learn to steer the *Heritage*—master of your own windship! Newest schooner to cruise the Maine coast, the 94-foot *Heritage* was launched in April 1983 at Rockland's North End Shipyard in which the Lees are partners—a yard committed to building or rebuilding 19th century sailing vessels. With the comfort of passengers in mind, the cabins (13 doubles, 2 triples, 1 single) were designed with standing headroom, electric lights, and running water sinks. A hot shower is forward, and a large skylight brightens the well-equipped galley. A powered yawl boat and two 18-foot sailing or rowing wherries ferry passengers to islands for a lobster bake or to explore. Jun.-Sep., $395/week; Jul.-Aug., $445/week. No children under 16. Shipyard near airport and bus station; free wharf parking.

DIRIGO CRUISES, Dept. G, 39 Waterside Lane, Clinton, CT 06413. Att.: Capt. Eben Whitcomb. (800) 845-5520 (ask for Mary) or (203) 669-7068.

Capt. Whitcomb makes sailors out of landlubbers on romantic, high-masted ships which sail the Maine coast and Long Island Sound, the Caribbean, and out of Key West. "Come aboard," he urges. "Slip away from homeport and glide from one exotic island to another. Bathe in the sea, the sun, and the trade wind breeze. Unwind and relax as we anchor each evening in a guiet lagoon." Good food, good companions, and as much sailorizing as you can digest are the order of the day as well as launch trips ashore. You'll soon talk about catting the anchor, hoisting sail, and even taking a trick at the wheel—unless, of course, you just lounge on deck. For a week of East Coast sailing in summer the rate is $450; and for a week of winter sailing from St. Thomas in the Virgin Islands, St. Maarten in the Netherlands Antilles, or Tortola in the British Virgins, rates are $475-$630. Day and sunset cruises out of Key West run $20-$35, less for seniors and children. The Schooners *Harvey Gamage, Charlotte Ann, Belle Blonde, Rachel & Ebenezer*, and *Appledore* are among the tall ships which Capt. Whitcomb is booking.

MAINE WINDJAMMER CRUISES, INC., P.O. Box 617-CA, Camden, ME 04843, Att.: Capt. Les Bex. (207) 236-2938.

"Our ships, the proud *Mattie* (veteran of the West Indies fruit trade) and the doughty *Mercantile*, are Yankee merchantmen, clipper-bowed and able, with billowing sails and hempen rigging," writes Capt. Bex, who has operated sailing vacations since 1935. "The area we cruise, Penobscot Bay and adjacent waters, is well protected. We sail the coastal waters, not the high seas." Discover Maine's magnificent islands and rugged coastline as you cruise through her bays and sounds. For seagoing appetites there are New England family-style meals—fish, chowders, chicken, roasts, ham—all cooked in the galley

A glorious way to cruise the Caribbean—*Capt. Arthur M. Kimberly for Kimberly Cruises, Virgin Islands.*

NEW ENGLAND   on a wood-burning stove. A lobster bake on shore is a highlight of the
cruise. Ships accommodate 26-29 people, with cabins for 2-4. Per
person rates for 6/day cruises are $395, Jul.-Aug.; $355, Jun. & Sep.
Minimum age: 12, accompanied by adult. Also special "vagabond
cruises" for 6 guests aboard the 40-foot *Mistress* ($420/person). No
minimum age on the *Mistress* if you charter the whole boat.

OUT O'MYSTIC SCHOONER CRUISES, 7 Holmes St., Mystic. CT
06355. (800) 243-0416.
Listen carefully for that little voice which says, "Really, who'll miss
you for just a few li'l ol' days?" That's the advice of P. J. Matthews,
owner of the *Mystic Whaler* which carries 44 passengers, and the
Mystic Clipper with quarters for 56. The two-masted, gaff-rigged
schooners sail from Mystic, CT, May through October, and from
Annapolis, MD, April to November. Cruise the sheltered coastal
waters of Long Island Sound with its historic ports of call. Or sail in
Chesapeake Bay—"a timeless estuary with crab fleets, skipjacks,
oyster fleets, and picturesque shoreline." Informality is the keynote.
Wear old clothes—dungarees, sneakers, a bathing suit, shorts. Loll in
the sun, read a good book, or get involved in setting sails, steering,
and handling lines aboard. Both schooners have private and coed
quarters, hot and cold running water wash basins, and tiled heads and
showers. The "Sneak Away" cruises are scheduled from overnight
($59 and up) to 5 days ($385 and up); dinner cruises weekends, $39.

SCHOONER AMERICAN EAGLE, Box 482-Y, Rockland, ME 04841.
Att.: Capt. John C. Foss. (207) 594-8007 or 7617.
Built in 1930 as a Gloucester fishing schooner, the 92-foot *American
Eagle* is Maine's newest restoration for passenger service. The grace
and history of a 50-year career at sea are complemented by 14
comfortable cabins for 28 guests, amenities such as running water, a
shower, rowboats for exploring, and space for your windsurfer. The
large galley forwards seat everybody, the panelled main cabin aft has
a potbelly stove. 1986 is her first year carrying passengers, and she is
expected to charge around the bay in grand manner. Typical cruising
ground includes Penobscot Bay area, Bar Harbor, Boothbay Harbor,
Mt. Desert, and up the coast. Per person rates for 6-day cruise,
$375-$450, Jun.-Sep. Or cruise with the Tall Ships to New York City
on Operation Sail over Fourth of July, 1986: $1,500. Free parking at
wharf in Rockland.

SCHOONER HOMER W. DIXON, Box 787-AG, Burlington, VT
05402. Att.: Capts. Doug Greason & Pegeen Mulhern. (802) 862-6918.
A new way to enjoy the Green Mountains, the Adirondacks, and
Lake Champlain: Sail aboard the Schooner *Homer W. Dixon* on the
only freshwater windjammer cruise in America. Expect invigorating
sailing, wonderful freshwater swimming, unbeatable mountain
scenery, and a region rich in history. The schooner accommodates 24
guests in 12 comfortable double cabins, and gives them outstanding
food plus "a crew and a pair of captains who truly care," comments a
recent new sailor. Sail, swim, sunbathe, or just relax. Anchor each
night in a different harbor. Enjoy a summer jaunt or take an autumn

Freshwater cruising on Lake Champlain—
Schooner Homer W. Dixon, VT.

foliage cruise, or a special cruise for birdwatching, lake history, and photography. Cruise 3, 4, and 6 days on Lake Champlain, Jun.-Oct., Rates: $235-$400. Burlington departures; easy access by car, ferry, plane, or train.

SCHOONER ISAAC H. EVANS, Box 482-G, Rockland, ME 04841. Att.: Capt. Edward B. Glaser. (207) 594-8007.

"Spend a relaxing week on an old-time sailing vessel," urges the captain. "We sail the Maine coast during the day and find a snug harbor for the night." The *Issac H. Evans*, built in 1886, spent years freighting and oystering in Delaware Bay. She has recently been rebuilt and rerigged. You board on Sundays for Monday sailings, and return on Saturday. Jun. & Sep., $360/week; Jul-Aug., $435/week. Free parking near the harbor. Arrive Rockland by air or bus.

SCHOONER LEWIS R. FRENCH, Box 482-G, Rockland, ME 04841. Att.: Capt. Dan Pease. (207) 594-8007.

Built in 1871 as a cargo vessel for Maine ports, the 64-foot *Lewis R. French* is New England's oldest two-masted schooner. Structurally, though, she's a new ship, having been rebuilt from the keel up in 1976 and gracefully refurbished for *sailing*—there's no inboard engine. Below deck are 10 small but comfortable cabins accommodating 2 guests each and "a galley forward and potbelly stove back aft in the main cabin," For going ashore, there's a 14-foot motor-powered yawl, also a sailing rowboat. Discover the beauty of Penobscot Bay from the deck. Enjoy home cooking from the wood-burning cook stove; luxuriate in hot showers; feast on a lobster cookout. For 3-day cruise, $245; 6-day cruises, $435 mid-season, lower rates Jun. and Sep. Whole boat charters available.

NEW ENGLAND   **SCHOONER NATHANIEL BOWDITCH,** Res. Dept., Harborside, ME 04642. (207) 326-4098.

"Discover the glory of Penobscot Bay with some salty characters who make their marvelous vessel yours for a week," encourages an enthusiastic vacationer. The 81-foot schooner, built in East Boothbay in 1922 and completely refitted in 1973, sails Maine's coastal islands where "the air is so clear and the sea so blue that you use all your film in one day," continues our vacationer. "You can help sail, and the food is terrific and never-ending. The captain spins yarns like a real Mainer." Wind and tide determine the itinerary, with each evening spent anchored in a new place—a deserted island, a fishing village, a deluxe yacht basin. Six-day cruises, boarding Sunday evening for Monday sailing are $350/person, Jun. & Sep.: $415 Jul. & Aug. Also charters and 3-day cruises, $225.

NEW YORK   **APPLEDORE,** P.O. Box 1414, Southampton, NY 11968. Att.: France Posener. (516) 283-6041.

The Schooner *Appledore* was built in Maine in 1978 along the lines of the famed New England ships of the 19th century: 86 feet long, beam of 20 feet, gaff-rigged, cabins for 16 passengers, 35 on day sails. On overnight cruises to Block island, RI, and Mystic, CT, passengers combine shipboard life with island sightseeing, cycling, and swimming. The *Appledore* follows the sun south in winter, with week-long fully-crewed cruises among various Caribbean islands. "Lay back and soak up the sun, sound and salt," urges Posener, "or help with setting the sails and heading into the wind. It's sheer beauty and contentment sailing the *Appledore*." Jul.-Aug., day and twilight sails from Montauk (eastern tip of Long island), $17. Dec.-Mar. 7-day inter-island cruise, $450 ($500 with scuba package).

The Schooner *Harvey Gamage* sails among Caribbean islands— *Dirigo Cruises, CT.*

BRITISH
COLUMBIA

BLUEWATER ADVENTURES, 1616 Duranleau St., Vancouver, B.C., Canada V6H 3S4. Att.: Dan Culver. (604) 689-7238.

On a luxuriously appointed 68-foot ketch with private staterooms, you sail up fjords to glaciers and spectacular waterfalls and among uninhabited islands of the fabled Inside Passage. Spot whales, porpoises, seals, and sea lions. Drop anchor around 4 p.m. to fish, swim, or explore the shore. It's a carefree life with gourmet meals, (May-Oct., 9 days, all-inclusive, $1,050.) Also, a 6-day cruise, May & Oct., to the Gulf Islands ($550) and a 10-day sailing adventure to see killer whales, totem poles, and a rich natural environment. "We loved every minute of it," says a couple from Vancouver. "We saw killer whales and dolphins, as well as dozens of bald eagles. All the scenery was magnificent, and the skipper and cook surpassed what was expected of them—they will be fondly remembered for years to come." Rates in U.S. dollars. Bring sleeping gear. Charters available. Arrival: Vancouver. (See also *River Running*—Whitewater Adventures.)

CARIBBEAN

KIMBERLY CRUISES, Box 5086-A, St. Thomas, VI 00801. Att.: Capt. Arthur M. Kimberly. (809) 776-8138 (evenings).

The 90-foot brigantine *Romance* is a spectacular re-creation in cordage and canvas of a 19th-century sailing vessel, with accommodations for 16 in 2- and 4-berth cabins. *Romance* offers leisurely 7-day Virgin Island cruises from Tortola, Dec.-Apr. and Jun.-Aug., visiting the caves of Robert Louis Stevenson's *Treasure Island*, the wondrous rock formations of the Baths, the wreck of the Rhone, the great barrier reef at Gorda Sound, and more. Nov. and May she cruises the Grenadines, Windward and Leeward Islands. Among the highlights: jungle rivers, virgin beaches, volcanic islands, whaling stations, and savory French-West Indian cuisine. Cruise rates, 7 days $500/person in 4-berth cabin, $550 in 2-berth. Single, group, & family bookings. Longer sail training, marine biology, and special-interest charters for colleges, camps, and clubs. "*Romance* has circumnavigated twice in the last few years," relates Capt. Kimberly, "who has sailed the ship for 20 years, "and our atmosphere, cuisine, and decor reflect the exciting island worlds of the South Pacific and the Orient."

CANOEING / KAYAKING

You are paddling down a slow, meandering river. A brimmed cap shades your eyes, a lifevest hugs your body. Your waterproof duffels with all your camping gear are securely tied to the canoe—easier to retrieve in case you should tip over. As you glide along, the scenery rolls by, one lovely sight after the next. You hear splashing water ahead—louder—then you see the rapids. Your companion points with his paddle to the smooth-water tongue, bordered by froth. Aiming for it, you slide into the turbulence, using your paddles to steer around rocks and maintain balance. You make it—and resume the gentle paddling rhythm.

These are the exciting moments that make canoeing on whitewater rivers sportier than paddling on lakes. Experts tell you that up to Class I or II water, canoeing is the way to go; beyond that, they paddle kayaks.

The easy accessibility of canoe waters and the liveries which service paddlers have turned some 11-million people into canoeists. But the largest single canoeing region in the world is not one with many rivers, but one with thousands of lakes.

A 100-mile watery boundary separates Ontario's Quetico Provincial Park from Minnesota's Boundary Waters Canoe Area (BWCA). For wilderness travel on smooth water, the BWCA is the canoeist's nirvana. The interlocking lakes, joined by not-too-difficult (usually) portages, cover over 1 million acres in Minnesota alone, with 1,200 miles of canoe trails.

Among the best known whitewater rivers are those down the rugged 92-mile corridor of Maine's Allagash Wilderness Waterway, in the churning waters of Appalachians, or through rapids of western rivers—the Snake, Salmon, Owyhee, Rogue, and rivers in California, and in Canada.

Whereas most canoe liveries on river systems are concerned primarily with equipment rentals and shuttle service to put-in and take-out points, the BWCA outfitters have developed ultra-light outfitting that is unmatched. So complete is it that you need arrive only with the clothing you want to take along. Park your car in the outfitter's lot, order canoeing and camping equipment, check off the menu list for the meals you want each day (they come freeze-dried or dehydrated), and within an hour of arrival you're on your way. If you prefer starting at a remote lake in the vast wilderness, they'll fly you in. At the rate of $30 a day or less, it's hard to find a better or less expensive vacation.

If you're a novice, you should be aware that the same streamlining that lets a canoe cut through the water with ease also makes it more likely to overturn. So lifevests are essential, and swimming skills come in handy. It's wise to put a change of clothing in a waterpoof duffel, tied down in case you get dunked. If you're worried about purchasing expensive gear, don't. You can rent everything you'll need for a vacation at moderate cost.

Not every canoe trip however, must be a do-it-yourself excursion with rental equipment. As the following pages indicate, some outfitters and guides take you on fully provisioned trips in great and wild areas—from the Allagash to the Everglades to the Rio Grande to Alaska's Brooks Range.

The sport of kayaking is equally rewarding, and not difficult to master with the proper guidance. Your waterproof cocoon carries you down the most turbulent of rivers—with plenty of opportunity to demonstrate the topsy-turvy Eskimo roll.

Many canoeing and kayaking programs

A glacial backdrop for kayakers and rafters alike—Hayden Kaden for Alaska Discovery, Inc., AK.

are structured to start with easy daily runs on gentle water before trying longer distances and rough water. To choose your kind of trip the criteria to consider are the length of the runs, the water levels, and the grade of the rapids. (Class I represents the easiest, and Class VI expert level.)

One of the prime delights of canoeing and kayaking is the stillness—broken only by the rhythmic splash of your paddle, the occasional noise of whitewater rapids, the call of the loon, the wind in the trees, or waves lapping on shore. It's a gentle, close-to-nature vacation.

Reminders
Proper safety for white water includes personal

flotation, a helmet, a spare paddle, proper clothing (wet suits when water or air temperatures are at 50 degrees), and grab loops. Can you handle a canoe or kayak? Set up a wilderness camp? If not, remember that guides are available even in areas where most trips are unguided. Doublecheck rates, tax, dates, canoeing skill needed, pre- and post-trip lodging and car parking. Find out about campsite facilities, maps, charts, and anticipated weather, fishing license, car or canoe shuttle service, safety equipment, and laws concerning wilderness camping in various regions.

Novices may want gloves to prevent blisters, especially for lake paddling. On rivers you get help from the current—sometimes too much! Never throw refuse overboard. Other rules, written or unwritten, on most waterways are: Wear lifejackets, don't mix booze with canoeing, and be sure your skill is equal to the water.

ALASKA

BROOKS RANGE WILDERNESS TRIPS, P.O. Box 40, Bettles, AK 99726. Att.: Dave Schmitz. (907) 692-5312.

"For five days we saw no humans, but we did see grizzlies, moose, caribou, and ospreys," writes a kayaker from Illinois. He paddled down the untraveled Reed River in the Brooks Range with Dave Schmitz, a veteran Arctic explorer who guides canoeing, rafting, and kayak trips in the region. On Noatak, Kobuk, and North Fork trips Dave uses Folbot folding 17' kayaks, sometimes preceding these journeys with backpacking expeditions. On the river floats you see much wildlife, supplement campfare with fresh fish (grayling, pike, sheefish, chum salmon), navigate some good rapids, and pass trappers' cabins as you approach the civilization of an Eskimo village. Most trips 7 days. Rates from $140-$170 and up/day including bush flights. Arrival: Bettles. (See also *Backpacking, Dog Sledding.*)

HUGH GLASS BACKPACKING CO., P.O. Box 110796-AT, Anchorage, AK 99511. Att.: Chuck Ash. (907) 243-1922.

"Our quality-of-service philosophy and the areas we take you to are what set us apart from other Alaskan wilderness companies," says owner Chuck Ash. "We operate our floats through roadless wilderness on the finest waters in Alaska. Our guides are trained in first aid, are experienced wilderness travelers, and Alaskan residents." Ash's kayak trips are in bluewater, mostly in the Kenai Fjords National Park and Prince Williams Sound. Canoe trips are run on road-accessible wilderness rivers in the Kenai Peninsula and in interior Alaska. Most trips are suitable for novices; Brooks Range trips require some canoeing experience. Choose from the John River (10 days, $1,395, Jul.); the Wild River in the Central Brooks Range (7 days, $1,050, Jul.); the Swanson River, an ideal family trip, (5-7 days, adults $125/day, children $95/day May-Oct.). Brooks Range trips originate in Bettles, AK; others start in Anchorage. (See also *Backpacking, Wilderness Expeditions.*)

Kayakers find an island of sea lions in the Kenai fjords—*Hugh Glass Backpacking Co., AK.*

M/V HYAK, Box 2071, Wrangell, AK 99901. Att.: Gary McWilliams. (907) 874-3084 .

With its protected waters, southeast Alaska is a sea kayaker's paradise. The *M/V Hyak* sailing from Ketchikan, offers 7- to 10-day tours to some of its most spectacular, pristine areas. The *Hyak* serves as a mother ship, offering warm lodging and hearty food after each day's kayak adventure. Expect to see glaciers, fjords, marine and terrestrial wildlife, early native American sites, abandoned gold mines, whales, hotsprings, and much more. "We provide an experienced local guide and top line kayaks and related equipment. Participants need bring only suitable clothing," Captain McWilliams explains. He recommends that kayakers be experienced, but this is not required. Trips can be tailored to the abilities of participants. Rate for 4 or less, $650/day including kayaks and guide. (See also *Boat Cruises.*)

SOURDOUGH OUTFITTERS, Box 18-AT, Bettles, AK 99726. Att.: David Ketscher. (907) 692-5252.

With mostly easy Class I water and occasional Class II rapids, the paddling is leisurely on these trips through the majestic Brooks Range wilderness. Sourdough offers 5- to 30-day excursions on the Noatak, Kobuk, Koyukuk, Nigu, Alatna, John, and Wild rivers for small groups. You'll see moose, wolves, black and grizzly bears on shore, and fish for grayling, lake trout, pike, char, salmon, and sheefish. It's a spectacular region of Arctic mountains, treeless tundra plains, steep canyons, and spruce forest. The Alatna, Koyukuk, and Noatak trips may be tacked on to scheduled backpacking trips in the Arrigetch

ALASKA

Peaks and Gates of the Arctic. Cost: $825-$1,980, for 5-16 days. Jun.-Sep. Arrival: Bettles, via Fairbanks. (See also *Backpacking, River Running, Dog Sledding, Ski Touring.*)

ARIZONA

JERKWATER CANOE CO., INC., Box 800, Topock, AZ 86436. Att.: Eloise Roche & Ernie Doiron. (602) 768-7753.

Let Dirty Ernie and Eloise "The Cockroche" arrange a peaceful paddle down a smooth stretch of the Colorado River through the red rock canyons of the Topock Gorge on the borders of California, Arizona, and Nevada year round. Their Jerkwater City Slicker trip is for paddlers who want to leave the city behind but not the comforts. On this 2-day trip spend your days paddling and your evenings in the Jacuzzi at Jerkwater's bunkhouse or at the casinos in Laughlin, a 35-minute drive from Topock. Including gourmet meals and accommodations: $100/adult, $50/child under 10, for 2-day trips (longer trips available). Trips for 2 to 20 persons. "Ernie and Eloise add just the right touch of spice and hospitality to make it a weekend you are happy to recommend to friends and look forward to repeating yourself," says one happy paddler. Canoe rentals/shuttles, too.

The indescribable beauty of kayaking among glaciers—*Alaskan Expeditions, CA.*

CALIFORNIA

ALASKAN EXPEDITIONS, P.O. Box 531, Santa Barbara, CA 93101. Att.: Ragan Callaway. (805) 687-0222.

"There's nothing more breathtaking than floating in a kayak amongst icebergs ridden by seals," writes a woman from Naucalpan, Mexico, who kayaked with Alaskan Expeditions last year. Michael Livingston of Anchorage, recalls waking a sleeping sea otter and her pup as he passed by in his kayak. "The mom dove into the deep blue water, but the little furry ball tried to crawl onto the kayak's slippery deck," he wrote. Outdoor lovers with a high sense of adventure are rewarded by the majestic fjords, glaciers, and indescribable beauty of Prince William Sound in south-central Alaska. You camp on islands and beaches, and at night hear the glacier ice falling into the ocean like the rumble of thunder; but the Sound is protected and the climate is mild for Alaska. Novice kayakers are welcome and will receive qualified instruction. Trips to Nellie Juan Glacier and Blackstone Bay, to Harriman Fjord, Jun.-Jul.; Cost $660/10 days, Jul.-Aug. $490/7 days, including train round trip, Anchorage/Whittier. For 2-8 participants. Discounts for families, groups, early reservations. Bring or rent sleeping bag.

CALIFORNIA RIVERS, P.O. Box 1140, Windsor, CA 95492. Att.: Ann Dwyer. (707) 838-7787.

Besides canoeing, Kiwi kayaking is Ann Dwyer's specialty. The Kiwi, imported from Australia, is a small, stable, easy-to-paddle 8-foot kayak. In spring and summer Dwyer schedules "Kayaking for Timid Souls" classes on a 14-mile stretch of the Russian River, remote yet close to the Bay Area (1-day, $45). Spring weekends kayakers and canoeists paddle a redwood canyon on the Navarro (2 days, $130). They gather on the Eel in June with a specialist in creative art (5 days, $325). In July, it's the Trinity with a 3-day Kiwi base camp ($205), as well as the Klamath for Kiwis and canoes (4 days, $265). Cache Creek in geothermal country near Clear Lake is the spot for 1- and 2-day Kiwi trips in Aug. ($50 & $130). Come alone or bring a friend or family.

MOUNTAIN TRAVEL, 1398-AG Solano Ave., Albany, CA 94706. (800) 227-2384 or (415) 527-8100.

"There are two ways to see Glacier Bay—by kayak or big cruise ship," explains Mountain Travel, "and there's nothing like being in a kayak." On their 8-day Glacier Bay trip—"an endless panorama of snow-covered peaks rising from coastal fjords"—you camp on beaches and explore the ice floes and wilderness in 2-person "non-tippable" kayaks (8 days, Jul.-Aug., $1,090). You can fish and kayak on the Kobuk River above the Arctic Circle—considered the best fishing trip in Alaska—and see Eskimo camps and wildlife (7 days, Aug., $1,775). On a 400-mile expedition along the Brooks Range north slope to Kotzebue Sound, paddle the broad Noatak River (20 days, Jul., $1,965). On another trek by canoe, explore the pristine lakes of Admiralty Island (7 days, $990). Rates cover all but sleeping gear and transport to departure points. No previous canoe or kayak experience necessary. (See also *Backpacking, Mountaineering, River Running-AK, Wilderness Living-AK.*)

COLORADO   **DVORAK EXPEDITIONS,** 17921-AG U.S. Hwy. 285, Nathrop, CO 81236. Att.: Bill Dvorak. (303) 539-6851 or (800) 824-3795 (in CO May-Sep.). [Oct.-Apr.: 1-A Blue Mtn. Rd., Lyons, CO 80540. (303) 823-5126.]

To teach the basics of whitewater kayaking or rafting, Dvorak

A skillful kayaker on the Selway River—*Dvorak Expeditions, CO.*

schedules instructional 6- to 9-day seminars in summer on the Green River through Desolation and Gray canyons (UT), on the Rio Grande (TX) in March, and 1- to 5-day sessions on the Arkansas, Dolores, and Colorado (CO & UT) in summer. The Arkansas River seminars feature pool training at their base in Nathrop. Rates range from $75/1 day to $640/9 days. For "special population" groups with physical or emotional disorders, kayak programs are available on request. Raft support for kayak trips is another Dvorak specialty, as well as supplying guides for competent kayakers not familiar with southwestern rivers. (See also *River Running* and *Youth Adventures*.)

CONNECTICUT   **OUTWARD BOUND, INC.,** 384 Field Point Rd., Greenwich, CT 06830. Att.: Pat Lyren. (800) 243-8520 or (203) 661-0797.

Outward Bound offers four very distinct locations for its canoeing and kayaking expeditions. Hike the Florida Trail and canoe down passages of the Wilderness Waterway into the clear blue waters of Florida Bay in the Everglades: 9 or 21 days, for $650/$1,075. Dec.-Mar. Or whitewater canoe down the Rio Grande River in the Big Bend National Park region on the Texas/Mexico border: 8-22 days, for $600-$950. Dec.-Apr. In Minnesota you'll learn flatwater and whitewater canoeing skills as you travel in the largest inland waterway system in the world: 8-29 days, from $500-$1,600, May-Sep. The remote backcountry lakes and rivers in Maine are ideal locations for canoe expeditions, while sea kayaking takes place off the Maine Coast: 7-22 days, from $700-$1,300, May-Sep. On Outward Bound courses, in addition to canoe and kayak instruction, you'll learn first aid and rescue techniques, navigation, and in some cases, will rock climb and rappel. Canoeing courses are also offered for the disabled, Jun.-Aug. (See also *Mountaineering/Rock Climbing, Wilderness/Nature Expeditions, Youth Adventures*.)

FLORIDA   **EVERGLADES CANOE OUTFITTERS, INC.,** 39801 Ingraham Hwy.,
               C-6, Homestead, FL 33034. Att.: Sheri M. Leach. (305) 246-1530.
               You must leave the road and enter the vast wilderness to truly
               experience Everglades temperate plants, 300 bird species, and
               numerous mammals. Everglades Canoe Outfitters schedule guided
               canoe explorations into the area. "We stress recreation, awareness,
               appreciation, and education," says Sheri Leach. "Most of our guides
               have worked as interpretive naturalists for the National Park Service."
               Special Tropical and Wilderness Waterway exploration trips.
               Oct.-May, 1-12 days. Average rate for guided trips is $65/day
               including instruction, sleeping gear, tents, food, waterproof dry box,
               shuttle service. Self-guided trips about $14/day. Recommends one
               canoeist: "They are very professional and our naturalist guide was
               extremely knowledgeable. He awakened an interest in things which I
               previously thought little about." (See also *Wilderness Living*.)

               FLORIDA TRAIL ASSOCIATION, INC., P.O. Box 13708,
               Gainesville, FL 32604. Att.: Member Services Coordinator. (904)
               378-8823.
               Canoes have carried people and materials on Florida's rivers, lakes,
               and streams for thousands of years. Today's canoeists paddle quiet
               waterways as did the Indians who used the rivers as highways. FTA
               advises members of liveries which provide canoes, paddles, and life
               jackets, and offers free trips to members for a day or longer with
               leaders who share their knowledge of the rivers. Participants bring
               their own canoes and equipment. There's little fast water—a boon to
               the novice. FTA membership: $23/single, $28/family. Canoe trail
               map, $1. (See also *Backpacking*.)

GEORGIA   **WILDERNESS SOUTHEAST,** 711-AG Sandtown Rd., Savannah, GA
               31410. Att.: Dick Murlless. (912) 897-5108.
               "A trip across the Okefenokee," Dick Murlless tells us, "Is a unique
               learning experience. No other swamp has its concentration of wildlife
               and wildflowers. We frequently see large alligators, white ibis,
               sandhill cranes, and osprey." Paddle 5-8 hours daily, with little or no
               current (avg. 11 miles/day) in this freshwater system. Or add the
               Suwannee River; its banks rise higher, channeling the water and
               producing a gentle current—exciting but easy to canoe. All WS
               programs in the swamp are done in cooperation with the U.S. Fish and
               Wildlife Service and the Okefenokee Natonal Wildlife Refuge. Trips
               3-7 days for 10-16 canoeists, average $50/day; bring or rent sleeping
               gear. (Okefenokee trips are not available in the summer.) Canoeing
               trips in the Everglades National Park, an estuary and salt-water
               system, are also offered in Jan. and Feb. Participants paddle among
               mangrove islands, sand beaches, and tidepools. Rates: $50/day
               include 2 guides, food, tents, canoes; bring or rent sleeping gear.
               Group and youth rates. (See also *Backpacking*, Scuba—FL,
               Wilderness Living, *Youth Adventures*.)

MAINE   **ALLAGASH CANOE TRIPS,** P.O. Box AG 713, Greenville ME
               04441. Att.: Warren Cochrane. (207) 695-3668.
               Since 1953 the Cochrane family has been outfitting and guiding

MAINE

trips on the St. John, Allagash, and Penobscot Rivers. Their trips are for all ages: 2-week canoe adventures for teenagers; trips through the Allagash Wilderness for families ("still the best canoeing area in the U.S." they say); excursions for adults; fly-in trips on the wild St. John for everyone; and trips to Quebec's Mistassini and Chamouchouane rivers for experienced canoeists. You receive thorough instruction in technique and handling of wood-canvas or Royalex canoes. The Cochranes provide wholesome meals (fresh produce from their garden and bread baked fresh in a reflector oven) and all equipment except sleeping gear. "Highlights were sharing this adventure with our children, excellent organic foods, learning how to paddle and live well in the wilderness, and conversations around the campfire," recalls one vacationer. Sample rates: Penobscot, 5 days, $205/adult, $135/child; Allagash, 8 days, $415 & $315; St. John, 7-day, fly-in trip, $450 & $350. Also 1- to 9-day custom trips. Experienced guides.

Skillfully maneuvering through some rough water—*Allagash Canoe Trips, ME.*

ALLAGASH WILDERNESS OUTFITTERS, Box 620-A, Star Rt., 76, Greenville, ME 04441. Att.: Rick Givens. (207) 695-2821 message relay via 2-way radio. [Dec.-Apr.: 36-A Minuteman Dr., Millinocket, ME 04462. (207) 723-6622.]

For 19 years, the Givens have been providing canoe/camping equipment and transportation for unguided trips in Maine's North Woods. The St. John River provides plenty of thrills for experienced whitewater canoeists, while the famous Allagash, with both flat water and moderate rapids, is a favorite with the less experienced. Both trips are 7 to 10 days in length. A fine 4-day trip with easy river and lake travel is the Upper West Branch of the Penobscot River. Canoeists also enjoy round trips on the lakes in the area. Complete outfitting, $33/day; canoe only, $13/day. Individual camping items available; transport or car-shuttle extra. Mid-May to Sep.

CHEWONKI FOUNDATION, R.F.D. 3 Wiscasset, ME 04578. Att.: Tim Ellis. (207) 882-7323.

"Building a close, small joyful community is a satisfying and important part of our canoe trips and sea kayaking." Tim Ellis explains. "Families find them especially rewarding." The foundation schedules 7- and 10-day excursions, Aug.-Sep., on Maine's premier wilderness rivers: the Allagash, St. Croix, and East and West Branches of the Penobscot; as well as on Maine's salt-water coast. All trips combine lake and river paddling, and all are open to "good swimmers of any age." Rates for 7 days, $300, 10 days, $400. Bring sleeping gear. "The food is perfect; the leaders' knowledge of campsites and pre-planning excellent. Chewonki runs fabulous vacations," writes a canoeist. (See also *Wilderness Living*.)

EASTERN RIVER EXPEDITIONS, Box 1173, Greenville, ME 04441. Att.: John M. Connelly III. (207) 695-2411 or 695-2248.

"We bring guests face to face with coves of seals, flocks of seabirds, and secret tide pools," relates John Connelly, whose ocean kayaking expeditioners spend nights island or coastal camping. Connelly offers canoe and kayak clinics. Kayakers learn basic strokes, whitewater technique, rolling, and water safety skills on the Penobscot and Kennebec rivers. In addition, overnight combination rafting and canoe trips. Rates: $65-$185 for day and overnight trips. May-Sep. Arrival: Bangor, ME. (See also *River Running*.)

KATAHDIN OUTFITTERS, P.O. Box 34-A, Millinocket, ME 04462. Att: Don Hibbs. (207) 723-5700.

"Canoe through the last great wilderness in the East today," invites Don Hibbs, referring to the North Woods of Maine. He outfits and guides small groups and families on canoe trips to beautiful and secluded rivers like the Allagash and the St. John, as well as to remote ponds for native brook trout fishing. As you are paddling the rugged backcountry, you'll learn canoe and camping techniques, how to use a map and compass, and something about the history of the region. These trips are open to everyone—singles or couples may join others on scheduled departures in Maine or on several new trips Don is offering in the Canadian wilderness. "It's a turnkey operation," he says. "All you do is arrive. We take care of the rest." Trips 3-10 days, up to 8 canoists, $60-$70/day, May-mid-Oct. Bring sleeping bag. Arrival: Bangor, ME, pickups arranged.

MAINE WILDERNESS CANOE BASIN, Springfield, ME 04487. Att.: Carl W. Selin. (207) 989-3636, ext. 631. [Sep.-Jun.: Box 62, Deer Isle, ME 04627. (207) 348-2339.]

Located on the northern shore of 4-mile Pleasant Lake amid the

MAINE   dense Maine forests, this canoeing base, Capt. Selin assures us, is the
                    ideal spot for beginning a canoe trip into the great variety of lakes,
                    streams, and rivers of eastern Maine. The entire Grand Lake Chain
                    opens with more than 40 miles of wilderness waterways—white water,
                    placid streams, and wilderness islands—for explorations and excellent
                    fishing. Special features of the operation are kayak outfitting and
                    progressive areas to learn kayaking. Complete outfitting, canoe, or
                    kayak trips, $18/day (bring sleeping gear). Group rates, pickup
                    service, backcountry tent sites, housekeeping, and outpost cabins.
                    Arrival: Bangor, ME. (See also *Sailing Schools, Youth
                    Adventures*—Maine Waterways Camps.)

NORTHERN OUTDOORS, INC., P.O. Box 100, The Forks, ME
04985. Att.: Wayne & Suzie Hockmeyer. (207) 663-4466.
     Kayaking is a big specialty with the Hockmeyers. On the
dam-controlled Kennebec and Dead rivers they run a professional
kayak school for beginners to advanced. "Kayaking is fun and we
approach it as a good-time vacation rather than a lot of work," they
explain. They consider American kayakers very fast, but prone to
penalty points in competition against the superior technique of the
Europeans. So they chose Russell Walters of England to run the kayak
school. "With his all-out effort and friendly manner he's a joy to be
with and a great instructor." Their lodge facilities for kayakers provide
such equipment as hot tub, sauna, and weight room. It's a kayaker's
dream—brand new lodge, food way above average, and miles of big
rapids that are challenging and pushy but not dangerous," writes an
enthusiastic kayaker from Norristown, PA. Rate for 2- to 5-day
course: $145-$350. Also canoe expeditions on Maine's wilderness
rivers, with empahsis on custom overnight trips for small parties, 1-7
days, $70-$450 with complete outfitting and deluxe meals. (See also
River Running.)

SUNRISE COUNTY CANOE EXPEDITIONS, INC., Cathance Lake,
Grove Post, ME 04638. Att.: Martin Brown. (207) 454-7708.
     Established in the early 70's as a traditional eastern Maine guiding
outfit, SCCE now offers trips from the Arctic Circle in northernmost
Yukon, to the mountains of Labrador, and the desert canyons of the
Rio Grande. "Our trips are run with integrity in respect to aesthetics,
instruction, and service," Marty Brown emphasizes. "We consider
canoe voyaging an art, and outfitting small private parties is a
specialty." He also schedules fall foliage trips (Sep., up to 10 people)
which individuals may join: 4-7 days on the St. Croix (ME),
Nepisiguit (New Bruswick), Bonaventure and Moisie (Quebec); and
weekly Rio Grande expeditions in the Lower Canyons, Mar.-Apr.
"Our system of coaching can turn almost anyone into a strong,
graceful, solo canoeist with both pole and paddle in just a few days,"
Brown promises. SCCE's outfitting service is complete to the extent
that you need bring only personal gear and sleeping bag. (See also
Canoeing—TX & Quebec, *Youth Adventures.*)

UNICORN RAFTING EXPEDITIONS, INC., P.O. Box-T, Dept 47,
Brunswick, ME 04011. Att.: Jay Schurman. (207) 725-2255.

Can you do an eskimo roll, a wet exit, or an eddy turn? These are some of the kayaking techniques offered during Unicorn's 1-, 3- and 5-day clinics. With its base camp at Big Moose campground in Millinocket, ME, Unicorn has an ideal location for its kayaking school, and plenty of variety with the Kennebec, Penobscot, and Dead rivers close at hand. Its kayaking director, Herbert Schreib, got his experience in the Austrian Alps and passes along his expertise in Class IV and V white water down the line. Unicorn also offers specially arranged trips in northern Maine and a 6-day Penobscot expedition: 4 days canoeing, 2 days whitewater rafting. Clinic rates: $65 to $325, including all equipment and a tent. For novice and intermediate kayakers. (See also *River Running*.)

MICHIGAN

KEWEENAW WATERWAY RESORT, Rt. 1, Box 241, Dept.-AT, Houghton, MI 49931. Att.: Bruce A. Barna. (906) 482-1109.

"It's a canoeists' paradise," Bruce Barna claims of Isle Royale—a wilderness archipelago in the cold, clear waters of northern Lake Superior. Its delicate ecosystem supports moose, beavers, red fox, hares, and other wildlife. There are miles of sheltered waterways and canoe-only campsites on the inland lakes and long bays. Excellent fishing. Barna's resort provides canoes and route planning. His rates for up to 15 are $10/day/canoe for two days, $8/day thereafter. Even getting to Isle Royale is fun. The park service boat, the *Ranger III*, leaves from Houghton (2 round trips a week, about $40/adult, $16/canoe), and the *Isle Royale Queen* leaves daily from Copper Harbor, 40 miles from the resort. Or take the Isle Royale Seaplane Service and let KWR drop-ship your canoes to the Island. May-early Sep.

Snapping a few photos before a gator takes a snap—*Wilderness Southeast, GA.*

MINNESOTA   **ANDERSON'S CANOE OUTFITTERS,** Rt. 3, Box 126-AT, Crane
Lake, MN 55725. Att.: Bob Anderson. (218) 993-2287.

The Anderson Outfitters of Crane Lake is your port of entry to the
western end of the BWCA and the Quetico Provincial Park. "Our
unique location and canoe shuttle service will allow you to be in the
BWCA in minutes or in Quetico Provincial Park in less than two
hours," says the outfitter. "One of Minnesota's best kept secrets is that
you will be on the Maligne River, Crooked Lake, McAree Lake or
other BWCA and Quetico super waters on the same day that you
depart from the Crane Lake Base." Anderson will make arrangements
for BWCA and Quetico permits and its shuttle service will check you
through American and Canadian Customs with expediency. Complete
outfitting, $20/day/person. Complete boat tow and outfitting, $209
for 7 days. Shuttle service only $68.50/person round-trip, with your
own canoe add $35/canoe.

BEAR TRACK OUTFITTING CO., Box 51, Grand Marais, MN
55604. Att.: David & Cathi Williams. (218) 387-1162.

Stressing personalized service and an ecological approach to the
wilderness, Cathi and David Williams offer complete or partial
outfitting for canoe trips in the Boundary Waters Canoe Area and
Ontario's Quetico Provincial Park. "The finest ultra-light equipment,
professional advice, and northern hospitality assure a truly happy and
unforgettable wilderness experience," David writes. At the outset,
Bear Track gives sound instruction in technique and planning for the
novice to the most experienced canoeist. Complimentary lodging for
complete outfitting guests the night before canoe trip in wood-heated
cabins. Bear Track also sponsors a solo canoe clinic: a 2-day on-water
seminar featuring Blackhawk and Mad River Canoes. Retail store has
complete fishing and camping equipment, accessories, and food
(dehydrated and freeze-dried). Complete outfitting, $30/day or less,
depending on length of stay and size of party. Group rates: May-Oct.
Arrival: Grand Marais. (See also *Backpacking, Ski Touring.*)

BILL ROM'S CANOE COUNTRY OUTFITTERS, INC., Dept. AT,
Box 30, Ely, MN 55731. Att.: Bob Olson. (218) 365-4046.

"We're one of the oldest and largest outfitters in the Boundary
Waters Canoe Area," Bob Olson, director of CCO, points out. His
guiding experience in these waters dates back to 1950, and each year
about 80% of the canoeists who use his service are either repeaters or
referrals. "Most come to get away from the big city rat race," he says,
"and most take a 6-day trip though we have outfitted people for as
long as a month." CCO plans routes for just the amount of travel and
layover time people want. The complete outfitting rate is $28-$37/day
(depending on number of people and days), $20-$23 for groups, and
20% off for under 16 years. CCO also offers partial outfitting, guides,
fly-ins, and housekeeping units and RV sites at Moose Lake. May-Oct.
Pickup arranged in Duluth or Hibbing.

BORDER LAKES OUTFITTERS, Dept.-AG, P.O. Box 8, Winton, MN
55796. Att.: Jack Niemi. (218) 365-3783.

This firm has offered complete and partial outfits for canoe trips

into the heart of the Quetico-Superior wilderness since 1929.
"Although there are larger outfitting companies than ours, we could
not maintain on a much larger scale the person-to-person sort of
operation we enjoy," explains Jack Niemi. "This is a real canoe
outfitter," reminisces one participant. "He knows all the routes and has
everything you need for a great trip. One highlight was following a
moose as it swam across a lake to an island." Located on Fall Lake, 3
miles east of Ely. Complete ultralight outfitting: as low as
$24.50/day/person. Also youth group rates, fly-in/paddle-out canoe
trips, overnight facilities. May-Oct.

GUNFLINT NORTHWOODS OUTFITTERS, Box 100 GT-AG,
Grand Marais, MN 55604. Att.: Bruce & Sue Kerfoot. (800) 328-3325
nat'l. or (800) 328-3362 in MN.
   "We're looking for people who care about our wilderness enough to
leave it a little better than they found it, folks who come to enjoy the
wildlife, sit around a campfire listening to the loons or watching the
Northern Lights," reflects Bruce Kerfoot. His family has been
outfitting for 55 years in the BWCA and Quetico Park. Gunflint is
centrally located to service over 50 canoe routes. It features careful
route planning, nourishing foods, and top-quality equipment as well
as a lodge with bunkhouses, meals, sauna, and a wide range of
facilities. Complete lightweight outfitting: $30-$40/day, $15-$20 for
children. Organized youth trips, $225-$295/week. May-Oct. (See also
Ski Touring, Wilderness Living.)

QUETICO CANOE ADVENTURES, INC., 194 S. Franklin St.,
Denver, CO 80209. Att.: Brooke & Eric Durland. (303) 722-6482.
   For a unique wilderness experience plan a 5-, 7-, or 10-day guided
trip in Minnesota's Boundary Waters or Ontario's Quetico Provincial
Park. The Durlands schedule trips for up to 8 canoeists according to
their interest and abilities: laid-back, strenuous, fishing, fly-in, or
family trips (geared down to 4-year-olds). "There are no passengers on
these trips, only crew. You'll help paddle your canoe, portage the gear,
and pitch in on the camp chores," explains Brooke. They provide all
food, equipment (canoes, tents, sleeping bags, foam pads), and guide.
Instruction and practice session in Ely before trip begins. Rates for
5-10 days, $350-$625, include airport pickup in Duluth, lodging
before and after trip, pontoon plane or boat tow to Canadian border,
and guide. Straight outfitting (no guide) also available. Jun.-Sep. In
Colorado the Durlands canoe the Gunnison, Yampa, and Colorado
rivers over Memorial Day, 4th of July, and Labor Day weekends,
$150/canoeist. (See also *Backpacking, Ski Touring*—Colorado
Adventure Network, CO.)

SUPERIOR-NORTH CANOE OUTFITTERS, 3586 114th Lane N.W.,
Coon Rapids, MN 55433. Att.: Jerry Mark. (218) 388-4416.
[Oct.-Apr. (612) 421-4053.]
   What's your preference: a base camp or moving each day? A
rugged, moderate, or easy trip? Walleye, northern pike, small-mouth
bass, or lake trout? Wildlife, remoteness, scenery, or waterfalls? From
his base on Saganaga Lake Jerry custom-plans your trip into the

MINNESOTA   BWCA, Quetico, and Northern Light Lake wilderness area. "The
Marks provide top-rate equipment, nutritious meals, and superior
service," a canoeist reports, "plus a happy family atmosphere."
Complete deluxe ultra-light outfitting: $30-$37.50/person/day.
Groups of 8 or more: $18-$25/person/day. Partial outfitting, tow,
pickup, and fly-in/paddle-back service available.

VOYAGEUR OUTWARD BOUND SCHOOL, P.O. Box 250, Long
Lake, MN 55356. Att.: Dee Dee Hull or Linda Larson. (800) 328-2943
(outside MN) or (612) 542-9255 (in MN).
   Paddling is the specialty at the Voyageur Outward Bound School.
Spring, summer, and fall courses take place in the spectacular
wilderness of the Boundary Waters Canoe Area and the Quetico
Provincial Park on the Minnesota/Canadian border. In winter,
whitewater canoe on the Rio Grande (Texas/Mexico border). Work
with a group of 8 to 10 participants and 2 instructors on 8-, 15-, 22-,
and 28-day courses for youth (14 and up) and adults of all ages.
Activities include paddling instruction, map and compass orientation,
portaging and expedition travel, emergency first aid, rock-climbing
and rappeling, individual and group dynamics. Special courses for
juniors, women over 30, life/career renewal adults, troubled youth,
corporate clients, the disabled or hearing impaired, and semester
courses (60-90 days) for those with greater interest. Rates: $600/8
days-$950/22 days. (See also *Ski Touring/Snowshoeing, Wilderness
Living.*)

Easy paddling in a kiwi
kayak on the Eel
River—*Ann Dwyer for
California Rivers, CA.*

WILDERNESS OUTFITTERS, INC., 1 E. Camp St., Ely, MN 55731. Att.: Jim Pascoe and Gary Gotchnik. (218) 365-3211.

The dip of the paddle, the splash of a fish, the call of the loon, the whispering of the pines, are the sounds of Canoe Country. Wilderness Outfitters, in operation since 1921, is the oldest canoe outfitting firm to service the BWCA and the Quetico park area with its vast, unspoiled lakes. "Our many years of outfitting experience assure you a successful, rewarding trip," says Pascoe. He offers complete deluxe ultralight outfitting, remote fishing camps on beautiful Basswood Lake, with daily camp service, fly-in/paddle-out canoe trips, fly-ins to Canadian outpost cabins, boat-ins to a remote Canadian resort. Canoe outfitting rates from $25/day including canoe, food, light equipment. Group rates, excellent fishing, canoe guides, partial outfitting, and airport pick-up service in Duluth or Hibbing, MN.

MISSOURI

AKERS FERRY CANOE RENTAL, Cedar Grove Rt., Box 90, Salem, MO 65560. Att.: Eugene & Eleanor Maggard. (314) 858-3224 or 3228.

In the heart of Big Springs country and Ozark National Scenic Riverways, Akers has canoe rentals, shuttle service, a general store, campground with hot showers, cafe, ferry boat, and inner tube rental year round on the pastoral, Class I Current River. The Maggards fill you in on details about the numerous caves and springs you'll run across. Canoes are always available during the week. Basic canoe rental, $20/day. Discount on weekdays and off season. Handles all group sizes.

BIG M RESORT, R7, Box 124, Licking, MO 65542. Att.: Daniel & Alicia Kuhn. (314) 674-3488.

The Piney river is basically a calm-water river with scenic views around every bend, occasional springs and caves, and excellent fishing. "To the observant canoeist, each mile has some unique features named by tie and lumber rafters at the turn of the century—such as Horseshoe Bend, Turkeyneck Eddy, and Ritz Rock." explains Dan Kuhn. Basic canoe rental fee is $12/day including paddles and life preservers; shuttle additional. Trips 1-7 days, 5-50 miles, 1-80 people, Apr.-Nov. Arrival: Licking, MO.

WILD RIVER CANOE RENTAL, Gladden Star Rt., Box 260, Salem, MO 65560. Att.: Jack Patton. (314) 858-3230.

Headquartered in Akers, 25 miles from the headwaters of the Current River, Wild River Canoe Rental is in the heart of the beautiful Big Springs country. "The Current is the most spring-fed of all the Ozark rivers and can be floated year round," Jack explains. The veteran outfitter with 20 years of experience offers free camping and bus service to and from the river for customers and has a general store and registered nurse. Canoe rentals are $22/day. Off-season and weekday discounts.

MONTANA

GREAT ADVENTURES WEST, 1401-B 5th Ave. So., Great Falls, MT 59405. Att.: Craig Madsen. (406) 761-1677.

Canoeing and canoe camping on most of Montana's scenic, historic, and whitewater rivers are specialties of Great Adventures—as are fly

MONTANA

fishing, rafting, horseback riding, and wildlife photography. In addition to their complete canoe rental service, they can provide professional guides, camping equipment, raft support, and "gourmet" camp meals for canoeists. From a comfortable riverside camp an avid angler can spend the day fishing while other members of the family explore in canoes or kayaks and take side hikes. Join a scheduled group or a custom-arranged trip, from $90/day, less for seniors and children. "You can expect spectacular scenery, excitement, personalized service, safety, generous and hearty meals, saunas, and comfortable camps," Madsen assures. Several different programs offered on the "wild and scenic" Upper Missouri River through the White Cliffs Area. (See also *River Running*.)

NEW
HAMPSHIRE

SACO BOUND/NORTHERN WATERS, Box 113, Center Conway, NH 03813. Att.: Ned McSherry. (603) 447-3002.

Saco Bound in Center Conway, and its Northern Waters outpost near Errol, offer complete canoe and kayak service for trips on the Androscoggin and Saco Rivers and Rangeley Lakes area, Apr.-Oct. Both outfitting centers can equip you for an exciting array of canoe-camping or whitewater possibilities—from short excursions on the Saco's gentle summer waters to closed-boat paddling on two fast Class IV rivers, the Magalloway and Rapid. Northern Waters' 5-day canoe and kayak clinics take place on Class II and III rapids on the Androscoggin. "Our basic concern," explains Ned McSherry, "is to teach techniques of safe paddling with that sense of quality we call 'style'." Clinics include 3-hour classes each morning and practice or rest sessions in the afternoon ($225/person, including equipment). Also single lessons, 2-day programs, and private instruction. Basic canoe and kayak rentals are $19.50/day. Also complete outfitting, guided trips, and car shuttle service. (See also *River Running*—Downeast Rafting Co.)

NORTH STAR CANOE RENTALS, R.R. 2, Rt. 12A, Cornish, NH 03745. Att.: John or Linda Hammond. (603) 542-5802.

"We make it possible for vacationers to enjoy the pleasures of Vermont and New Hampshire in a very special way—the canoe way," says John Hammond. "You can explore the cool, clear waters of the North Country's Connecticut River and enjoy the serenity and magnificence of this historic river." North Star offers a leisurely one-day trip that is excellent for families with young children. Overnight canoe camping is also available through the unspoiled back country, with camping sites along the river's banks and islands. North Star provides base camp, parking, river map, free one-day trip shuttle, paddles, life jackets, and canoes. Rates: $24/canoe for day trips; $18/each additional day. Group rates; youth discounts. Excellent perch, bass, and trout fishing. Mid-May to Nov.

NORTH
CAROLINA

NANTAHALA OUTDOOR CENTER, US 19 West, Box 41, Bryson City, NC 28713. (704) 488-2175.

Fifteen national champions, four world champions, two U.S. team coaches, and half the Olympic whitewater canoeing team (a 1972 event) have been or are now on the NOC staff. The result is high-quality whitewater instruction for all levels of canoeists and kayakers, beginner to competition. Choice of clinics: weekend, 3, 4, or 5 days, or a "Week of Rivers"—a course of intermediate paddlers split into groups according to skill levels, with training on several rivers during the week. Clinic rates, including meals, lodging, and equipment: weekend $165, 3 days $245, 5 days $400. With previous whitewater experience, canoe rentals for paddling on your own are $29/day. "The instructors were excellent, and praise and criticism well balanced," reports a kayaker. "The student/instructor ratio was never more than 5 to 1—important for optimum learning. Meals were all-you-can-eat and very good. All of our group made significant improvement." Arrival: Asheville, NC or Chattanooga, TN (See also *Backpacking, Mountaineering, Cycling, River Running*.)

Paddling churning waters of a North Carolina river— *Outward Bound, Inc., CT.*

OREGON

SUNDANCE EXPEDITIONS, INC., 14894 Galice Rd., Merlin, OR 97532. Att.: Judo Patterson. (503)479-8508.

"Nationally acclaimed as the 'College of Kayaking,'" states Sundance, "this is the West's largest and most comprehensive kayak school." With an instructor for every 4 students, the teaching includes whitewater reconnoitering, boat handling, and wilderness camping in an intensive 9-day hardshell kayak program on the Rogue. Students spend the first five nights at the riverhouse (equipped with sauna and hot tub) with daily instruction on the river. Instruction continues as they kayak down the river for 4 days, camping along the way. "The food is beyond gourmet," according to Judo. "Outstanding!" says a canoeist. Tuition: $785 for 9-day course including lodging, equipment, food. Advanced and intermediate programs in May. Arrival: Medord or Grants Pass, OR. (See also *River Running*.)

SUNRISE SCENIC TOURS, 3791 Rogue River Hwy., Gold Hill, OR 97525. Att.: Ted & Sheri Birdseye. (503) 582-0202.

"For those ready to graduate to the ultimate river craft, the

OREGON   hardshell kayak," writes Ted Birdseye, "we have qualified instructors
                  for 1- to 10-day courses in rolling, river reading, and overall running
                  skills. if you prefer inflatable kayaks, we'll give you a thorough
                  orientation on some easy stretches of water before you set off on one
                  of our trips." SST runs 1- to 5-day inflatable kayak trips with raft
                  support on the Klamath, Deschutes, Umpqua, Rogue, and Illinois.
                  Trip rates: 1-5 days, $40-$335. Kayak school: 1-5 days, $45-$330, $60
                  each additional day. Rates include equipment, camping gear, meals.
                  For B&B in an 1870 setting. $35-$50/night. Arrival: Medford, OR.
                  May-Sep. (See also *River Running*.)

PENNSYLVANIA   **KITTATINNY CANOES,** Dept. AT, Dingmans Ferry, PA 18328. Att.:
                  Frank & Ruth Jones. (717) 828-2338 or 2700.
                       Frank and Ruth Jones cover more than 100 miles of the river
                  between Hancock, NY, and the Delaware Water Gap in the Poconos.
                  "We have one of the largest as well as the most experienced liveries on
                  the Delaware, with over 1,200 canoes, rafts, kayaks, and tubes," says
                  the outfitter. In addition, they have six rental bases and two
                  campgrounds on the river. There are whitewater trips for rafters or
                  experienced canoeists or quiet water for beginners and families.
                  Excellent fishing. Family owned and operated for over 32 years. Rates
                  are $11/day/person weekdays or multiple-day rentals; $13 for
                  Saturday or Sunday. Group rates. Radio-dispatched van service, car
                  shuttle, base-to-base trips. Mid-April through Oct.

                  POINT PLEASANT CANOE OUTFITTERS, P.O. Box 6, Point
                  Pleasant, PA 18950. Att.: Tom McBrien. (215) 297-8181.
                       With four main bases along the Delaware—at Martin's Creek near
                  Easton, Reigelsville, Upper Black Eddy, and Point Pleasant—this
                  service specializes in canoeing, rafting, tubing, and pedal/paddling, a
                  cyling and canoeing combination. Their shuttle buses take
                  participants upriver to put-in points and drive them back from
                  take-outs. This provides the flexibility to choose smooth or white
                  water stretches, whichever you prefer. "Tubing is the biggest craze on
                  the East Coast," they say, "and you can choose 2-, 3-, or 4-hour tubing
                  floats." You also can choose from a variety of tubes. Designed in Italy,
                  they come in 4 sizes and 4 colors applied by silk screen mat. For those
                  who want to do some cycling along with canoeing, there are 80 miles
                  of off-road bike trails starting at points on the river. Rates: canoeing
                  for 2, $26/day; rafting for 4, $30/day; tubing, $8/person; pedal/
                  paddling, $15/person, weekender canoe/island camping for 2, $50.

                  WHITEWATER CHALLENGERS, INC., Box AT, Star Rt., 6A1,
                  White Haven, PA 18661. Att.: Ken Powley. (717) 443-9532.
                       For those getting their first taste of kayaking or canoeing and for
                  experienced boaters who want to improve their technique and skill
                  level, Whitewater Challengers offers beginner and intermediate
                  whitewater clinics. Available in 1- or 2-day sessions, these clinics
                  include ACA certified instructors, classroom sessions, in-water
                  instruction, movies, video tapes, all equipment, "and lots of fun,"
                  Powley adds. The instructors combine years of whitewater boating
                  and river guiding experience. Their enthusiasm makes the learning

experience all the more enjoyable and rewarding. Beginner clinics: daily, Jul.-Oct. Intermediate clinics: weekdays, Apr.-Jun. 1-day clinic $50/person, group of 6 $47/person. For 2-day clinic $95/person, group of 6 $90/person. (See also *River Running*.)

TEXAS

OUTBACK EXPEDITIONS, P.O. Box 44, Terlingua, TX 79852. Att.: Larry G. Humphreys. (915) 371-2490.

"We provide instruction in basic boating skills and wilderness camping," explains Larry Humphreys. He runs year-round canoeing and kayaking trips in the Southwest and in Mexico. On the Rio Grande (TX) you travel from Redford to Langtry though 6 "exceedingly beautiful canyons" for up to 300 miles, from 1-21 days. On the Pecos River (TX) you may run 45 miles (3 days) from Independence Creek to Pandale, or 50 miles (4 days) from Pandale to Langtry, with over 30 Class II and III rapids that require sound canoeing skills. He also runs 4-day trips on the Concho River in northern Mexico. Rates are $55-$85/day, including boating and camping equipment, shuttles, and meals; for 4-16 participants; group discounts. (See also *Backpacking, River Running*.)

SUNRISE COUNTY CANOE EXPEDITIONS, INC., Cathance Lake, Grove Post, ME 04638. Att.: Martin Brown. (207) 454-7708.

Martin Brown chooses March and April for paddling the Lower Canyons of the Rio Grande, designated a "Wild and Scenic River." He calls it one of America's last frontiers—"stark, lonely hills, then massive peaks rising from the desert flats, miles of sheer, subtly hued canyon walls thousands of feet high, and Class II to III rapids. It's a mellow trip," he adds, "leisurely paced with time for easy hikes up bluffs and side canyons, bathing in hot springs, and maybe catfishing." Whitewater technique, especially solo paddling and poling, is SCCE's specialty which you can learn within a few days. Including pickup and return to Odessa: 9 days, $745 ($1,339 for 2); rate covers 2 nights lodging in Odessa, 7 days on river, all equipment, meals, guides, transport. (See also *Canoeing*—ME & Quebec, *Youth Adventures*.)

TEXAS CANOE TRAILS, 121 River Terrace, Dept. AG, New Braunfels, TX 78130. Att.: Betty Walls. (512) 625-3375 or 0662.

"The rivers and wilderness areas of the Southwest are now accessible to people of all ages," says Wayne Walls, founder of Texas Canoe Trails. "Our professional guides make the backcountry a safe, affordable experience for the entire family. Slow down and enjoy the clean air, solitude, peaceful surroundings—and make new friends! "Paddle through high, sheer-walled canyons along the Rio Grande River through incredible gorges once roamed by Apaches and Comanches, starting from the colorful "old west" town of Lajitas. A canoe or kayak trip is really the way to experience the awesome immensity of this region. From San Antoino, take the Guadalupe River, either the Lower or Upper area, to enjoy the scenic Hill Country. From Durango, Colorado, canoe on the Animas River, observing wildflower meadows and cottonwood forests. Trips range from easy to intermediate. Both canoes and kayaks are supplied by this service, which specializes in teaching all skills necessary. Half-day to 10-day trips. $30-$40/day; longer runs, $65 and up/day. Group discounts. Year round. (See also *River Running*.)

UTAH

SLICKROCK KAYAK ADVENTURES, P.O. Box 1400, Moab, UT 84532. Att.: Cully Erdman. (303) 963-3678.

Enjoy the ultimate river experience by learning to kayak in the Rocky Mountains. Slickrock Kayak Adventures runs instructional kayak trips for the beginner and intermediate boater, with professional instruction from some of the country's top kayakers. "Our state-of-the-art clinics and trips are conducted in a variety of wilderness settings, from the magnificent red-rock canyons of Utah to the majestic peaks and deep forests of Colorado and Idaho," Cully Erdman explains. He runs how-to-kayak on the Green, Arkansas, Dolores, Colorado, San Juan, Rio Grande, and other rivers, and has appeared in a number of TV sports shows. (SKA also runs expeditions in Mexico, Chile, Nepal, and New Zealand.) Rates run from $295-$525 for 5-10 days trips, all inclusive from Moab, Utah. Group discounts.

VIRGINIA

DOWNRIVER CANOE CO., Rt. 1, Box 256-A, Bentonville, VA 22610. Att.: John Gibson. (703) 635-5526.

It's only an hour and a half drive from Washington to Downriver's headquarters for a single-day trip on the South Fork of the Shenandoah. "This is a mellow, gentle river," John Gibson assures his customers, "with enough white water to make it fun and exciting." This 8-mile run is known not only for its beauty but for some of the "best fishing in Virginia." If you tip over, don't worry. The water is waist deep and you can get things reorganized with little trouble. For 2-day weekend trips Gibson provides a private campground on the riverbank. His trip-planning service is used by couples as well as groups. Basic canoe rental: $36/day including shuttle service and campground.

SHENANDOAH RIVER OUTFITTERS, Dept. AT, RFD 3, Luray, VA 22835. Att.: Nancy Goebel. (703) 743-4159.

Just two hours from Washington, DC, this "oldest and largest outfitter in the Mid-Atlantic states" puts you on the Shenandoah River with its rugged cliffs and secluded clearings where Indians once lived. SRO is active in a "help-preserve-the-Shenandoah" campaign and offers free canoeing in exchange for two filled trash bags. SRO's director, Joe Sottosanti, designed and built the sturdy canoe they use. Made of flexible vinyl rubber (Royalex) especially for whitewater canoeing, it is named the "Shenandoah" after the river that has damaged many a craft with its tough rapids and side-bending rocks. Rate for complete outfitting, $75/canoeist for 2 days, $100 for 3 days. Guide, $40/day. Day trips, $30/canoe; tubing, $8/person; including life jacket and shuttle. Also partial outfitting and group discounts. "The peace of gently floating along, the excitement of Compton Rapids, and the beauty of Shenandoah Valley make these trips a welcome break from everyday living," says a vacationer.

WASHINGTON **LIBERTY BELL ALPINE TOURS,** Mazama, WA 98833. Att.: Eric Sanford. (509) 996-2250.

"For sheer fun and excitement there's nothing like kayaking," says director Eric Sanford. His popular 5-day classes start you from scratch and have you flying through the rapids before you know it. Learn the basics in a warm lake, then head down the Methow River with more challenging rapids each day. Nights at base camp with hearty meals and fireside stories ($345, Sun p.m. to Sat. a.m.). Also Weekend

Some smiles before taking a splash on the Methow River—Eric Sanford for Liberty Bell Alpine Tours, WA.

Kayaking Seminars—quiet inland paddling, seals, whales, exotic birds, sheltered crossings between islands—accompanied by a naturalist/guide ($425, Sun p.m. to Sat. a.m.). Liberty Bell also schedules Boardsailing Weekends ($125) and a Kayaking/Boardsailing Week ($325). Jul.-Aug. (See also *Backpacking, Mountaineering, Cycling, River Running, Ski Touring.*)

WEST VIRGINIA **APPALACHIAN WILDWATERS, INC.,** P.O. Box 126-AG, Albright, WV 26519. (800) 624-8060 or (304) 329-1665.

"If you've ever seen kayaks or canoes in action and had a yen to try your talents—this is the way to start," claims Imre Szilagyi, who started AW nearly 15 years ago. He offers a 1-day, low-key introductory clinic to whitewater canoeing. The emphasis is on having fun while paddling the Upper New and learning the fundamentals under the supervision of American Canoe Association-certified instructors. "We select outstanding individuals and develop their talents with the industry's most sophisticated training program," says Imre. AW provides 2 days of intense canoe instruction for Class I and

WEST
VIRGINIA

II streams. Kayak beginners can learn technique as well during a 2-day school, with the first day on flat water concentrating on strokes and the Eskimo roll and the second day on Class II to III water. Instruction $80/day including equipment, shuttle, and lunch; May-Sep. From Jun.-Sep., test your talents with 3 days of canoeing on the New from Hinton to Thurmond (41 miles), with a fourth day rafting on the Lower New. (See also *River Running*.)

CLASS VI RIVER RUNNERS, INC., P.O. Box 78-AT, Lansing, WV 25862. (304) 574-0704.
   "Our kayak trips are designed to teach ability and skill along with safety," states Class VI. They have 2- to 9-day kayak clinics for beginners and intermediates. Most people take the 2-day course—the first day on a lake and the second on upper sections of the New or Gauley Rivers. For extra days they may go to the Greenbrier River and camp out. Kayak school rate is $60/day with equipment, meals, transport, and instructors. (With your own kayak, $48.) Class VI's canoeing service involves rental canoes, usually for accompanying whitewater raft trips on the New or Gauley. Guided trips, $40/day; non-guided, $25/day. Says one river runner: "Particularly positive aspects of the trip included the flexibility of the people-oriented guides, and great food." (See also *River Running*.)

ALBERTA

TOMAHAWK CANOE TRIPS, 11035-64 Ave., Edmonton, Alta., Canada T6H 1T4. Att.: Greg Hunter. (403) 436-9189.
   "We offer a variety of canoeing adventures ranging from half- to 9-day trips for all experience levels," notes Greg Hunter. "Our trips are on rivers and lakes in the Rocky Mountains and foothills near Jasper Park, with calm water for beginners and white water for experienced canoeists or those eager to learn. Hunter has guided canoeists in these waterways for more than 15 years, and is an examiner of other instructors in Jasper Park. He offers trips from a full day to 9 days on the Miette, Athabasca, Berland, McLeod, Brazeau, Kakwa, and Smoky rivers, and Maligne Lake. Prices range from $22/person for a day trip $175/3 days, to $500/9 days, (Canadian funds) including guide, canoes, paddles, life jackets, waterproof packs, transport and meals. Jun.-Aug. "The trip was enjoyable, exciting, educational, and unstructured. Our guide was extremely knowledgeable and organized, but in a relaxed way," says one beginning canoeist.

MANITOBA

NORTH COUNTRY RIVER TRIPS, Berens River, Man., Canada R0B 0A0. Att.: Jack & Georgia Clarkson. (204) 382-2284 or 2379.
   "The area east of Berens River has great canoe routes," say the Clarksons, "but they were always thought to be too inaccessible until we started assisting canoers in the planning stages and with fly-outs when required." The Clarksons will mail maps, advise on routes, and arrange to transfer canoeists' cars from put-in to take-out point, or they'll fly you and your canoe in and out. "Try a trip from the Red Lake, Ontario area to the Berens River settlement," they suggest. "Or Wallace Lake to the mouth of the Pigeon River." They can advise, too, on the Hayes, God's River, and others in Manitoba. Complete outfitting service. "Clarkson's service was impeccable, and the

equipment we rented was in good shape. We recommend the service highly," write two contented canoeists. (See also *River Running*.)

NORTHWEST TERRITORIES

SUBARCTIC WILDERNESS ADVENTURES LTD., Box 685, Fort Smith, N.W.T., Canada, X0E 0P0. Att.: Jacques & Ruth van Pelt. (403) 872-2467.

"What I like doing most is planning trips for people in small groups so that they have a personal relationship with the wilderness. I would never want to get too big because this North Country with its silence and vastness would be spoiled by too many visitors," says naturalist

An unforgettable arctic wilderness camp—Lyn Hancock for Subarctic Wilderness Adventures ltd., N.W.T., Canada.

and trekker Jacques van Pelt, explaining his approach in designing Subarctic adventures. Van Pelt's low-key, personalized approach is evident in his canoeing/kayaking trips. Adventurers can take a nomadic canoe exploration, paddling streams, rivers and lakes, camping, and fishing alone or in small escorted groups in unspoiled areas of Wood Buffalo National Park, the Tazin Highlands, or the Canadian Shield. Some put-ins reached by road; others by floatplane. Price: $99/person/day/escorted; $69/unescorted. Or paddle the Slave River Rapids, retracing the route of early explorers on a 2 1/2-day trip. You have a chance to photograph some of North America's most spectacular big water. Guide is mandatory; bow paddling experience necessary. Rates; 1-4 persons, $239/person, single supplement $50. Jun.-Sep. (See also *River Running, Dog Sledding, Wilderness Living*.)

ONTARIO

CANOE CANADA OUTFITTERS, P.O. Box 1810-A, Atikokan, Ont., Canada P0T 1C0. Att.: Bud Dickson or Jim Clark. (807) 597-6418.

"We're centrally located on the remote northern edge of Quetico Provincial Park and outfit into the entire 2,000-square-mile area," says

Bud Dickson. "Our specialty is ultralightweight outfitting for self-guided wilderness trips. The finest equipment and food pack, knowledgeable trip planning, and careful routing are the highlights of our service." Detailing trip routes to match your interests is another specialty. It's an area of abundant wildlife and sport fishing where artifacts of the voyageurs and loggers may be found. Rates for complete ultralightweight outfitting are $34/day, $230/week (U.S. funds). Youth and group rates: $25/day, $165/week. CCO also has fly-in, paddle-out service and cabin-canoe trips. They'll pick you up at Thunder Bay (Ont.) or International Falls (MN) airports.

CARIBOU WILDERNESS CANOE OUTFITTERS, Box 1390. Atikokan, Ont., Canada P0T 1C0. Att.: JoAnne or Bob Bigwood, (807) 597-6888.

"Very personal service and our own special food packing," are features of the Caribou canoe trips through Quetico Park and surrounding wilderness areas. No experience is necessary as Caribou plans your route before each trip and gives pointers on equipment, usage, campsites, fishing, and outstanding area features. Complete lightweight outfitting for 3 or more days includes campsite with showers (motel accommodations optional) before and after trip, truck portage to and from park, camping permit. Also partial outfitting, guides, and fly-in, paddle-out trips. Dinner or breakfast before or after trip by reservation. May-Oct. Arrival: Atikokan Airport or Thunder Bay, bus or Caribou's limo to Atikokan.

WANAPITEI WILDERNESS CENTRE, 7 Engleburn Pl., Peterborough, Ont., Canada K9H 1C4. (705) 743-3774.

Situated in Temagami country—a land of sparkling waters, rugged shorelines, beautiful islands, and magnificent forested hills—Wanapitei offers canoeing adventures for adults, novice to expert. They experience the Temagami, Lady Evelyn, and fabled Nahanni, and run the Spanish, Bazin, Coppermine, and the spectacular Dumoine whitewater rivers. Wanapitei leads expeditions to the Hudson and James Bay, the Yukon and Northwest Territories. "For the canoeist," they promise, "northern Canada is unique, with vast areas still in their primeval state." Expert instruction allows participants to gain skills and environmental awareness. Fees depend on distance and transport. Base rate per week (Canadian funds) is about $350/person. In spring there are workshops in Temagami and on the Madawaska River. May-Sep. Says one repeat canoeist, "both Bruce and Carol are two of Canada's best whitewater experienced canoeists. Their trips have been an unsurpassed wilderness experience." (See also *Ski Touring, Youth Adventures*.)

WILDWATERS NATURE TOURS & EXPEDITIONS. P.O. Box 2777, 119 N. Cumberland St., Thunder Bay, Ont., Canada P7A 4M3. Att.: Bruce T. Hyer. (807) 345-0111.

There are 200,000 square miles of wilderness between WildWaters' wilderness lodge at Shawanabis Lake (150 miles north of Thunder Bay) and the North Pole. It's a rugged land, "uninhabited and unpolluted," Hyer writes, "and rewarding to anyone prepared to understand its ways." On a 12-day *Voyageur* trip ($600/canoeist), fairly rigorous paddling alternates with fishing, swimming, and photography. There's more time for relaxing and instruction on 7-day *Wilderness Nature* tours ($375). Most strenuous are Hyer's *Trailblazer* expeditions. "A canoe tripper's dream," he calls the 15-day Fawn/Winisk rivers trip over 1,000 miles of bush flights and 270 miles of arctic river with big rapids and falls, speckled trout, sandhill cranes, caribou, polar bear, and beluga whales ($1,500). A 13-day trip on the Upper Albany River is $950. (Rates in U.S. funds, include bush flights.) Hyer also runs a canoe trip leaders' school, whitewater training course, and offers sea kayaking on Lake Superior. Authorized topgraphic maps provided. High quality rentals/outdoor gear at Thunder Bay store. Trippers use superlatives to describe Hyer's expeditions and leadership skills.

QUEBEC

QUEBEC SUNRISE COUNTY CANOE EXPEDITIONS, INC., Cathance Lake, Grove Post, ME 04638. Att.: Martin Brown. (207) 454-7708.

   The only outfitter to offer a commercial expedition on the Moisie River in Quebec's Central North Shore region, SCCE schedules a 10-day expedition for 12 canoeists with 5 guides in mid-September. "One of the world's ultimate whitewater trips," Marty Brown calls it. It's an arduous run through remote and inaccessible territory, but the rewards are great. The dramatically beautiful Moisie rises off the Labrador plateau and cuts an incredible glacial canyon with sheer cliffs up to 2,000 feet. A steadily dropping gradient gives the canoeist a continuous series of long but navigable rapids—and some rugged portages. Start in Sept Illes, Quebec; float plane to river. Rate: $1,190/person. SCCE offers several itineraries in Canada—in Quebec, New Brunswick, and the Yukon. (See also *Canoeing*—ME & TX, *Youth Adventures*.)

RIVER RUNNING

There you are, relaxed and at ease, lifejacket snugly strapped around your torso, drifting slowly down the river on your rugged inflatable raft. Off in the distance you hear a rumble, and you know that tranquil moments are soon to end. You glimpse white water ahead, and grab hold of the ropes that crisscross the boat as you move closer, closer, louder. Then you're crashing, rising, floating, flying, pounding, and twisting through a turbulent, frothy boil. You squint, blink, and hold on as the walls of spray pummel you, one after another. You've never felt so alive!

Suddnely it's over. You're drifting smoothly on, reveling in the canyon's beauty, wondering how soon it will give you another wild ride.

That's the lure of running big water, a sport which manages to combine the thrill of a world-class rollercoaster ride with experiencing up close some of the earth's most compelling land- (or canyon-) scapes.

Take for example the classic run through the Grand Canyon of the Colorado in Arizona. Start at Lees Ferry near the Utah border, and raft nearly 300 river miles—12 days in oar-powered rafts or 9 to 10 days in motorized boats—to Lake Mead on the Nevada border. The water ranges from slow, gently-moving currents to the wildest, most powerful froth imaginable. And you see the spectacular canyon in a way that only river runners do—from the inside, looking up.

Because of the ever-increasing popularity of river running, nearly every waterway with enough current for a raft is serviced by an outfitter. You can find a river as mild—or as wild—as you wish. It's safe to take a baby along on the Snake above Jackson, Wyoming—a scenic half-day run through Grand Teton National Park. Below Jackson the Snake is a different story—another half-day run, but this time, hold on! Or if you're going for raging, unpredictable white water, well, there's plenty of that, too.

Options abound—from a few hours to a week or more. From single-person Sportyaks to 4-person paddle rafts to motorized craft holding up to 16. From Alaska to Georgia, from Maine to California. Or you may opt for a run that specializes in a particular activity—side canyon hikes, nature walks, archaeology, painting, photography. in short, the choice is yours.

Aside from the obvious joys of rafting, there are also the more subtle, yet undeniable, pleasures. On the river you are *totally* involved. As one river runner drolly notes, "While hanging on to a rubber raft for dear life, with waves breaking ten feet over your head, there is little time to mull over the cares of the workaday routine."

As you may have gathered, most rafting on whitewater rivers is *not* for the faint-of-heart. And, with the exception of brief runs, it's not for the lazy. Rafters are often expected to haul gear, help set up camp, bail the boat, pitch in as part-time chefs, and leave the campsite in pristine condition. "It is a participation sport," one rafter wryly observes, "where you pay big money to work."

Not only will you work; you may also experience heat, cold, bugs, mosquitoes, drenchings, bruises, scratches, rain, wind, lightning, dunking, or exhaustion. But, say dedicated river rats, it's all worth it.

"We had our boat ripped badly on the rocks in the Middle Fork," one western rafter reports. "Another raft in our party got hung

Drifting through the grandeur of the Grand Canyon—*John Blaustein for Grand Canyon Dories, CA.*

up on a rock, and the people and gear were dumped into the river. But even with being uncomfortable at times, this trip will be a lasting, happy memory, and our entire group wants to go again soon."

Being "uncomfortable at times" is a mild understatement, but one that doesn't dampen the enthusiasm of a confirmed river runner one bit. "Just hang loose and roll with the punches," encourages an aficionado, "and you'll have the time of your life."

"To anyone who has ever considered this crazy sport as a possible holiday, I have only this to say: Do it!"

Reminders

The details that follow tell whether boats are oar-powered or motor-powered. Check whether you pay extra for transport to and from the river, car shuttle, waterproof duffel, camera container, sleeping gear, or accommodations before or after the trip.

Choose the type of trip you really want—a scenic pleasant run, or a rugged whitewater adventure. Check limits on weight or bulk of personal gear, minimum age for taking the trip, physical fitness required, anticipated weather, and fishing regulations. For rafting trips especially for young people, see the chapter, Youth Adventures.

ALASKA

ALASKA DISCOVERY, INC. P.O. Box 26, Gustavus, AK 99826. Att.: Hayden & Bonnie Kaden. (907) 697-2257.

For an "unparalleled wilderness adventure," raft the Tatshenshini and Alsek rivers which carve their way through the magnificent peaks of the Fairweather-St. Elias Range to the Gulf of Alaska. You'll maneuver exciting rapids and wide-braided estuaries filled with glacial ice. A spectacular bush plane flight back to Gustavus ends the 11-day trip ($1,575). ADI also rafts the Stikine River, used as a highway by gold seekers at the turn of the century. John Muir called its valley "a Yosemite 100 miles long." In 7 days ($900) you float and paddle calm waters from semi-arid volcanic mountains to lush rainforests and see abandoned settlements, wildlife, and hot springs. Return to Juneau by plane or ferry. Group discounts for 4 or more. Jul.-Aug. (See also *Backpacking, Ski Touring, Wilderness Living.*)

NOVA RIVERRUNNERS OF ALASKA, SRC Box 8337, Palmer, AK 99645. (907) 745-5753.

With Anchorage as the starting point, NOVA takes river runners on the Matanuska, "for the entire family," and on LionsHead, "the most exciting commercial river day trip in Alaska." Both trips about $45/person, or $80 with transport between Anchorage and the rivers. For the wildwater of the Chickaloon you shuttle by helicopter—or by horseback—to the remote headwaters camp, and next day make the unforgettable run. Cost: $245/person. NOVA also schedules expeditions on the Yukon River in Yukon/Charley National Preserve (10 days, $1,645), on the Copper in Wrangell-St. Elias National Park (7-9 days, $1,095-$1,195), and on the Kobuk in Gates of the Arctic National Park (12 days, $2,250). Rates are all-inclusive, except for sleeping gear. A well-established outfitter—now in its 12th year of operation.

SOURDOUGH OUTFITTERS, Box 18-AT, Bettles, AK 99726. Att.: David Ketscher. (907) 692-5252.

"Experience the real wilderness with us," invites Dave Ketscher. "See caribou, moose, black and grizzly bears, predatory and migratory birds. Fish for arctic char, grayling, pike, salmon, sheefish, and lake

trout. Visit Eskimo villages and archaeological sites." He runs
wilderness rivers of the Brooks Range by raft, canoe, and
kayak—Class I and II water through "beautiful untouched Alaska."
His 1- to 3-week trips, some of which combine with Sourdough's
backpacking treks, are on the Noatak, Kobuk, Koyukuk, Nigu,
Alatna, John, and Wild rivers. Rates range $950-$1,980, 7-21 days,
and include bush flights from Bettles to and from put-in and take-out
points. Jun.-Sep. Arrival: Bettles via Fairbanks. (See also
Backpacking, Canoeing, Dog Sledding, Ski Touring.)

ARIZONA

ARIZONA RAFT ADVENTURES, INC., P.O. Box 697-R, Flagstaff,
AZ 86002. Att.: Robert Elliott. (602) 526-8200.
   "Participation and diversity are what distinguish us from the other
outfitters who run the Grand Canyon," Rob Elliott remarks. He offers

Discovering the exhila-
rating effort of oar-
powered
rafts—*Arizona Raft
Adventures, Inc., AZ.*

8-day motorized trips and 6- to 14-day oar-powered and paddle trips.
The emphasis is on involvement: rowing, paddling, hiking, swimming
the small rapids, helping in the kitchen, learning the natural history,
and flat-out relaxing. Trips Apr.-Oct. Rates: $90-$115/day including
round trip to and from Flagstaff. Camping gear rentals, $25.
Discounts for charter groups and groups of 10. A vacationer praises
the guides as "versatile, witty, fun, and hard-working. I was impressed
by their strong concern for maintaining the canyon environment."
Another remarks, "Five months later, I'm still excited and eager to do
it again."

ARIZONA

ARIZONA WHITEWATER EXPEDITIONS, P.O. Box 26028, Tempe, AZ 85282. Att.: Jerry Van Gasse. (602) 838-7428.

"We offer the largest selection of raft trips in Arizona," emphasizes Jerry Van Gasse. With paddle and oar-powered rafts he runs the Verde River (January-April), starting at Camp Verde or Childs—good rapids, enticing side canyons, hot springs, Indian ruins, and wildlife. On the 35-mile run through the Salt River Canyon Wilderness (February-June) you encounter many whitewater rapids. Begin on the White Mountain Apache Reservation—or take the milder 16-mile trip from Horseshoe Bend to Roosevelt Lake. "Casual and humorous guides. Great food and beverages," writes an enthusiastic participant from Scottsdale, AZ. Trips 2-5 days, for 12-16 participants who are competent swimmers, minimum age 10 (12 on the Salt). Rates $135-$150 for 2 days, about $300 for 5 days: sleeping bag, tent and wet suit rentals. Transport from Phoenix or Tuscon to put-in extra. May-Aug.: AWE also runs the Chama River in New Mexico.

CANYONEERS, INC., P.O. Box 2997, Flagstaff, AZ 86003. Att.: Gaylord Staveley. (602) 526-0924 or (800) 525-0924.

"Our trips are planned to be fun, a restful change of pace, instructive, conveniently arranged, and your money's worth," emphasizes Gaylord Staveley. This is his 31st year of passenger-carrying whitewater operation—and his company's 50th anniversary! For his 7-day motorized trips through 280 miles of the Grand Canyon of the Colorado River the rate is $859. Those willing to hike or ride saddle mules into or out of the canyon (at Phantom Ranch) may take the first 2 days (87 miles) for $336, or the next 4 days (193 miles) for $684. Canyoneers also takes river runners on the full 280-mile trip in oar-powered boats: 14 days, $1,325. Among the highlights for a river runner from Ponca City, OK, were the "very adventurous side trips...outstanding food...totally knowledgeable guides on the canyon and all of its history. An excellent company. I'd love to take the same trip again."

Rafting through monumental beauty in the Grand Canyon—*Del E. Webb Wilderness River Adventures, AZ.*

DEL E. WEBB WILDERNESS RIVER ADVENTURES, P.O. Box 717, Page, AZ 86040. For downriver trips, call collect: (602) 645-3296; for 1-day floats, call (800) 528-6154, in AZ (602) 645-3279.

Wilderness River Adventures is a veteran river running company with its roots in the first commercial whitewater operation in the Grand Canyon. They offer both motorized and oar-powered trips from 3-10 days, May to September. "What better way can you imagine to experience and appreciate the rare beauty of the Grand Canyon?" asks Del Webb's manager, Dean Crane. "We've got the experience it takes to make every river trip safe, smooth-running, comfortable, and action-packed." You can put-in at Lees Ferry, AZ, mile zero; Phantom Ranch, mile 86 (hike in or out of the Grand Canyon); or Whitmore Wash, mile 188. Del Webb recommends special 3-day "Weekend Escapes" for first-timers or people on a tight schedule. A 1-day float between Glen Canyon Dam and Lees Ferry has no white water, and is a perfect side trip from Page or Lake Powell. (See also *Houseboating*—Lake Powell Resorts & Marinas, AZ.)

DIAMOND RIVER ADVENTURES, P.O. Box 1316, Page, AZ 86040. (602) 645-8866.

"On a Diamond River Adventure it takes a very short time for a real feeling of togetherness to develop," says Bill Diamond, who runs trips down the Colorado River through the Grand Canyon. "By the time a river run is over each tour group is a family." He offers 5- to 12-day oar-powered trips, ($514-$998), and 4- to 8-day motorized ($413-$805), providing everything needed including pop and beer, tents and pads (oar-powered trips), and cots and tarps (motorized trips). Trips run from Lees Ferry to Diamond Creek, ending at Grand Canyon Caverns. Also part-way trips for those willing to hike in or out on the Bright Angel Trail. Full-length trips include briefing in Page and a drive to Lees Ferry. Discounts for children. "I haven't had a more relaxing and enjoyable vacation in five years," writes a rafter from Fort Collins, CO. "I came out of that canyon a different person than when I went in...I'd like to thank your people who made it so special.

EXPEDITIONS INC./GRAND CANYON YOUTH EXPEDITIONS, R.R. 4, Box 755, Flagstaff, AZ 86001. Att.: Dick & Susan McCallum. (602) 774-8176 or 779-3769.

Family vacation trips through the Grand Canyon are a specialty with the McCallums. These are 5- to 18-day oar-powered journeys in boats specially designed by Dick. "I've been down the Canyon at least 150 times in everything from a kayak to a 30-foot raft," he says. "Each trip is a rich, rewarding new adventure." Some are hiking/rafting adventures and raft support trips for kayakers running the rapids. Rates: $500-$1,200 for Grand Canyon trips; all gear and transportation from Flagstaff provided. Apr.-Oct. (See also *Youth Adventures.*)

WILD & SCENIC, INC., P.O. Box 460, Dept. AT, Flagstaff, AZ 86002. Att.: Patrick & Susan Conley. (602) 774-7343.

With 15 years' experience on rivers, the Conleys are convinced that the greatest fun in river running is rowing your own boat. This they

ARIZONA

do on the Green and San Juan rivers in Utah using 1-person Sportyaks—7-foot skiffs made of tough, durable plastic and virtually unsinkable. "You learn and practice boating skills on a stretch of quiet water before the rapids begin," Patrick explains. "You 'read the water,' chart your own course, and have a full share of the fun. The river gives you something extra in exchange for a little spunk!" You need not be a strong swimmer or experienced boater or camper to qualify. Their 7-day (6-night) San Juan trip starts and ends in Bluff, UT, $575. Green River trip, 8 days, 7 nights, from town of Green River, UT, $675. Through Westwater Canyon of the Colorado, 3 days, 2 nights, from Moab, $225. Rates include transport to and from river, pre-trip motel, sleeping bag, foam pad, ground cloth, tent. May-Sep. (See also *Van Camping*.)

CALIFORNIA

ACTION ADVENTURES WET n WILD, INC., Box 13846, Sacramento, CA 95853. Att.: Loren L. Smith. (916) 662-5431; in CA, (800) 238-3688.

Loren Smith speaks of over 20 years' experience leading groups through some of the West's most majestic wilderness areas while maintaining "an unequalled safety record—not a single reportable personal injury claim." His trips are for varied experience levels on California's American, Merced, Salmon, Tuolumne, and Klamath; Oregon's Rogue. They offer the excitement of shooting rapids, Loren notes, and the chance to "drink in the beauty of sparkling beach campsites, encounter wildlife in its native habitat, or glide amid majestic redwoods for up to 6 days of uninterrupted natural beauty." Rates: $39-$200/day including all but personal gear. Apr.-Oct. trips; all year on American River.

ALL-OUTDOORS ADVENTURE TRIPS, 2151 San Miguel Dr., Walnut Creek, CA 94596. Att.: George Armstrong. (415) 932-8993 or 932-6334.

"We put adventure in your life," say the Armstrongs. On California's whitewater rafting rivers run Meatgrinder Rapid on the American, test Hell's Corner Gorge on the Klamath, battle Ike's Rapid on the Salmon, endure Quarter Mile Rapid on the Merced, or take the ultimate challenge on the magnificent Tuolumne River. Apr.-Oct., 1- to 6-day trips. Rates/person: $50-$100/day. (See also *Backpacking, Cycling*.)

AMERICAN RIVER TOURING ASSOCIATION, 445 High St., Oakland, CA 94601. Att.: Steve Welch. (415) 465-9355.

"Who guides your trip is as important as where you're going," advises ARTA's director, Steve Welch. His non-profit organization specializes in hiring "excellent guides who enjoy the personal aspect and educational participation more than the white water." ARTA runs dozens of oar-powered and some motorized trips on 14 rivers throughout the West and Northwest from April to October, 1- to 16-day trips. Most are scheduled to fit convenient vacation dates. For example, they run the Rogue (OR), Green (UT), Colorado (UT and AZ), and 7 rivers in CA. Sample rates: 4 days, Green River, $350; 13 days, Grand Canyon, $1,250; 6 days, Main Salmon, $550, or Middle Fork, $665. Bring or rent sleeping gear.

ECHO: THE WILDERNESS COMPANY, AG, 6529 Telegraph Ave., Oakland, CA 94609. Att.: Joseph Daly or Richard Linford. (415) 652-1600.

ECHO schedules trips on some the West's finest waters: Idaho's Middle Fork and Main Salmon and the Snake through Hells Canyon (6 days); California's Tuolumne, American, and Merced (1-4 days); and Oregon's Rogue and Owyhee (5 days). A typical ECHO fleet consists of 4 or 5 boats, 4 to 6 people in each, and sometimes a kayak or two. Oars and paddles provide the power, and passengers develop whitewater skills, instructed by guides who win kudos for being "alert, able, and intelligent." Try their Birds of Prey trip on the Snake in May—they spotted 112 species last year! According to a Berkeley professor who ran the Middle Fork, "The trip was great in every respect; the river is incredibly beautiful, scenery spectacular, and the guides pleasant, friendly, and above all very competent. I appreciated their willingness to share the art of reading the water and running the rapids." Sample rates: Main Salmon, 6 days, $719 (including transport to/from Boise); American, 2 days, $139-$147; Owyhee, 5 days, $524 (with van service to/from Boise). Bring sleeping gear. Group and youth rates. Charters.

Dories below Diamond Peak in the Grand Canyon, 224 miles downriver from the put-in—*Martin Litton for Grand Canyon Dories, CA.*

GRAND CANYON DORIES, Box 7538, Menlo Park, CA 94026. Att.: Martin Litton. (415) 854-6616.

On all his river trips—whether it's the Grand Canyon (AZ), Main

CALIFORNIA and Lower Salmon River (ID), Owyhee and Grande Ronde (OR) or the Snake River through Hells Canyon (OR-ID)—Martin Litton uses the motorless dory: a compartmented rough-water boat of aluminun, Fiberglas, or taut marine plywood. "It rides higher and drier than a raft, and doesn't bend or buckle in the waves or get soft when it's cold," he explains. There's a guide in each boat, but participants may take the oars and learn to run the rapids or try one of the 2-person inflatable kayaks Martin takes on all trips. Sample rates: Main Salmon, 8 days/$696, 13 days/$1,144; Hells Canyon, 6 days, $548; Lower Salmon, 5 days, $436. May-Sep. Litton's Grand Canyon excursions of 18 days ($1,676) or longer are for those who want a relaxed, quieter voyage, with guided hikes along the way. Bring or rent sleeping gear. "As if the spectacular scenery wasn't enough, our boatmen had to be the finest. They made us feel that our enjoyemnt and safety were their primary concerns," says one trip member.

HENRY & GRACE FALANY'S WHITE WATER RIVER EXPEDITIONS, INC., P.O. Box 1269-D, Mariposa, CA 95338. (209) 742-6633.

The Falanys offer 7-day deluxe and super-deluxe trips on the Colorado River through the Grand Canyon on motorized rafts which they consider "the most complete and deluxe packages available" on this spectacular run. On their deluxe trip ($895) you meet in Las Vegas and travel by motorcoach to the Lees Ferry put-in. The super-deluxe trip ($1,125) takes you to Lees Ferry on a scenic flight over the Grand Canyon, and includes a geologist and musician with every group, a cocktail bar and hors d'oeuvres, and sleeping bag and duffel. Satisfied vacationers cite the excellent crew, interpretative program, food and beverages, safety record and good equipment among the features they appreciate. Arrival: Las Vegas, NV.

KERN RIVER TOURS, P.O. Box 3444, Lake Isabella, CA 93240. (619) 379-4616. Att.: Mary Jo Roberts.

"The newest and most exciting white water in the U.S. is the 20-mile stretch called the Forks of the Kern" according to this outfitter. They pack river gear by mule into the canyon for a 3-day adventure designed for experienced rafters. KRT also runs 1-hour to 2-day trips down the Upper and Lower Kern; the American, which flows out of the High Sierra; and the Merced, which flows out of Yosemite National Park. Rates from $15 to $365 per trip. Special Bare Bones run on the American—weekdays only, no meals or frills, $40/day. Apr.-Sep. There's also a 1-week High Adventure mini-camp for 13- to 18-year-olds, which includes rafting, mountaineering, and mountain biking, at an "affordable" rate.

KLAMATH RIVER OUTDOOR EXPERIENCES, P.O. Box 369, Orleans, CA 95556. Att.: Bob Hemus or John Torres. (916) 469-3391 or 469-3351.

Deluxe trips on the Klamath for small groups, with good food and attention to detail, is the specialty of this locally owned and operated company. They use inflatable kayaks and durable boats with top quality equipment. For the novice, KROE recommends 1-, 2- or 3-day run on the Lower Klamath where white water and flat stretches blend with steep rock walls, lush green banks, and lots of wildlife. The Upper Klamath runs and Cal Salmon provide two days of heavy white water, challenging currents, and accelerating shoots. "Good people—and good at what they do," writes a satisfied river runner from Smithtown, NY. "All I could have wished for." Trips are from 1-5 days, for 2-15 people, May-Sep.; Rates: 1 day, $30-$40; 2 days, $100-$150; 3 days, $200-$245; group discounts. From Sep.-Mar.: Steelhead fishing "in the most productive stretches of river" using McKenzie style drift boats. Airport pickup at Eureka, CA, or Medford, OR, extra.

LIBRA EXPEDITIONS, P.O. Box 4280-A, Sunland, CA 91040. Att.: Jon Osgood. (818) 352-3205.

A weekend getaway to raft a wild river is a breeze for anyone in the LA area. Just get yourself to Libra's pickup point in Irvine, Torrance, San Fernando, or Anaheim on Friday afternoon and board their comfortable well-equipped motorcoach. That night you'll be camping under the stars in the heart of Gold Rush country beside a turbulent river that will give you two days of exciting, drenching, whitewater rafting before you return to the city Sunday night. Once you've run the South Fork of the American River, you'll want to go back for "the utmost in thrills" on the Middle Fork. Both trips are scheduled every weekend from May to Oct. (And on weekdays with your own transportation.) For even bigger water, raft the North Fork or the Giant Gap run any weekend from Apr. to early Jun. Rate including meals, campfires, entertainment, guides, and all: $150-$175/person/weekend, $45 for bus roundtrip. Corporate and group rates. Gourmet and handicapped trips midweek only.

MOUNTAIN TRAVEL, 1398-AG Solano Ave., Albany, CA 94706. (800) 227-2384 or (415) 527-8100.

Known as one of the world's great wilderness trips, the Tatshenshini and Alsek run takes rafters through mountains where glaciers flow right down to the river banks. "It's a strange, spectacular feeling," says Mountain Travel. "You feel insignificant next to such immense natural wonders." With a put-in at Dalton Post in Canada, the trip covers nearly 100 miles of rivers from the spectacular St. Elias Range to the quiet bays of the Pacific. You float past mountains of icebergs, hike on immense blue-white glaciers, and observe grizzlies, Dall sheep, and bald eagles. A float plane takes you back to civilization. Trips start and end in Juneau. 12 days, $1,590. No previous experience necessary. (See also *Backpacking, Mountaineering, Canoeing—AK, Wilderness Living—AK.*)

O.A.R.S., INC., P.O. Box 67-G, Angels Camp, CA 95222. Att.: George Wendt. (209) 736-4677.

Oars only on these trips—no motors to destroy the serenity. George Wendt also believes in small groups: 16 maximum in the Grand Canyon, where he plans plenty of leisurely hikes to explore rare natural wonders and Indian ruins. "Floats on Utah's San Juan River,

Oar power takes these rafters through the Grand Canyon—*Liz Hymans for O.A.R.S., Inc., CA.*

Oregon's Rogue, and Idaho's Salmon are geared for families," he says, "while young adults enjoy the exciting rapids of the California rivers and the Middle Fork of the Salmon." Something for everyone on 14 different rivers throughout the western U.S., from 1-18 days. Sample rates: Grand Canyon, 5 days, $811, 13 days $1,500, Rogue, 5 days $480. Main Salmon, 6 days, $748. Youth rates. Most trips Mar.-Oct. Bring sleeping gear. An experienced river runner from Houston calls OARS "an extremely impressive organization...a group of the most mature, most interesting, and most knowledgable guides I have ever encountered."

CALIFORNIA **OUTDOOR ADVENTURES,** 30 Golden Gate Dr., San Rafael, CA 94901. (415) 453-8422.

"We run trips on the most challenging stretches of white water in the country," Outdoor Adventures reports. "Drop for drop, nothing tops the incredible Forks of the Kern (Class V), just 3 hours from Los Angeles, or the Tuolumne near Yosemite National Park (2- to 30-day trips, $258-$328). Or try a thrilling 6-day paddle down the Middle Fork in Idaho ($895/adult; $795/youth). For family vacations, they recommend Idaho's Main Salmon with its big rapids, sandy beaches, quiet pools, pine groves, and hikes to old cabins (6 days, $695/adult, $595/youth). On some Salmon trips one kid (8-16) with one adult floats free. Other trips, 1 and 2 days, on the Kern, Merced, East Carson, and American rivers ($74-$198). Mar.-Oct.

OUTDOORS UNLIMITED, Dept. A, P.O. Box 22513, Sacramento, CA 95822. Att.: John Vail. (916) 452-1081.

"Each day brings delights—the splash, spray, and tumult of rapids, and the tranquil, reflective stillness that only the wild places can provide" John Vail writes. His aim is to make each trip everything you anticipated—from your suntan to your drive home. Choose a 5-, 8- or 12-day oar-powered run through the Grand Canyon of the Colorado ($625-$1,145); 5 days on Oregon's Rogue ($385); 3 or 6 days on the Klamath ($230-$405); or 2-3 days on California's Tuolumne, American, or Merced Rivers ($165-$315). Boats carry 5 people and are manned by qualified oarsmen who double as expert chefs and guides. Paddle boat option on all trips. Discounts for charters and children under 13. May-Sep. Bring or rent basic camping equipment.

SOBEK EXPEDITIONS, Dept. AG, Angels Camp, CA 95222. (209) 736-4524.

SOBEK recommends "the intoxicating ride through the wild and scenic corridor of the Tuolumne River, an ideal 2- or 3-day immersion in California whitewater." Excellent meals, scenic side-hikes, and Gold Rush history highlight the trip. Mar.-Oct., 2 days/$245, 3 days/$350. Their 12 days on the Tatshenshini River in Alaska, which they ran first in 1976, is one of the continent's most beautiful river trips, with bald eagles, grizzly bears, moose and mountain goats, as well as ice-draped peaks and wildflowers galore. "Gorgeous scenery, total, unspoiled wilderness—not another human seen for 12 days," comments a guest from Haines, AK. Jul.-Aug., 12 days, $1,650. SOBEK also arranges river trips on every major North American river, including the Colorado through the Grand Canyon, the Rogue, the New in West Virginia, and the Nahanni in the Yukon; see their Adventure Book for details. (See also *Combo Trips.*)

TRIBUTARY WHITEWATER TOURS, 55 Sutter Street, Suite 65, San Francisco, CA 94104. Att.: Dan Buckley. (415) 428-2035.

This small flexible company offers trips on many of California's scenic rivers. Convinced that "there's a river for everybody," Dan Buckley welcomes rafters of varying interests, and gives you the option of joining a paddle crew or relaxing in an oar boat. He features 1- to 3-day runs on the Yuba, American, Scott, Salmon, and Carson early in the season (Mar.-Jul.), and from summer through October on the American, Trinity (Burnt Ranch Gorge), and Klamath (Hells Corner). Trips on other Sierra and coastal rivers can be arranged. All Tributary guides undergo rigorous training—safety is a prime concern—and are extremely knowledgeable about the rivers' natural features, Dan reports. Group size: 8-30. Sleeping bag and tent rentals. Rates: 1 day, $49-$110; 2 days: $120-$180; 3 days: $200-$230. Also 6- to 8-day river-guide school: $240. "Our group, 15 of us, have had three trips with Tributary and we're planning more," says an experienced river runner from Mountain View, CA. "The guides are excellent—want us to have a good time, but safety comes first."

TURTLE RIVER RAFTING CO., 507 McCloud Ave., Mt. Shasta, CA 96067. Att.: David Wikander. (916) 926-3223.

Nearly everyone gets involved in paddling, boat preparation, and camping activities on these trips. David Wikander believes wilderness and rivers should be accessible to all. To this end he keeps prices low and runs special trips for children, senior citizens, disabled persons, women's groups, men's groups, and others. Some trips are for "little,

CALIFORNIA

little kids." For those who have never gone on a river because of their fears, but always wanted to, he has "trips for timid water-lovers." Runs are on the Upper Klamath and the Klamath, American, Upper Sacramento, Owyhee, (California) Salmon, Smith, Scott, Rogue, and Eel. Rates: $45-$75/day. Apr.-Oct.

WILLIAM MCGINNIS' WHITEWATER VOYAGES, P.O. Box 906, El Sobrante, CA 94803. Att.: Bill McGinnis. (415) 222-5994.

"Our trips are excursions into a world which few people realize exists," declares Bill McGinnis, author of *Whitewater Rafting* and *The Guide's guide*. "We go to see and taste the wild places, to merge a bit

Surging water brings shouts of excitement— *Sally Holstrom for William McGinnis' Whitewater Voyages, CA.*

with the surging flow—and also to enjoy the conversation, the personal contact, the whole sense of adventure." His extensive program encompasses runs on California's Kern, American, Carson, Merced, Yuba, Klamath, Scott, Salmon, and Trinity, and the Rogue, Owyhee, and Crooked rivers in Oregon. Also the Colorado through the Grand Canyon. Paddle rafting emphasized; some oar boats and inflatable kayaks. A writer for *People Magazine*, tells us: "Bill's guides are the absolute best! They're courteous, safety-conscious, entertaining, and professional." And speaking of his "exciting and safe" run down the South Fork of the American, a Sonoma, CA participant recalls fondly, "We swam in the river with the local beavers, slept under the trees, watched sunsets, and relaxed." Sample rates: Kern, $168 up/2 days; American, $644 up/day; Lower Klamath, $246 up/3 days; Trinity, $182 up/2 days. Apr.-Oct. Bring tent and sleeping bag.

ZEPHYR RIVER EXPEDITIONS, P.O. Box 3607, Sonora, CA 95370. Att.: Robert Ferguson. (800) 431-3636 (in CA) or (209) 532-6249.

Name a raftable California river and chances are ZRE runs it. The Tuolumne, American, Kings, East Carson, Merced, and Eel are all on the agenda, with the choice of oar-powered or paddle boats up to you. What's the best month? "Mid-May to mid-June has the highest water level for the ultimate ride," says Bob Ferguson. "Mid-June to August is ideal for swimming and exploring, and early fall is beautiful in this land of canyons and limestone cliffs." Sample rates: 1 day, $75, 2 days, $145-$185. Jun.-Sep. Skilled guides, meals for hungry adventurers, quality equipment, and shuttle service from meeting points to the river are all standard. Bring sleeping gear. Group, family, and charter rates.

COLORADO

ADVENTURE BOUND, INC., 649 25 Road, Grand Junction, CO 81505. Att.: Tom Kleinschnitz. (303) 241-5633.

One of the largest rafting outfitters in Colorado, Adventure Bound has over 20 years' commercial river-guiding experience. Professionally led trips include the mountain canyons of the Colorado and Gunnison rivers, and major canyon-country runs on the Colorado (Ruby, Horsethief, Westwater, Cataract), Green (Lodore, Whirlpool, Split Mountain, Desolation, Grey), and Yampa (Dinosaur National Monument) rivers. Competent vacationers should not expect "just a river trip," advises Bob Rothe, a physicist from Boulder who ran Westwater Canyon. There's time for hiking, swimming, even "riding a waterfall" or "river-bottom walking." Paddle, oar, or motor-powered trips, May-Sep., 1-6 days, $46-$595/trip. River bag, poncho, and sleeping bag rentals. Departures from Craig and Grand Junction, and Steamboat Springs, CO.

COLORADO ADVENTURES, INC., P.O. Box 3088, Steamboat Springs, CO 80477. (800) 332-2439 natl., (800) 332-3200 in CO.

"We're the largest and oldest whitewater rafting company in Colorado," the Griffiths report, having started their company in 1972. Besides scheduling trips for individuals to join, they specialize in custom trips for conferences, seminars, and groups. With well-trained guides, a fleet of over 40 vehicles for pickup points, a kitchen which caters "to anything you desire," sleeping gear rentals, and reservations for off-river lodging, their company handles any size group—up to 250 on some single-day runs—May-Sep. Choose from single-day trips on the Upper Colorado, Arkansas, and North Platte rivers; 2- or 3-day trips on the Upper Colorado, North Platte, or Westwater Canyon; or 3- to 6-day runs through the Green River Wilderness or Cataract Canyon (the upper stretch of the Grand Canyon). The choice gives you every-thing from easy and exciting rapids where you just want to have fun, to challenging white water for experienced rafters. Oar-powered and paddle boats. Rates (including air charters as needed): single-day trips $50 up; multi-day trips $80/day up; youth and group rates.

DVORAK EXPEDITIONS, 17921 U.S. Hwy. 285, Nathrop, CO 81236. Att.: Bill Dvorak. (800) 824-3795 or (303) 539-6851.

COLORADO [Oct.-Apr.: 1 Blue Mtn. Rd., Lyons, CO 80540. (303) 823-5126.]
Bill considers the river canyons in Utah, Colorado, New Mexico, and Texas perfect for the variety of trips different individuals and groups want. Using paddle and oar-powered boats, his approach to river running is to share wilderness knowledge, whitewater skills, and encouragement. He does this on 26 canyons of the Colorado, Green, Dolores, Rio Grande, North Platte, Poudre, Arkansas, and Gunnison Rivers. "You explore your own limits, get thoroughly involved, and as a result gain great satisfaction," he explains. Families with 5-year-olds take his trips on the Green. On other rivers minimum age is 10 or 12. He also has developed a service for "special populations"—people with physical or emotional impairments or in trouble with the law. Mostly 2- to 5-day trips, around $80/day, less for groups and 16 years or under. Half- and 1-day trips $25-$50; group discounts. (See also *Canoeing, Youth Adventures*.)

ECHO CANYON RIVER EXPEDITIONS, P.O. Box 1002, Colorado Springs, CO 80901, Att.: David & Kim Burch. (303) 275-3154 (summer) or (303) 632-3684 (year round).
Choose between paddles (group participation) and oars (hang on and enjoy!) on these half- and full-day whitewater rafting adventures down the Arkansas River above and through the Royal Gorge (May-Sep., $25 or $46, children less). Also 3- and 5-day trips on the Dolores River through Slickrock and Dolores canyons, including the infamous "Snaggletooth" rapid ($210 or $325). You'll explore picture-worthy side canyons and historic ruins, and round out your days with hearty campfire meals. Two-day scenic trips on the Rio Chama in northern New Mexico are perfect for groups and families (May-Jul., adult $130, child $115). Wet suits recommended on early-season trips (bring your own or rent from ECRX). Group rates with 6 or more. Bring sleeping gear. Arrival: 8 Mile General Store, 45000 U.S. Hwy. 50 West, Canon City, CO 81212 (8 miles west of Canon City).

FAR FLUNG ADVENTURES/TELLURIDE WHITEWATER, P.O. Box 685, Telluride, CO 81435. Att.: Bill White. (303) 728-3895.
"Telluride specializes in putting people and rivers together. "Our highly trained guides share a respect for the river and a commitment to make your trip enjoyable, safe, and memorable," says Bill White. "As part of our philosophy, we practice river conservation and zero-impact camping." He offers whitewater rafting, kayaking, and canoeing on four wilderness rivers that rush from southwestern Colorado through the great mountain ranges and nudge into the Four Corners area. Choose from a half-day to a 2-day trip on the San Miguel ($35-$130), 3-6 days on the Dolores ($85/day), 1-3 days through the Black Canyon of the Gunnison ($95-$400). These are oar or paddle trips in Class II-IV waters, mid-Apr. to Oct. Telluride also offers special fishing, geology, naturalist, and photography trips, as well as family and children-oriented outings, free shuttle service, and rental boats. Arrival; Telluride, CO; (optional for Gunnison trips—Ouray or Montrose. (See also Far Flung Adventures in TX & Taos Whitewater in NM, this chapter, *Combos*.)

FOUR CORNERS EXPEDITIONS, Box 1032-AT, Buena Vista, CO 81211. Att.: Reed & Karen Dils. (303) 395-6657. Toll free CO: (800) 332-7238. [Oct.-Apr.: (303) 395-8949.]

A family from Georgia might have been nervous on their first whitewater rafting adventure down the powerful Arkansas River. "Instead," they report "an easy-going and knowledgeable guide made the river seem friendly." Since 1976, Four Corners has been taking people down Colorado's Arkansas and Dolores rivers in 15-foot rafts. On the Dolores, you camp at the bottom of a 2,000-foot canyon, below an ancient Anasazi Indian ruin, then wake up to the cry of "Coffee!" and the prospect of another day of exciting rafting. Oar trips are recommended for families with young children or adults who want a relaxing ride; paddle trips for those who want "a piece of the action." Cost: $25-$75/adult and $18-$75/child for half-day to overnight. Custom trips 3 or 6 days, $70/person/day, and fishing trips. Can service groups up to 110. Experience with handicapped customers. May-Sep.

OUTDOOR LEADERSHIP TRAINING SEMINARS/ARKANSAS RIVER TOURS, P.O. Box 20281-A, Denver, CO 80220. Att.: Rick Medrick. (303) 333-7831. [Summer: (303) 942-4362.]

Exciting 1- to 3-day trips on the Arkansas River require constant attention and teamwork as you paddle roaring Class III and Class IV rapids. Other OLS river adventures include the Dolores in southwestern Colorado—a primitive region of wilderness canyons; an unbelievably beautiful stretch of the Upper Rio Grande Gorge in New Mexico; and the canyons and moderate rapids of the Lower Rio Grande in Texas. Sample rates: Arkansas, 2-3 days, $145-$210; Dolores, 3 days, $235; Lower Rio Grande, 7 days, $495. Day trips on the Arkansas, $55-$75. Bring sleeping gear. May-Aug. Both paddle and oar-powered rafts. In operation since 1973. Licensed Colorado River outfitters. (See also *Backpacking, Mountaineering, Ski Touring, Wilderness Living.*)

RIVER RUNNERS LTD., 11150 Highway 50, Salida, CO 81201. (800) 525-2081 nat'l. or (800) 332-9100 in CO.

With 15 years of service River Runners Ltd. has taken more people down the Arkansas River than any other raft company. They report "the most rigorous and thorough training available," for their boatmen—"no substitute for experience." The Salida to Parkdale section of the river is a good introductory trip for those wanting beautiful scenery and the fun of floating the river. The Browns Canyon section offers continuous exciting whitewater rapids for beginners or experienced rafters wanting to "meet the challenge." For thrilling and exciting water, the Royal Gorge area is "the ultimate—a continuous series of thunderous rapids that test the mettle of even the most experienced boatman." With half-day and all-day trips in each section, rates run from around $20-$40 per adult, less for children. The Royal Gorge all-day trip is $70, adults only. The trips are by oar boat or paddle boat as requested. On 2- to 3-day raft trips you camp on the riverbank under the stars, hike, swim, and enjoy western cooking. (See also *Jeeping.*)

COLORADO

ROARING FORK RIVER COMPANY, 6805D East Arizona, Denver, CO 80224. Att.: Bill Kelso. (303) 759-9599.

This outfitter goes where the water flows—on the Roaring Fork, the Upper Colorado, the Arkansas, and the Dolores. You choose: white water to "mellow," paddle- or oar-powered, fishing or lolling. As the Colorado slices through the Rocky Mountains it exposes fascinating geological strata and gives some rapid excitement through Gore and Christmas Canyons and Red Gorge. Four days on the Colorado, with riverside campsites and hearty, Old-West-style meals, costs $290; 1-3 day trips, $39-$125. On the Dolores, raft between deep walls of red sandstone, shoot numerous rapids, and sight wildlife. Six days/$435. On the Roaring Fork 1-day runs are $39 with lunch.

SILVERCREEK EXPEDITIONS, P.O. Box 4001, SilverCreek, CO 80446. Att.: Bob Bingham. (800) 526-0590, ext. 154, or (303) 887-2131.

Skilled professional guides who are "friendly and willing to share their knowledge" pilot rafters through an 11-mile stretch of minor class rapids and scenic flat water—an excellent trip for first-timers. You depart from the luxurious Inn at SilverCreek at 8:30 a.m. and return about 5 p.m. Lunch is purchased en route to the private put-in, giving rafters a chance to request their preference in breads, coldcuts, fruits, and pop. For up to 24 people, $40/adult, $35/8-14 year-olds. Group discounts. Jun.-Sep. Arrival: Granby (via Amtrak), or Denver plus 2-hr. drive. (See also *Pack Trips*—C & R Stables.)

ULTIMATE ESCAPES, LTD., M-115 S. 25th St., Colorado Springs, CO 80904. (800) 992-4343 or (303) 578-8383.

"Wild and untamed, like the Old West itself, the Rio Grande below Big Bend National Park cuts through immense canyons with spires, arches, and rugged walls stretching 1,000 feet overhead," says Gary Ziegler, head of Ultimate Escapes. "It's a true wilderness river on the U.S./Mexican border, cutting through desert country as primitive as it was a century ago." Spend 7 days rafting and canoeing 80 miles of the Lower Canyons, running whitewater rapids, exploring side canyons, visiting prehistoric archaeological sites, camping alongside a large hot spring at the foot of a rapid, and just plain enjoying this larger-than-life frontier. For 7 days, $499, Nov.-Mar. (See also *Hiking with Packstock, Pack Trips, Combos.*)

WILDERNESS AWARE INC., P.O. Box 1550-A, Buena Vista, CO 81211. Att.: Joe or Susan Greiner. (303) 395-2112.

Wilderness Aware has been operating since 1974. The Greiners run small, personalized trips on the Dolores, Arkansas, Colorado, Gunnison, and North Platte rivers. Rafts are oar- and paddle-powered, depending on river conditions and guest preference. There's whitewater excitement and breathtaking canyon scenery on all the rivers. "We use only the best equipment and the most qualified guides," reports Joe. "Safety is our primary concern and our safety record is perfect. Participation is welcomed and encouraged. Our leisurely schedule allows the time for hiking and exploring." Sample rates: 1 day, $55/person; 2 days, $130; 3 days, $195; 6 days, $380. Bring sleeping gear. Wet suit rentals available.

GEORGIA

A team of paddlers tackles rapids on the Chattooga River— *Robert Harrison, Whetstone Photography, for Southeastern Expeditions, Inc., GA.*

SOUTHEASTERN EXPEDITIONS, INC., 1955 Cliff Valley Way N.E., Suite 220-B, Atlanta, GA 30329. (404) 329-0433.

"Our most popular and challenging trip is Section IV of the Chattooga (NC), with over 40 rapids (Class III and IV) in a 6-mile stretch," Claude Terry explains. "This is where most of the movie *Deliverance* was filmed." The Chattooga flows through panoramic mountain scenery, and SEE's guides are well versed in the area's flora and fauna. Minimum age: Chattooga, Section III, 10 years; Section IV, 13 years. "No experience necessary—we train you on the river," Terry says. Trips on the Ocoee in Tennessee are for 12 years or over. They also lead adventurous groups (10 or more students) through 1- or 2-day Ropes Course at their Chattooga outpost. Such obstacles as "The Tar Pit" and "Leap for Life" stimulate resourcefulness. Chattooga trips run all day: with a smorgasbord lunch, $30-$55; overnight wilderness campout trips, $130-$145; 30 people maximum. Ocoee River, $22-$28/half day. Ropes Course, $60/day. Canoeing is another SE specialty with fall and spring trips on 90 miles of the Rio Grande in Texas ($600 per canoeist), and an August trip for both kayakers and rafters on the Colorado through the Grand Canyon ($1,155/person).

IDAHO

BARKER-EWING IDAHO, INC., P.O. Box 3032-AT, Jackson, WY 83001. (307) 733-1000.

"Our extended whitewater trips through the Main Salmon gorge on Idaho's 'River of No Return' provide first-class outdoor adventure for all ages," exhorts Frank Ewing, "whether you prefer the more active involvement of running the rapids by paddle raft, or the relative security of our large sweep rafts which carry all the amenities for comfortable camp life." Packages for 7 days/6 nights (adults, $795; under 18, $695) from Jackson, WY, or Idaho Falls, ID, include ground transportation to Salmon, ID, comfortable accommodations and

IDAHO   dinners there first and last nights, plus 4 leisurely downstream days
                      through the central Idaho wilderness, ending with an exciting upriver
                      return through the rapids and canyons by jetboat on the 5th river day.
                      "You'll like this country!" reassures Wayne Johnson, partner-guide on
                      most trips. "Superb mountains, sparkling water, and good
                      companions will make this a memorable experience through the years
                      to come."

HAPPY HOLLOW CAMPS, Star Route Box 14-A, Salmon, ID 83467.
Att.: Martin R. Capps. (208) 756-3954.
    Marty Capps, who has run Idaho rivers for 20 years, believes you
haven't had a real western vacation until you've floated the beautiful
Main Salmon. He uses sturdy nylon neoprene boats, oar-powered and
designed for wild rivers. His 1- to 3-day trips feature panning for gold,
visiting Indian caves, spotting wildlife, swimming, fishing,
experienced guides, and good wholesome meals. Rates are $45/day,
overnight $65, all-inclusive. Mar.-Oct. (See also *Pack Trips*.)

HIGH ADVENTURE RIVER TOUR INC., Box 222, Twin Falls, ID
83301. Att.: Randy McBride. (208) 733-0123.
    The Middle Fork of the Salmon cuts through the heart of Idaho's
Primitive Area. From start to finish the water is crystal clear, fed from
mountain springs and melting snow, Randy explains. "Your adventure
will cover 95 miles of river through country that changes daily,
dropping 2,600 feet in elevation. You encounter 80 rapids, with many
serene stretches in between. Our guides are experienced and our food
incredible." Explore natural hot springs, abandoned cabins, Indian
writings, and isolated ranches from camp areas in forest or on sandy
beaches. Rates: $795 including all but sleeping bags and personal gear,
(or $895 including round trip from Boise).

IDAHO ADVENTURES RIVER TRIPS, P.O. Box 834-AT, Salmon, ID
83467. Att.: Hank Miller (208) 756-2986.
    "Sometimes the river is so noisy you can't hear yourself scream,"
says veteran rafter, Hank Miller. "Sometimes the river is so quiet the
dip of an oar sounds like a waterfall." One of the oldest, largest, and
most experienced companies, Idaho Adventures operates on the three
major rivers in Idaho. It provides a complete trip package that
includes all transportation between the river and Boise (which is
served by major airlines), as well as food, camping equipment, and
sleeping gear. Four-day whitewater raft trips on the Snake River
($595) through Hells Canyon, the deepest gorge in North America and
consistently the biggest rapids in Idaho; 4- and 6-day float trips on the
mighty Middle Fork ($575 or $895); 6-day raft trips on the scenic
Salmon River through the "River of No Return Wilderness" ($725) are
their specialties. For those wanting just a taste of rafting...from half-
to 3-day trips. ($40-$240) are offered on the Salmon River. Family
rates. Apr.-Oct. Average four passengers per raft, maximum 24 per
trip. "The gear was first class; the food was super first class!" writes
one float tripper.

Sweep boat supports
rafters on Idaho's
Middle Fork—*Jay
Krajic for Middle Fork
River Expeditions, ID.*

MIDDLE FORK RAPID TRANSIT, P.O. Box 2368, Ketchum, ID
83340. (208) 726-5666; summer (208) 774-2263. Att.: Phil Crabtree or
Dr. Bob Porter.

The ultimate experience—river running. Phil and Bob personally
oversee the planning and leadership of your excursion down the
beautiful and exciting 96 miles of straining, surging rapids of the
Middle Fork of the Salmon River in Idaho. The experienced boatmen
insure a safe, exciting trip using custom-rigged rafts. Your trip is
further enhanced by gourmet meals, scenic campsites, and a history of
the canyon. Rate: 6 days, 5 nights, $825 plus 4% tax. Meet at
Village Lodge in Stanley the evening before trip for briefing and to
pick up dry bags and ammo cans (for cameras). Back at 8 a.m. on
launch day to drive to the put-in. Trips Jun.-Sep. A travel consultant
from Chester, CT, reports…"equipment the best, food superb, guides
experienced, knowledgeable, talented, and interesting, scenery
spectacular, and thrills unforgettable." Arrival: Stanley.

MIDDLE FORK RIVER COMPANY, P.O. Box 233, Sun Valley, ID
83353. Att.: Steve Lantz & Betsy Barrymore. (208) 726-8888.

"We're known for our quality of service, for attention to every
detail, and for the wonderful meals we serve on the river," reports
Steve Lantz. On these trips you have the option of an oar boat where
the guide rows and you relax, or paddle rafts where you grab a paddle
and join the action. Lantz calls the run on the Middle Fork of the

IDAHO

Salmon "the most popular alpine river rafting in America's Wild and Scenic River System with unparalleled white water, abundant wildlife, pristine beaches, Indian pictographs and natural hot springs." (Jun.-Sep., 3 days/$650 including fly-in, 6 days/$995.) In spring they run the Bruneau and Owyhee "like floating through natural wonders as inspiring as Bryce and Zion." (Apr.-Jun., Bruneau 4 days/$750, Owyhee 6 days/$850.) From Memorial weekend through Sep., day and evening floats take you down the scenic headwaters of the Salmon near Sun Valley. (3 hrs./$30, 1 day/$60 adult, $50/child.) Another specialty is steelhead fishing in McKenzie drift boats on 150 miles of the Salmon. (Spring and fall, $200/boat/day for 2 persons, 1 guide, fishing equipment and lunch.) "We are the most complete river outfitting service in Idaho. Absolutely everything you need is provided."

MIDDLE FORK RIVER EXPEDITIONS, Box 199, Stanley, ID 83278. Att.: Patrick & Jean Ridle. (208) 774-3659. [Sep.-May: 1615 21st E., Seattle, WA 98112. (206) 324-0364.]

"Come float in uninterrupted solitude through wilderness lands explored by Lewis and Clark," urge the Ridles. They call their trips the ultimate whitewater adventure. "We specialize in personalized service, superb gourmet food with home-baked delights, the only black-tie champagne brunch on the river, and a farewell banquet at trip's end." You're off the river each afternoon with plenty of time for hiking, soaking in natural hot water springs, trout fishing, finding Shoshone petroglyphs, observing wildlife, swimming—or just savoring the pure mountain air. "Holding tight, shrieking, groaning, then sighing with relief and cheering when a turbulent passage is safely over develops a real esprit de corps," promises Pat. "All part of the unabashed fun." Trips are 3, 4, 5, and 6 days. Jun.-Sep.; $450-$795; also children's and group rates.

Relaxing in calm water on "The River of No Return"—*Salmon River Lodge, ID.*

SALMON RIVER LODGE, P.O. Box 348, Jerome, ID 83338. Att.: Dave Giles. (208) 324-3553.

In the comfort and ease of safe, custom-made, heavy rubber float boats, you float for three days down the Main Salmon Canyon, a fifth of a mile deeper than the Grand Canyon. Expert guides set up camp on sand bars and produce campfire meals you'll not forget. On the fourth day, Dave's powerful jet boat takes you back up stream to the lodge. (Rate: $500/4 days, $600/5 days.) As early as April and May, and on through the summer, these are favorite trips for fishermen, families, wilderness enthusiasts. You spot bighorn sheep, deer, elk, mountain goat, and sometimes black bear in the canyon, and catch trout in the swift, clear side streams (and steelhead in fall). For an easy 1- or 2-day trip, begin upriver from the lodge and float down. ($50/1 day, $150/2 days with overnight at lodge.) To reach Dave's lodge, charter from Boise or Missoula to Salmon, and request pickup to the river where a jet boat takes you across. (See also *Pack Trips, Jet Boating.*)

MAINE

EASTERN RIVER EXPEDITIONS, Box 1173, Greenville, ME 04441. Att.: John M. Connelly III. (207) 695-2411.

"We have a reputation for running the safest trips possible on the East's biggest whitewater rivers," observes John Connelly. He runs the Kennebec, Dead, and Penobscot (ME); the Hudson and Moose (NY); and the Gauley (WV). "Our equipment, staff, and guides not only meet, but exceed the most stringent of rafting codes," Connelly asserts. Each trip begins with coffee and a thorough orientation before crews board rafts and paddle through challenging drops and narrows. Most trips feature steak cookouts. Rafting overnights may include caving in West Virginia or hiking in Maine. Mar.-Nov., from $25/half-day family trips to $185 overnight. Also weekday rates and trip organizer discounts. Arrival: Bangor, ME; Charleston, WV. (See also *Canoeing.*)

MAINE WHITEWATER, INC., Gadabout Gaddis Airport, Bingham, ME 04920. Att.: Jim Ernst. (207) 672-4814.

"Our 1-day whitewater adventures on the Penobscot and Kennebec Rivers (May-Sep.) offer a breathtaking experience for the entire family," reports Jim Ernst, a veteran guide of western rivers with over 20,000 miles to his credit. The Kennebec trip from West Forks, includes 12 1/2 miles of Class III-V rapids, a steak cookout, and exploratory hikes to Moxie Falls and Dead Creek. The Penobscot trip (weekends, from Milinocket, take you through the lush wilderness of Baxter State Park. Rate: $70/day, group discounts. One former tripper writes: "Jim gives you a total picture of the river world—the history, environment, attractions. You feel that you've spent a day not on the river but with the river." Group discounts.

NORTHERN OUTDOORS, INC., P.O. Box 100, The Forks, ME 04985. Att.: Wayne & Suzie Hockmeyer. (207) 663-4466.

It's your choice on these Kennebec River trips—a rowing or a paddle raft with a guide as the river plummets through deep canyons on the longest, steepest drop of any river in the East. Even more challenging is the West Branch of the Penobscot, a spectacular river

MAINE

with both turbulent whitewater and quiet stretches. "We are Maine's number 1 outfitter," claim the Hockmeyers. "We were the original pioneers on the Kennebec, Penobscot, and Dead rivers in Maine, and on the Hudson River Gorge in New York." They emphasize that these are not float trips, but are geared for those who are adventurous and want lots of excitement. 1985 is their 10th anniversary of taking people down these whitewater rivers. Most are 1-day trips, but they also provide a kayak clinic, overnight raft trips, and mini-vacation packages. Rates average $70-$90 for the 1-day trips (group discounts), including a steak lunch and shuttle to and from the river. May-Oct. in ME. (See also *Canoeing/Kayaking.*)

ROLLING THUNDER RIVER CO., P.O. Box 291-A, Kingfield, ME 04947. Att.: Chuck Dunn & Steve Longley. (207) 265-2001.

"We provide whitewater rafting trips in Maine that are exciting for people of all ages, especially for families and kids," says Chuck Dunn, Rolling Thunder's owner and operator. The runs are on the Kennebec and Penobscot rivers."Both rivers can be enjoyed by people young and old, provided they are in reasonably good health and feel comfortable in and around water," says Dunn. On the Kennebec, Dunn uses 15-foot, custom-made Moravia sport rafts for a guide, a 7 paddlers. This run is from Harris Station Dam to West Forks, and has 12 uninterrupted wilderness miles through rock-walled canyons and cascading water. On the Penobscot, Dunn uses 18-foot boats for the 13-mile run from Ripogenus Dam through Exterminator, Telos Hole, Crib Work, and other great rapids. Typical rates run from $60/weekday or $75/weekend for a full day of rafting and a riverside lunch, or a $179 package price which includes the river run and 2 nights and 4 meals at off-river country inns, condos, or hotels. Group discounts. Apr.-Oct. Also runs on Dead and Rapid rivers in spring. Dunn recommends booking raft trips early as prime weekend space goes quickly. Most popular trips are 1 and 2 days on the Kennebec and Penobscot.

UNICORN RAFTING EXPEDITIONS, INC., P.O. Box-T, Dept. 47, Brunswick, ME 04011. Att.: Jay Schurman. (207) 725-2255.

"The Kennebec, Penobscot, and Hudson Rivers are now recognized as the premier whitewater rivers in eastern America," claims Jay Schurman. "We've combined western- and eastern-style rafting and give each participant first-class, individual treatment—including gourmet meals with steaks on 1-day trips and lobster on our overnight expeditions." Schurman offers a wide variety of trips to suit everyone: families, singles, groups, first-timers or experienced river runners. For exploring the Maine Wilderness, plus riverside camping with friendly companions, Unicorn offers 5- and 6-day river adventures. For experienced rafters seeking a real challenge—"a highly exciting and dangerous river"—Unicorn recommends its 1-day Moose River Run (NY). Rates for 1- to 6-day trips: $60-$450. (See also *Canoeing/Kayaking.*)

MONTANA

DOUBLE ARROW OUTFITTERS (AG), Box 495, Seeley Lake, MT 59868. Att.: Jack Rich. (406) 677-2411 or 2317.

Blackfoot and Clearwater River float trips are conducted from the ranch with motor vehicles to haul guests to and from the river. On the South Fork of the Flathead trips, you spend 1 1/2 days packing in on horseback to the junction of Young's and Danaher Creeks, then 4 days floating to the take-out point at Meadow Creek. It's a magnificent area for riding and rafting. Group size: 4-12. Rate for 6-day trips: $950. Bring sleeping gear. Jun.-Aug. Arrival: Missoula, MT (See also *Hiking with Packstock, Pack Trips, Youth Adventures.*)

Rafting the Middle Fork of the Flathead through Glacier National Park—*Bill Hofmann for Glacier Raft Company, MT.*

GLACIER RAFT COMPANY, P.O. Box 264-J, West Glacier, MT 59936. Att.: Darwon Stoneman. (406) 888-5541.

Spectacular Glacier National Park is the setting for half- to 4-day trips on the Flathead River system. There are rough-and-tumble whitewater runs, quiet trips for scenery buffs, and fishing trips. The 4-day trip on the Middle Fork of the Flathead begins with a scenic flight over the Great Bear Wilderness to the put-in for whitewater rafting through Spruce Park Gorge ($450). On a 3-day North Fork float you have fine views of Kintla and Vulture Peaks and some good trout fishing ($195). A 5-day combination horseback/rafting adventure brings accolades from everyone ($495). For more challenging whitewater, try Idaho's Lochsa River when the water is high (May-Jul.). "We run 50 miles with over 60 rapids ranging from

MONTANA

Class III to V," says Stoneman. Trips 1-3 days, $60-$230. Group and children's rates. (See also *Combos.*)

GREAT ADVENTURES WEST, 1401-B 5th Ave. So., Great Falls, MT 59405. Att.: Craig Madsen. (406) 761-1677.

Craig Madsen, a native Montanan, likes to put people on rivers to enjoy the pristine beauty of his state. "On just one river trip it's not unusual to see deer, antelope, bear, mink, beaver, hawks, eagles, waterfowl, and small mammals," he says. He is ready to arrange either whitewater excitement, tranquil scenic floats, or historic journeys, whichever you prefer, on the "wild and scenic" Upper Missouri River

Pristine beauty on the "wild and scenic" Upper Missouri River—*Great Adventures West, MT.*

through the White Cliffs area, the Yellowstone, Blackfoot, Clark Fork, Smith, Flathead, and other rivers. Some trips are pre-scheduled for individuals to join. Others are customized to your requirements. Fly-fishing trips or instruction with experienced fishing guides are also a specialty, and 5- to 7-day combination rafting, fishing, horseback riding, wilderness trips are available, too. Rates start around $90/day (discounts for seniors and children) and include professional guides, food, all camping gear. Bring or rent sleeping bags. "Rafts and drift boats have ample room and carry many luxiries, making river travel and camping very comfortable and pleasant," Madsen point out. May-Oct., 1- to 7-day trips. Arrival: Great Falls, MT. (See also *Canoeing.*)

GREAT NORTHERN RAFTING, Box 278, West Glacier, MT 59936. Att.: Reno & Deedee Baldwin. (406) 387-5340.

Raft the Flathead River in Glacier National Park through pristine high country with the help of Great Northern's trained guides. Navigate the river in May when the snow melts from the glacier's rugged peaks and stirs the water into a frenzy. Or wait until summer when the river has calmed—perfect for a relaxing day's float on your 15- to 18-foot raft. Half- to 3-day trips, $23-$150/adult, $15-$120/child. (Min. age varies according to trip.) For a total wilderness experience, the Baldwins offer a "Great Bear Adventure," combining horse packing, fishing, and floating with optional lodging for $560/person for 5 days (additional days available). Also, guided fishing trips, 1 to 4 days. Fly to Kalispell, MT. May-Sep. Arrival: Kalispell or West Glacier.

NEW
HAMPSHIRE

DOWNEAST RAFTING CO., INC., c/o Saco Bound, Box 113, Route 302, Center Conway, NH 03813. (603) 447-3002.

April runoffs start the rafting season on New Hampshire's Swift River and East Branch Pemigiwasett River. Then in late May, as spring waters subside, Downeast moves to their West Forks base camp near the dam-controlled waters of northern Maine and runs the famous 16-mile Lower Dead River with its Class IV and V water. Special 2-day trips on the Rapid River (Rangeley Lakes area) include overnight lodging ($120-$230, Jul.-Aug.). Daily trips on the Kennebec and Penobscot, Class IV and V, are scheduled Jun.-Sep. A special package combines 2 days of rafting the Kennebec with 2 nights (dinner, breakfasts) at Sugar Loaf Inn Resort ($149-$168); and 2 days on the Penobscot with nights at Squaw Mountain ($149-$159). Downeast uses 6- to 8-person rafts for 1-day trips, $55-$80/day including equipment, guides, and steak fry. (See also *Canoeing*-Saco Bound.)

NEW MEXICO

NEW WAVE RAFTING CO., Rt. 5, Box 302-A, Santa Fe, NM 87501. Att.: Steve & Kathy Miller. (800) 552-0070, ext. 265, or (505) 455-2633.

Paddlers have a chance to participate on New Wave's runs on the Rio Grande and the Rio Chama in New Mexico, and the Royal Gorge in Colorado. They also run the Big Bend section of the Rio Grande in Texas, the Rio Antigua in Mexico, and the Pacuare, Reventazon, and Chirripo in Costa Rica. On full-day trips you have exciting Class IV water in the Taos Box section of the Rio Grande, designated a Wild and Scenic River ($65-$70). Add to this run overnight camping in the Rio Grande Gorge State Park with the second day on the Racecourse run (Class III, 2 days, $150). Another overnight trip is scheduled in the La Junta section of the Rio Grande, starting with a 1-mile hike down

NEW MEXICO

to the river, with mules carrying the gear ($180). Also an overnight run is available on the Rio Chama, Class II water, perfect for families, through a canyon made famous by artist Georgia O'Keefe ($150). "On our paddle trips," the Millers promise, "you're part of the action. You run the river—and that makes all the difference."

RIO GRANDE RAPID TRANSIT, Box A, Pilar, NM 87571. Att.: Patrick Blumm. (505) 758-9700.

"The Rio has been our home for many years," Patrick says. "This means we can give you the quality river experience you are looking for." He offers half- to 4-day trips with a fleet of river-craft ranging from 2-man torpedoes to 10-man rafts. There are trips for everyone. Paddle yourself in a 2-person torpedo boat on a classic run starting at Rio Grande Gorge State Park, following a guide down the rapids. Let a professional boatman row you through the legendary rapids of the 17-mile Taos Box, on America's first designated "wild and scenic" river. Or take a relaxing flatwater sunset dinner float through scenic desert canyons. (Rates: $25-$65/day.) An alternative is the 2- or 3-day, 35-mile run on the Rio Chama, which Patrick calls "the prettiest stretch of river in the Southwest," ($150-$195). A rafter from Albuquerque tells us that the people at RGPT "are professionals in every way, be it skillfully guiding through Class IV whitewater, passing along some bit of history as you float through the canyon, or preparing your pleasant and always filling meal." Arrival: Taos, Santa Fe, or Albuquerque.

TAOS WHITEWATER, P.O. Box 707, El Prado, NM 87529. Att.: Steve Harris. (505) 758-2628 Apr.-Sep., (915) 371-2489 other months.

"Our expeditions through the Rio Grande Gorge near Taos offer an exciting acquaintance with the vibrant character of the river and its deep, lava canyon setting," says Harris. On a 3-day, 30-mile trip down the gorge, packmules tote your gear to the put-in. At night you camp among the pines. (May-Jul., $250.) Or run the Rio Grande's Taos Box Canyon and Pilar "Racecourse" rapids on a 2-day trip that covers 27 miles, camping overnight at Rio Grande Gorge State Park. (May-Jul., $150.) Another option for several weekends is 2 days running 24 miles of the Rio Chama down Class III rapids. It's a fine mix of forest camping, trout fishing, shore exploration, and alpine canyon country. (May-Oct., $150.) Trips include river guides, shuttles, safety gear, meals, and waterproof storage. Group and weekday discounts. Also 1-day trips through the Lower Box Canyon, $45-$70. (See also Telluride Whitewater in CO and Far Flung Adventures in TX, this chapter.)

NORTH
CAROLINA

NANTAHALA OUTDOOR CENTER, US 19 West Box 41, Bryson City, NC 28713. (704) 488-2175.

The outdoors people who operate NOC provide year-round instruction, guides, and equipment to help people enjoy the mountains and rivers. They offer rafting on five rivers: half days on the Nantahala, ideal for first-timers and families with Class II to III rapids, $17, full-day excursions on the Chattooga's churning Class IV and V water, $34-$50 half days on the Ocoee, with big, continuous rapids, $27; and full days on the French Broad, a good family trip, $32, or the Nolichucky, with crashing water and extraordinary gorges, $42. Rates include transportation between rivers and NOC outposts and a picnic lunch on all-day trips. Group rates. (See also *Backpacking, Mountaineering, Cycling, Canoeing/Kayaking*.)

OREGON

EAGLE SUN, INC., P.O. Box 873, Medford, OR 97501. Att.: Bill F. Smith. (503) 772-9910.

"You'll discover the rare satisfaction of challenging the natural forces of a river and living in complete harmony with the environment on raft and paddle boat trips," says Bill Smith. Eagle Sun recommends some river runs for beginners and others with Class III to V white water for experienced rafters. Choose a trip on the Rogue, Klamath, Scott, or Salmon rivers in northern California and Oregon. Rates: from half day/$30 to 5 days/$350; group and youth rates. On most trips you camp out with an option for lodge overnights on the Rogue and Salmon. "Guides orient and instruct you in boat handling techniques and water safety," Smith explains. "You become part of a highly personalized team which works together to master the thrills of river exploration." Guides, food, camping gear provided. Bring tent and sleeping bag. Rogue and Klamath trips, May-Sep.; Scott and Salmon, Apr.-Jun. Fishing trips in drift boats on the Rogue are another Eagle Sun specialty, $75/day.

LUTE JERSTAD ADVENTURES, LJA, INC., P.O. Box 19537, Portland, OR 97219. (503) 244-4364.

This long-established outfitter offers the learn-to-row-yourself concept. Guests have the option of rowing Hopi rafts or riding with a guide. "Meals are superb outdoor creations at camps along the riverbanks, and repeat guests year after year speak for the quality and fun of the trips," Lute Jerstad tells us. Each of his 3-day trips on Oregon's Grande Ronde, John Day and Deschutes rivers, and 5-day trips on the Owyhee, Hells Canyon or the Snake, and the Rogue rivers, has its own character and thrills. Sample rates from $275 for 3-day trips, and from $480 for 5-day trips. Early season Owyhee trips begin in April. Rogue, Snake and Deschutes trips run to mid-September. Lute also offers an exciting combination trip of horsepacking and whitewater rafting. (See also *Pack Trips*.)

O.R.E. INC., 30493 Lone Pine Dr., Junction City, OR 97448. Att.: Bob Doppelt or Peggy Bloom. (503) 689-6198.

"We are the Pacific Northwest's second largest outfitter, and we offer unique participatory river trips in Oregon, Idaho, and northern California," reports Bob Doppelt. "Our trips focus on involvement with three options—row it yourself, paddle raft, or ride with guides." O.R.E. uses light, easy-to-maneuver rafts and provides expert supervision on more than 9 rivers—the Salmon, Rogue, Deschutes, McKenzie, No. Umpqua River, Grande Ronde, John Day, Owyhee, and Klamath. Trips range from 1-5 days on the Salmon (shuttle not included). Limit, 30 participants; minimum age, 8. Bring sleeping bag and tent. Education trips also offered with geologists, naturalists, birding experts, photography instructors. One rafter summarizes his

OREGON

trip: "We had a great time with these people who are congenial, organized, informed about the rivers they run and the environment they love, educators of those they host, professional in their approach to rafting safety, and wizards of outdoor cuisine." (See also *Wilderness Living, Youth Adventures*.)

ORANGE TORPEDO TRIPS, P.O. Box 1111-G, Grants Pass, OR 97526. Att.: Don or Mryna Stevens. (503) 479-5061.

"Our company pioneered the use of inflatable kayaks on whitewater rivers 18 years ago," say Don and Mryna Stevens, "and we are one of the most experienced outfitters in the Pacific Northwest." Their guests challenge the rapids in one-person inflatable kayaks under close, expert supervision. These are stable, easy-to-maneuver boats and OTT's systems of instruction make it possible even for first-timers to have an exciting yet safe run in Class III whitewater. Trips are designed as fun, family-oriented experiences with challenges for everyone. Congenial guides are experts in the local history, flora, and fauna. Trips in northern CA: Klamath or Eel, 3 or 4 days/$245-$355; Salmon (in Idaho), 4-6 days/$435-$775. In OR: Rogue, Deschutes, and North Umpqua, 1-3 days/$45-$395. Group rates. Lodging on some trips, camping on others. Raft option. May-Sep.

PACIFIC CREST OUTWARD BOUND SCHOOL, 0110 S.W. Bancroft, Dept. AT86, Portland, OR 97201. (800) 547-3312 or (503) 243-1993.

Outward Bound is "learning through doing," and you'll quickly be in harmony with sights and sounds of the river canyons as you paddle through some of the best white water in the country on Oregon's Rogue and Deschutes rivers. Participants work as a team, navigating through rapids and learning from skilled instructors. These are small-group courses, with participants involved every bit of the way. You need not be an experienced athlete in order to have fun. Most memorable moments for one river runner: "A hike to canyon rim at daybreak, a leisurely 1 1/2-mile jog, then a dip in the 60-degree water to complete the shaking of the cobwebs." Courses for adults and teens Apr.-Oct. Cost: $675 for 7 days. Financial aid available. (See also *Backpacking, Youth Adventures*.)

RIVER TRIPS UNLIMITED, INC., 4140 Dry Creek Rd., Medford, OR 97504. Att.: Irv Urie. (503) 779-3798.

Running wild rapids with a "pro" is unforgettable, according to Irv Urie, a full-time outfitter and fishing specialist on Oregon and California rivers. His 1- to 4-day excursions include swimming, inner-tube riding, rock hunting, gold panning, and wildlife sighting. On overnight trips, you stay in comfortable lodges along the river. Irv uses deluxe rubber rafts, inflatable kayaks, and McKenzie drift boats and can also take kayaks along for extra fun. Rates on the Klamath and Smith (CA): $60-$75/day; on the Rogue and other Oregon rivers: 1 day/$45, 3-4 days/$325-$425, including meals and overnight lodging. For 3 days on the Klamath in kayak or raft, lodge overnights, $300. Salmon and steelhead trips another specialty. Writes an enthusiastic participant from Chiloquin, OR: "Have nothing but the best to say of Irv Urie's trips. Excellent food and guides. Enjoy every trip with Irv."

ROGUE EXCURSIONS UNLIMITED INC., P.O. Box 855, Medford, OR 97501. Att.: Paul E. Brown. (503) 773-5983.

After a day of shooting the Rogue's thrilling rapids, rock hunting, and swimming, relax at a rustic riverside lodge to enjoy a sumptuous meal and hot shower before sinking into bed. Paul's trips offer all this—and a leisurely pace for absorbing the quiet beauty of the surroundings. His boats and equipment are "the best money can buy." Says a repeat guest, "An absolutely perfect trip. Fishing was great, food super and the guide service couldn't have been better." Usually 2-4 rafts per trip, 3 days, $330/person, including river lodge or camping out (your choice), May-Sep. Hardshell drift boats for steelhead trips, 2 per boat plus guide, 4 days, $1,400, Sep.-Nov.

SUNDANCE EXPEDITIONS, INC., 14894 Galice Rd., Merlin, OR 97532. Att.: Judo Patterson. (503) 479-8508.

In Sundance's home "turf" are two of Oregon's finest whitewater rivers: the Rogue and the incredible Illinois, both in the Federal Wild and Scenic Rivers Act. Sundance runs 4-day trips on the Rogue in oar-powered, paddle rafts, and inflatable kayaks all summer, starting every Thursday. Everyone participates in maneuvering the raft downstream through the exciting whitewater rapids. "I enjoyed the personal attention, considerate response to our requests, and the encouragement to go for it!" comments a river runner. "The most fun I've ever had." Rate for 4 days, $340. The Illinois is runnable in April and May—high adventure for whitewater enthusiasts with a 65-foot drop each mile and a paddle boat option. For 3 days, $335; 4 days, $395. Group and family rates. Arrival: Medford or Grants Pass, OR. (See also *Canoeing*.)

SUNRISE SCENIC TOURS, 3791 Rogue River Hwy., Gold Hill, OR 97525. Att.: Ted & Sheri Birdseye. (503) 582-0202.

For beginners the Birdseyes recommend 1- to 5-day trips on the Rogue or Klamath Rivers. More experienced river runners will appreciate the swift water and high Cascades scenery of the Umpqua or the large swells and desert country of the Deschutes. In late May SST challenges the brawling Illinois River through the Kalmiopsis Wilderness Area. "All our trips are tailored-made," stresses Ted. "We match guests with the river craft of their choice—big people rafts,' inflatable one-person kayaks, or drift boats for fishing." Trip rates: 1-5 days, $40-$335, including river equipment, camping and sleeping gear, hearty meals. B&B (1870 setting) $35-$50/night. Discounts for 5 or more. May-Sep. Arrival: Medford, OR. (See also *Kayaking*.)

WALKER RIVER EXPEDITIONS, Rt. 1, Box AG, Enterprise, OR 97828. Att.: Jim Walker. (503) 426-3307.

"The Snake River in Hells Canyon has three distinct personalities in the 80-mile stretch we travel," notes Jim Walker. "The upper third has the most challenging rapids, the middle third is more open with evidence of the pioneers' struggle to eke out a living from the steep slopes, and the lower third closes in again to steep-walled sides." He runs the Owyhee and Grande Ronde rivers. Rubber rafts and inflatable kayaks on all trips. If you really want to get in on the action, you may sign up to row 13' rafts under a guide's direction. Rates include round trip transport from Enterprise. Hells Canyon: 4 days, $369; 5 days, $450; 2 1/2-day fly-out, $275. Combo horseback 3 days/rafting 4 days, $695. Bring or rent sleeping gear. May-Sep. Arrival: Enterprise, OR.

PENNSYLVANIA **CANYON CRUISE,** R.D. 4, Box 155, Wellsboro, PA 16901. Att.: John & Cindy McCarthy. (814) 435-2969.

Running Pine Creek through Pennsylvania's Grand Canyon, provides over 60 miles of "swift, clean white water, stunning beauty, wildlife, and majestic scenery," says Canyon Cruise. They offer 1- and 2-day tours—the first day through the upper canyon from Ansonia to Blackwell, and the next day from Watrous to Ansonia, or 25 miles beyond, weather and group permitting (no camping). Experienced river rats rent equipment (Grumman canoes, Avon inflatable rafts) and go without guides. In its 26th year of operation, CC specializes in family and youth groups, and clubs. "It's a very safe river and the scenery is breathtaking," says Canyon's Cindy McCarthy. For ages 5 and up, Mar.-Jun.; 1 day, $28; 2 days, $45. Includes hot midday cookout, transport to river, and equipment (bring raingear).

POCONO WHITEWATER RAFTING, Rt. 903, Jim Thorpe, PA 18229. Att.: Doug Fogal. (717) 325-3656.

"You'll laugh, scream, get soaked—and love it," warns Doug Fogal. He's talking about his 6-hour trips through the Lehigh River Gorge where every day, spring and fall, paddlers bounce, splash, and skim through one rapid after another. "It's an exciting introduction to whitewater rafting for individuals, families, youth groups, anyone," Fogal claims. Rate: about $39/person. In the lower summer water, floats and duckies take over, floating the "family-style rapids" in 3-4 hours ($19-$29/person). Fogal also runs spring and fall trips on 16 miles of thrilling, tumultuous Class III, IV, and V water of the Upper Hudson Gorge—"some of the best white water in the East." These are guided trips; rates, $65/person, including lunch, guide, and transport to/from river. Lehigh trips start at Jim Thorpe, PA (2 hours from NYC or Phila.) off Rt. 903, "Pennsylvania's hiway to adventure." Hudson River trips start near Indian Lake, NY.

WHITE WATER ADVENTURERS, Box 31-A, Ohiopyle, PA 15470. (800) WWA-RAFT (outside PA); (412) 329-8850 (collect in PA).

"This river is one of the most impressive attractions at Ohiopyle State Park," writes WWA of the Youghiogheny, "but until you've tried to conquer it with raft and paddle you'll never feel its real magnetism. Then you'll want to try and try again." They also run 11 miles of the Cheat River through its memorable canyon. "With 4-10 people to a raft you're so busy that all of life's cares are forgotten," one river runner remarks. Each excursion lasts about 6 hours, with time out for lunch, swimming, and splash fights. 1-day trip on Youghiogheny,

$22-$40; 2 days, $38-$48. Cheat River trips: $35-48. Pickup in
Ohiopyle for Youghiogheny trip (Mar.-Oct.). In Albright, WV, for the
Cheat (Mar.-Jun.).

Sunset Rapid offers one
of many challenges on
the New River—*Robert
Harrison, Whetstone
Photography, for
Wildwater Expeditions
Unlimited, Inc., WV.*

WHITEWATER CHALLENGERS, INC., Box AT, Star Rt. 6A, White
Haven, PA 18661. Att.: Ken Powley. (717) 443-9532.
   "The Lehigh River is an excellent introduction to white water,"
remarks Ken Powley. "The numerous Class III rapids along this
stretch of the Lehigh can be handled comfortably by first-timers, yet
provide plenty of excitement for more experienced paddlers." Acres of
rhododendron surround this isolated river gorge, and deer, beaver,
and red fox can be seen on the banks. "It's virgin terrain, and only a
short drive from New York or Philadelphia," writes a river runner.
"The people at Whitewater Challengers are all very friendly and
positive. Their motto is 'Go with the pros!'" Open Mar.-Nov. Rates
from $15-$39. Bring lunch. Discounts for groups. Whitewater
Challengers claims it is "America's largest whitewater outfitter,
serving some 50,000 rafting guests annually." Also trips through the
Hudson River Gorge, 1 day, $65, Mar.-Jun.
(See also *Canoeing*.)

WHITEWATER WORLD, LTD., Rt. 903, Jim Thorpe, PA 18229. Att.:
Paul Fogal. (717) 325-3656.
   Whitewater World has complete rafting facilities on four great

rivers in three states and two countries. "Each river offers its own brand of raw adventure in a remote wilderness setting," says Paul Fogal of WW. "Either they offer rumbling, frothing, surging currents; slam-bang rapids that thunder through towering gorges; or unexpected swirls, rises, and plunges..." You can raft the Hudson River Gorge in the Eastern Adirondack Mountains starting near Indian Lake, NY in Apr., May, Sep., Oct. Day rate, $65. Or choose one of three distinct runs on the Lehigh River from Mar.-Nov. (a less demanding float trip in summer months). The Cheat River in northern West Virginia offers still more excitement with its 35 separate, diverse rapids. "It has more rapids in its 12-mile stretch than any other river in the East," notes Fogal. Apr. and May. Day rate, $49. Or if you're looking for huge waves and endless eddies and whirlpools, the Riviere Rouge in Quebec is your answer to excitement. Day rate, $38-$47; 2-day trip, $103. Youth rates; group discounts for 15-plus.

SOUTH CAROLINA

WILDWATER LTD., Dept. A, P.O. Box 100, Long Creek, SC 29658. Att.: Jim Greiner. (803) 647-9587.

People learn about conservation on these trips on the Chattooga and the Ocoee, according to Jim Greiner, as well as discovering the excitement of running white water. "We reach the put-in for the Chattooga with a short hike down a mountain," he explains. "During the day we pass only one spot where man has intruded—a bridge. The canyons, falls, rapids, huge rocks, virgin timber, and wildlife are our companions." Any active person, with or without previous rafting experience, enjoys navigating Section III of the Chattooga, a National Wild and Scenic River (a full day trip, $30-$40 including lunch). But the challenging rapids of Section IV are not for the first-timer (full day, $38-$55 with lunch). On the Ocoee River, the five miles of continuous white water is fun for everyone (half day, $20-$27). In winter Wildwater offers trips in Costa Rica and Hawaii, and sailing in Georgia's barrier islands.

TENNESSEE

OCOEE OUTDOORS, INC., P.O. Box 72, Ocoee, TN 37361. Att.: J.T. Lemons. (615) 338-2438.

"We were the first full-time outfitter on the Ocoee River," states J.T. Lemons, "and since our start in 1977 have logged over 50,000 miles and 11,000 trips while maintaining a flawless safety record." He recommends these 1-day trips in paddle rafts for everyone—even the 5-mile stretch of Class IV water which has gained a reputation as "one of the most challenging in America." The Hiwassee River, with Class I and II water, offers a perfect setting for family floats and trout fishing, or for paddlers wanting to hone their canoe and kayak skills. From Mar.-Nov. Ocoee rates: $23-$28/day, group and special event discounts. Hiwassee rates: rafts, $8-$9/person; canoes, $22-$28/canoe. The London Times travel editor describes his Ocoee trip: "Crash-helmeted and life-belted, we paddled along strenuously under the captaincy of a fit expert and finished the voyage soaked but triumphant."

OUTLAND EXPEDITIONS, P.O. Box 397, Benton, TN 37307. Att.: Lamar Davis. (615) 338-2107.

For daily trips on the Ocoee River from March to November, Outland Expeditions specializes in groups—up to 76 people—and for 15 or more provides a picnic lunch (chicken, baked beans, potato salad, drinks) for $4.50 per person. "We have an outstanding rapport with church groups and other activity groups," reports Lamar Davis. He runs both the upper and lower canyons, including the 5-mile stretch "through the heart of the Cherokee National Forest with almost continuous whitewater action and Class III and IV rapids—ideal for beginners yet challenging for experts." Rates: $20-$24.50 depending on number in group, weekday, or weekend.

SUNBURST WILDERNESS ADVENTURES, P.O. Box 329A, Benton, TN 37307. Att.: Marc Hunt. (615) 338-8388.

"An Ocoee River raft trip is the ideal way for anyone to learn what white water is all about in just half a day," writes Marc Hunt. "The 5 miles we run is one of the most continuous white water stretches anywhere, with a good, dependable water flow all season long." Most people, he reports, think the trip is the most exciting thing they've done. "It's high-powered and high-quality but done within the saftey framework of a guide with each boat." Sunburst requires that rafters be at least 12 years old. No previous paddling experience necessary. Rates for half-day trips: $25 weekdays; $27 weekends. Apr.-Oct. Meet at Sunburst headquarters near Benton, TN.

TEXAS   **FAR FLUNG ADVENTURES,** Box 31, Terlingua, TX 79852. Att.: Mike Davidson. (915) 371-2489.

Far Flung has been putting people and rivers together in Big Bend country for 6 years. Year-round trips explore rough-hewn canyons, warm springs, and tumbling rapids on the Rio Grande (and other rivers from Mexico to Alaska). Choose a 1-day run through Colorado Canyon ($50/person), 2 days in Santa Elena Canyon ($150), or 7 days through the isolated Lower Canyons ($500). FFA runs fall and winter trips on Mexico's Rio Usumacinta (10 days, $1,300), Rio Antigua (6 days, $500), and others. In May and June it runs the tumbling white water of New Mexico's Rio Grande Gorge (1-3 days, $60-$250) and schedules whitewater-rafting schools on the Rio Grande and Rio Chama (7 days, $500). In summer, Alaska expeditions: Copper (10 days, $1,300), Chilikadrotna (12 days, $1,350), and others. Experienced naturalist/guide/instructors; oar- or paddle-power option. Bring sleeping gear. "A fantastic trip with excellent food and guides," writes a Texas couple. "It was true escapism." (See also Taos Whitewater in NM, and Telluride Whitewater in CO, this chapter.)

OUTBACK EXPEDITIONS, P.O. Box 44, Terlingua, TX 79852. Att.: Larry G. Humphreys. (915) 371-2490.

"Leave your preconceptions behind," urges Larry Humphreys, "and discover pleasure in the unexpected." The unexpected usually occurs on his trips down the Rios Moctezuma, Usumacinta, Balsas, and Grande de Santiago in Mexico. You travel on Class III and IV water, past ancient Indian ruins, natural springs, and waterfalls, or through dense jungle brightened with tropical toucans, macaws, parrots, and flamingoes. Some trips involve a truck ride or carrying your gear

TEXAS

down a steep jungle trail to the put-in. Dec.-Feb., 5-14 days, $85/person/day. In Texas, year-round trips on the Rio Grande (1-9 days, $75/person/day), between Redford and Langtry, through Big Bend National Park and the entire Wild and Scenic section (the Lower Canyons). Groups are kept small. River runs may be combined with backpacking. (See also *Backpacking, Canoeing*.)

TEXAS CANOE TRAILS, 121 River Terrace, Dept. AG, New Braunfels, TX 78130. Att.: Betty Walls. (512) 625-3375 or 0662.

The Rio Grande waters around Big Bend National Park challenge the adventurous or satisfy the beginners, depending on which section of the river you choose. From the TCT base in Lajitas, run an easy 8 miles in half a day. Or choose 14 to 25 miles of the Colorado Canyon, a leisurely 2 to 5 days. Further downriver, the Santa Elena Canyon offers 1,500-foot sheet canyon walls and tricky rapids; Mariscal Canyon presents an easy 2-day trip (10 miles); Boquilas Canyon provides a scenic family trip beneath 2,300 canyon walls (30 miles, 3-4 days); and the Lower Canyons challenge "water rats" with fast, exciting rapids on a 100-mile stretch (7-10 days). Other rivers serviced by TCT: the Lower and Upper Guadelupe (near San Antonio—good trout fishing), the Animas (near Durango), and the Dolores, Piedra, and San Juan rivers in Colorado, as well as the Moctezuma and Rio Santa in Mexico. Half-day or overnight trips, $30-$40/day; longer runs, $65 up/day. Group discounts. Year round. (See also *Canoeing*.)

UTAH

ADRIFT ADVENTURES, P.O. Box 81032, Salt Lake City, UT 84108. Att.: Myke Hughes. (801) 485-5978.

The river runs in Utah's Canyonlands are favorites with everyone. Choose Cataract Canyon of the Colorado River through Canyonlands National Park for a 3-day motorized or a 5-day oar-powered trip—especially wild and exciting in May and June with spring run-offs; (May-Sep., $330-$490 including charter flight). The run on the Green River through Lodore, Whirlpool, and Split Mountain canyons takes you over 60 rapids, ranging from light to medium, in either oar or paddle rafts (Jun.-Sep., 4 days, $325). Labyrinth Canyon of the Green River offers a wilderness wonderland for rafting or canoeing—no rapids on the 45-mile section past sandstone cliffs and sculptured landscapes (May-Aug., 3 days, $220). A spring ski and rafting package is a specialty of this outfitter (Apr.-May, 8 days, $639), as is an overland/rafting combination. (See also *Comb Trips*.)

ADVENTURE RIVER EXPEDITIONS, INC., P.O. Box 96, Green River, UT 84525. Att.: Skip Bell. (801) 564-3648. [Oct.-Mar.: (801) 277-9569.]

"In the Green River Wilderness participants live the thrill of coursing whitewater rapids, explore the wonders of desert spire, red sandstone cliffs and multi-colored canyons, and marvel at our western heritage of prehistoric rock artwork, Indian ruins, and the relics of early explorers and outlaws," according to Skip Bell. The company runs 1- to 6-day whitewater rafting trips on the Green and Colorado Rivers through Canyonland National Park. Boats are paddle- and oar-powered. Day trips, $30/person; overnights, $70/person/day, including guides, rafts, and food. Bring your own tent and sleeping bag, or rent. Limit: 25 rafters—novices and experienced welcome. Apr.-Sep.

FASTWATER EXPEDITIONS, Box 365-A, Boulder City, NV 89005. Att.: Bill & Fran Belknap. (702) 293-1406.

"Why should river guides have all the fun?" the Belknaps ask. "If you love water, try our Sportyak trips for doers who'd rather row

Omelets for breakfast on the Green River—
Bill Belknap for Fastwater Expeditions, UT.

than ride." With one to a boat, the fleet of Sportyaks glide and splash through rapids and everchanging beauty on the 100-mile stretch of the winding Green River. It's exciting, challenging, and a real thrill to navigate thundering rapids without flipping. On canyon hikes you discover Indian petroglyphs and fossils and poke around an abandoned ranch where Butch Cassidy once used to stop. Bill (a photographer and writer) adds a photo seminar to some trips. "Superb guiding and supervision," writes a Sportyakker. "Learning to 'read' the river and run the rapids is a great experience." Green River (UT), Desolation/Gray Canyons, Jul.-Oct., 9 days, $825; "Autumn on the Green," Oct., 10 days, $895; San Juan River (UT), May-Jun., 7 days, $650. Rates include sleeping gear. Up to 16 per group.

UTAH

GRAND CANYON EXPEDITIONS, Dept. AG, P.O. Box O, Kanab, UT 84741. Att.: Ron & Marc Smith. (801) 644-2691.

On 9-day motorized raft trips, GCE runs the entire 300 miles of the Grand Canyon from Lees Ferry to Lake Mead. In first-class comfort and safety, you negotiate nearly 200 exciting rapids while traveling through what Ron calls "the most spectacular geological exhibit anywhere in the world. We refuse to rush you," he says. "It's a once-in-a-lifetime vacation and should be unhurried." With over 20 years of river running, GCE has run trips for the National Geographic Society, Smithsonian Institution, Chicago Field Museum of Natural History, World Cinemax, and others. Special-interest expeditions highlight canyon history, geology, photography, ecology, and fine arts. Rates: $1,100/adult, $990/ages 8-14. Apr.-Sep. Charter rates. Arrival: Las Vegas, NV.

Rafting under a full moon—*Holiday River Expeditions, UT.*

HOLIDAY RIVER EXPEDITIONS, 544 East 3900 South, ATG, Salt Lake City, UT 84107. Att.: Dee Holladay. (800) 624-6323 or (801) 266-2087.

For the greatest wilderness experience, Dee Holladay prefers oars to motors, keeps his groups small, and is always on the lookout for new areas to explore. Dee knows his business thoroughly, according to river runners—Holladay has been in operation for 20 years—and his boatmen are knowlegeable about the geology and history of the rivers. They'll show you their favorite places; a short walk up a side canyon to a private waterfall, a picnic on a cliff overlooking what seems to be the entire world, soft, sandy beaches where you'll be sleeping under the stars. Dee offers a wide selection of trip dates, especially on Utah rivers: 5 days in Cataract Canyon (every Monday, $500: 4 days in the Green River Wilderness, $280 includes flight to put-in; 4-5 days, Dinosaur National Monument, $340-$390; 2-3 days, Westwater, $175-$250; 4 days, San Juan River, $300.) He also runs the Main Salmon in Idaho, 6 days, $550; and the Lower Salmon River Gorge, 3-4 days, $250-$300. Group and family rates. Bring or rent sleeping gear. May-Sep.

SIERRA WESTERN RIVER GUIDES, P.O. Box 7129, University Station, Provo, UT 84602. Att.: Verle Duerden. (800) 453-1482 or in UT (801) 377-9750.

"Super guides, quality outfitters" is the comment of vacationers on Sierra Western's trips. With custom-designed equipment (rafts and rigging) they run some great rivers—the American (CA); the Colorado (in CO) and through the Grand Canyon (AZ); the Arkansas and Roaring Fork (CO); and the Main Salmon (ID). On Main Salmon trips there's extra fun with paddle rafts and inflatable kayaks. Most trips May-Sep., from 2-6 days. Rates range from $125/adult for 2 days on the American, to $595/adult ($545/child) for 6 days on the Main Salmon or $895 for 6 days in the Grand Canyon. A deluxe 3-day whitewater special with lodging and breakfasts in Aspen includes rafting each day and time for golf or tennis—$275/adult, $215/child.

STEVE CURREY EXPEDITIONS, INC., P.O. Box 1574, Provo, UT 84603. Att.: Steve Currey. (801) 224-6797.

With 20 years of running famous rivers of the West—the Main Salmon and Middle Fork, Selway, Owyhee, the Colorado through the Grand Canyon, and others—Steve has built a reputation for "trips of consistently high quality." He considers his guides "the best...chosen for their personality, leadership, and enthusiasm to work with people." His equipment is designed for the specific requirements of each river. From April to June SCE runs 4-day trips on Oregon's Middle Owyhee, $750. In June, Idaho's Selway River, 5 days, $645. From July to September, 5 days on the Main Salmon with paddle boat option ($645), and the Middle Fork ($695), with transportation,($130 extra) from Boise to the put-in and back at trip's end. Grand Canyon trips are scheduled from April-September: 8-day motorized trips, Lees Ferry to Lake Mead, $895; 13-day oar-powered trips, $1,250; and 5-day oar trips in the Upper Grand Canyon, $500; or 9 days in the Lower Canyon, $900.

UTAH

TAG-A-LONG TOURS, P.O. Box 1206, 452 N. Main St., Moab, UT 84532. Att.: Paul M. Niskanen. (800) 453-3292 or (801) 259-8946.

"Our expeditions are planned to allow guests to kick back and relax," writes Paul Niskanen. His 3- to 6-day Cataract Canyon trips on the Colorado assemble in Moab and include a scenic flight back from Hite Marina at trip's end. Or continue on with a 4-day jeep expedition into the Canyonlands. For 2-day trips in the Westwater Canyon of the Colorado, rafters meet in Grand Junction. If you prefer more moderate rapids, raft the Green through Gray and Desolation Canyons. Or enjoy lazy floating, swimming down river with the boats, and some fine rapids on 1-day trips through Professor Valley just up river from Moab. Tag-A-Long uses oar-powered rafts on all runs, and motors, paddleboats, and Sportyaks on some. Trips scheduled Apr.-Oct.; charters only on the San Juan, May-Jun. Special river expeditions for associations and business groups complete with bar and musical entertainment. Sleeping gear rental. (See also *Jeeping, Van Camping*.)

WESTERN RIVER EXPEDITIONS, INC., 7258 Racquet Club Drive, Salt Lake City, UT 84121. (800) 453-7450 or (801) 942-6669.

"Motorized and oar-powered trips take rafters on some of the West's most fabulous river runs," WRE tells us. Expeditions vary from 1-10 days and include the Green River (in UT, with optional stay at Tavaputs Ranch); Westwater and Cataract Canyons on the Upper Colorado (UT); the Grand Canyon (AZ); the Middle Fork and Main Salmon (ID); the Fraser River in British Columbia; and various rivers and trips in Alaska. WRE is especially proud of river menus featuring "steaks, seafood, fresh fruits, and superb salads." It also provides a raft and canoe rental outlet in Moab, UT. Sample rates: Green River, 4-5 days/$550; Westwater Canyon, 3 days/$345; Grand Canyon, 6 days/$945. Children's discounts. Transport to and from river included. Trips Apr.-Oct.

WEST
VIRGINIA

APPALACHIAN WILDWATERS INC., P.O. Box 126-AG, Albright, WV 26519. (800) 624-8060 or (304) 329-1665.

"Quite simply, we have the finest whitewater staff in the business," claims Imre Szilagyi who started this company nearly 15 years ago. "The rivers we run provide trips for novices on up to grizzled veterans seeking a world-class challenge." AW fits equipment to each day's water level, and adds a touch of class with "plastic bags to keep wet tennis shoes from migrating into your sleeping bag." They run the Class III-V water of the Cheat and Tygart rivers, Class V on the New, and Class IV-VI on the Gauley. The Upper Youghiogheny in western Maryland is a run for adventurous experienced rafters, Class VI. Trips on various rivers are scheduled Mar.-Nov., usually with 10-person guided rafts, or with duckies (small inflatable kayaks for extra fun) when water is low. Average rates around $40-$50 weekdays, higher weekends; special rates for groups, off-season, consecutive 1-day trips. Family trips (1-2 days) and 3-day retreats on the Lower New. (See also *Canoeing*.)

CHEAT RIVER OUTFITTERS, Box 196-AG, Albright, WV 26519.
Att.: Eric Neilson. (304) 329-2024.

"We give you 13 miles of some of the best white water in the eastern
U.S.," says Eric Neilson. "There are at least 30 major rapids on the
Cheat of Class III, IV, and V difficulty. You'll shoot Cue Ball, Big
Nasty, High Falls, Even Nastier, and Coliseum—and lurch to the top
of exploding 10-foot waves. We take anyone 13 years and up willing
to challenge this fantastic river." Rates are $50/day on weekends;
$35/weekdays. Apr.-Jul., Sep.-Oct. CRO also runs trips on the North
Branch River (Jul.-Aug.). Adds Eric: "We use top-quality 4- to 8-man
rafts with trained, experienced river guides."

CLASS VI RIVER RUNNERS, INC., P.O. Box 78-AT, Lansing, WV
25862. (304) 574-0704.

"America's most condensed area of challenging and diverse white
water" is Class VI's description of West Virginia's New and Gauley
rivers. And with rapids named "Mash" and "Heaven Help You" you
know you're in for some big water. "We run small, personal trips in
16-foot rafts with a special combination of oar and paddle power,"
explains director David Arnold. "Our guides are highly qualified and
our meals are the best." Rates: New River, 1-6 days, $45-$500, Upper
Gauley or Lower Gauley, 1 day, $75. A 2-day, 28-mile trip on the
Gauley ($75/person) includes all river equipment, 4 hearty meals, and
50 major rapids. "It's man against the elements in its rawest form,"
writes a 3-time veteran of Class VI trips. "One reaps a sense of
satisfaction seldom experienced." (See also *Canoeing*.)

MOUNTAIN RIVER TOURS, INC., P.O. Box 88CA, Hico, WV
25854. Att.: Paul W. Breuer. (304) 658-5266.

"There you are, paddling along in a big rubber raft and enjoying the
incredible beauty of the Appalachians," writes Paul Breuer. "Then you
hear the rumble of churning water, see froth ahead, and suddenly
you're flying, rising, floating, bouncing, shooting through the rapids."
With 16-foot rafts and a team of whitewater experts he offers 1- and
2-day adventures on the New River (WV) from April to
mid-November and on the Gauley in spring and fall. Also half-day
floats on the Cumberland River (KY), and the French Broad and
Nolichucky Rivers (NC). Rates for day trips $43 and up; 2-day trips
on the New, $129; on the Gauley, $165. Group and weekday
discounts. Bring sleeping gear. MRT also offers customized fishing
trips. Their headquarters are in Hico at the interchange between US 19
and 60, just north of the New River Bridge on Sunday Road.

NORTH AMERICAN RIVER RUNNERS, INC., P.O. Box 81, Hico,
WV 25854. Att.: Frank M. Lukacs, Jr. (304) 658-5276.

In 8-person paddle rafts, NARR challenges three of West Virginia's
most exhilarating rivers—the New, Gauley and Cheat—as they carve
their way through spectacular canyons. Each has its own special
thrills. There's the awesome canyon of the Cheat (Apr.-May); the
huge waves and mountain scenery along the New (Apr.-Oct.); and the
churning, continuous rapids of the Gauley (Sep. & Oct., for
experienced rafters only). Rates for 1-day trips: $45-$80 weekends,

WEST VIRGINIA $44-$60 weekdays. Also overnight trips on the Gauley and New, group rates, campgrounds, custom trips, kayak and canoe instruction. Minimum age: 14 on the New and Cheat, 16 on the Gauley. Last year NARR initiated a new program for trips on the Upper Youghiogheny in western Maryland. A 9-day whitewater trip in Costa Rica is also offered.

WILDWATER EXPEDITIONS UNLIMITED, INC., Dept. AT, 1 Riverfront St., Thurmond, WV 25936. (304) 469-2551.

Raft through history as well as rapids in the scenic canyons of the turbulent New River—"some of the most challenging water there is." From March to October: 1- and 2-day runs with paddle-powered rafts and a 5 to 1 participant/guide ratio. An exclusive riverside base camp provides overnight camping and meals. In spring (Feb.-Apr.) trips feature the folklore and ghost towns of the New River—6 rafters per trip. Wildwater's rugged fall trips on the Gauley are for those with prior whitewater experience. Gear provided; special trips on request. Rates: $60-$160/day, depending on river, time of year, and service required. An Ohio attorney calls his 15 years of rafting with Wildwater "unparalleled primarily because of their degree of professionalism...the thoroughness of preparations...the well-trained guides. So peel off your 3-piece suit, don your river gear, and prepare for an experience that will bring you back again and again," he advises.

BRITISH   **FRONTIER RIVER ADVENTURES**, 927 Fairfield Rd., North
COLUMBIA   Vancouver, B.C., Canada V7H 2J4. Att.: Tom Randall. (604) 929-7612.

The Thompson and Fraser rivers in British Columbia offer the largest rapids in North America. The Thompson, with lots of white water flows through beautiful semi-desert country and narrow rockwalls. The Fraser is dramatically different with rugged, lush scenery and growing rapids, among them the world-famous Hells' Gate. Choose a 1- or 2-day trip on either river (Apr.-Oct.), or spend 3 days experiencing the wildest of both (Aug.-Sep.). Meeting place is Boston Bar, B.C. If you have 8 days, try what Tom Randall calls "a true frontier adventure" following the route of the Gold Rush miners of the 1800's on the Fraser. Raft approximately 350 miles, explore old homesteads and Indian sites, maneuver challenging rapids, and see "breathtaking hoodoos, awesome canyons, and beautiful beaches" (May-Oct. pickup in Vancouver). Motorized and paddle boats. Youth rates; tent and sleeping bag rentals. Rates (Canadian): 1 day $55, 2 days $125-$130, 3 days $185-$195, 8 days $650.

WHITEWATER ADVENTURES, 1616 Duranleau St., Vancouver, B.C., Canada, V6H 3S4. Att.: Vern Whittle. (604) 669-1100.

"This is outdoor adventure made easy," says director Dan Culver of these 1- to 7-day trips on the mighty Thompson and Fraser rivers. On the Thompson, you float past sand beaches and rolling hills to startling white canyons and breathtaking waterfalls. Towering rock faces and cascading streams form spectacular scenery on the Fraser. The many huge rapids on both rivers produce cries of "more!"

(Apr.-Oct.) In U.S. dollars: 1 day, $60; 2 days, $150; 7 days, $600,
including transport back to Vancouver. Bring sleeping gear. Dan also
offers 12-day trips on the seldom-visited Nahanni River in the
Northwest Territories where you see some of the steepest canyons in
the world and portage Virginia Falls, twice the height of Niagara.
(Jul.-Aug., $1,500 including bush flights.) "Food you'd never dream
could be cooked so beautifully over a campfire," comments a tripper.
WA also runs a 6-day Chilco River Expedition—"the biggest
whitewater in North America, and a magnificent train ride back to
Vancouver"—$715; including bush flight, and exploratory trips on the
Coppermine River, 14 days, $1,665; and 11 days on the Tatshenshini,
$1,500. Culver started his rafting service in 1974. (See also
Windjammers—Bluewater Adventures.)

Fantastic ice ridges
dwarf rafters in
Alaska—*Bart Hender-
son for Sobek Expedi-
tions, CA.*

MANITOBA   **NORTH COUNTRY RIVER TRIPS,** Berens River, Man., Canada,
                R0B 0A0. Att.: Jack & Georgia Clarkson. (204) 382-2284 or 2379.
                     "We are the first and only whitewater rafting outfit in Manitoba.
                We operate on the Berens, Pigeon, Gods, and Hayes rivers as well as
                the Bloodvein which is Manitoba's only Heritage River," notes Jack
                Clarkson. Rates: $225/2 days, $325/3 days, and $425/4 days, in
                Canadian funds. Some trips originate at Hecla Island, a Provincial
                Park. Try the historic river trip to York Factory—now being made into
                a park, it encompasses the Old Hudson Bay Co. Fort. You have a
                chance to see polar bears, beluga whales, and seals on return jet boat
                service to Gillam. (10 days, $1,295.) "For great speckled trout fishing,
                the Gods River is a must for a float fishing trip," says Jack. (7 days,
                $895.) Canoeing also, with floatplane put-in service. There's plenty of
                excitement on these river trips, as one rafter can vouch: "Once we had
                a pack of timber wolves come into camp; we also had a bear raid; and
                another time our canoe was 50 feet from a bull moose that was tearing
                up the bush!" (See also *Canoeing.*)

NORTHWEST   **SUBARCTIC WILDERNESS ADVENTURES LTD.,** Box 685, Fort
TERRITORIES   Smith, N.W.T., Canada, X0E 0P0. Att.: Jacques & Ruth van Pelt.
                (403) 872-2467.
                     "You don't run the river, the river runs you," points out Jacques van
                Pelt, and once you're rafting on the Slave River in North Country
                you'll understand what he means. Subarctic offers 5 rafting excursions
                on various parts of the Slave. You can travel the entire rapids
                corridor—the Drowned, Mountain, Pelican, and Cassette Rapids—or
                run a section of the course. Trips range from a half to 4 days. Rates:
                $110/person/day for multi-day trips; half-day trips $55/adult,
                $45/child under 13. Family and charter rates. Groups from 4-24.
                Jun.-Sep. For those unfamiliar with rafting on the Slave, Jacques
                offers a poetic description: "If the Slave were only rapids to raft it
                would be just another hectic North American experience. But it has a
                beautiful rhythm: fast waters and then quiet pools, exciting battles
                with rapids and then leisurely drifting. In between the turbulence, you
                have time to think about what you are doing in life." (See also
                Canoeing, Dog Sledding, Wilderness Living.)

ONTARIO   **WILDERNESS TOURS,** Box 89, Beachburg, Ont. K0J 1C0. Att.: Joe
                & Jack Kowalski. (613) 582-3351.
                     Spectacular scenery and big wild rapids characterize the majestic
                Ottawa River. It offers a unique combination of warm water and
                powerful rapids all summer long. Just 75 miles west of Ottawa, this
                whitewater paradise is in easy driving distance of major northeast
                population centers. Rates for day trips are $65 weekends and $55
                weekdays (Canadian dollars), May-Sep. The 2-day whitewater
                package, $135-$164, includes 2 days of rafting, 2 nights camping, and
                all meals and equipment except sleeping bags. Tent rental is extra.
                Also a 4-day vacation package, $249. Complimentary kayaks and
                windsurfers are available at WT's base camp. The outfitter also
                features weeklong rafting expeditions on the Harricana River flowing
                into James Bay. From Matagami, 580 miles north of Montreal, you fly

west to the put-in. A real adventure: "Wild, beautiful country—50-odd rapids to navigate—some portaging—not a trip for cream puffs," comments a participant. "Our guides were uniformly high caliber."

QUEBEC

ADVENTURES EN EAU VIVE, LTEE., R.R. 2, Chemin Riviere Rouge, Calumet, P.Q., Canada J0V 1B0. Att.: Gil or Phyllis Landry. (819) 242-6084.

Just an hour from Montreal, the Riviere Rouge flows with powerful Class IV and V waters all summer—10 magnificent miles of lively foam-capped rapids; stretches of swift free-flowing current swirling into placid, reflective pools; and each turn of the river bringing new challenges. "But the run is deceptive," Gil Landry reports. "It starts quietly...suddenly a 10-foot drop...exhilarating 'rapides' hot streamside lunch...sandy swimming beach...then a dramatic end through Rogue River Canyon with one magnificent rapid through the staircase." Two-day trip with free shuttle service, rafting equipment, and four hearty meals starts at $125. (Jun.-Sep.) One-day "express" trip also offered, with prices starting at $38. Adventures En Eau Vive also has a 25K run on the Hudson River near Lake George. Price: $60/person. Discounts for group of 16. (Apr.-May)

SCUBA DIVING/SNORKELING

The boat is anchored inside the reef. You've learned four important hand signals from the instructor for communicating under water. You've tried a back roll, the way divers plunge in, encased in your cumbersome wet suit, boots, fins, mask, gloves, weight belt, and air tank harnessed on your back, with still more gear dangling. Now you roll into the calm surf.

You are engulfed in color—the blue of the water, the white sand bottom strewn with waving yellow and purple sea fans, fat pink conches, and unworldly formations of coral in a liquid world. You flipper silently with multi-colored parrot fish, red snapper, yellow tails, and bright jewel, angel, and butterfly fish. It's an enchanting underwater world, and when your instructor signals that your 30-minute dive is over, it's too soon.

Training for scuba certification is available through the YMCA, YWCA, and local dive shops and schools throughout North America. At many diving areas and for all diving expeditions, certification is required. The total training time ranges from 24 to 50 hours or more, spread out over a number of weeks and divided into pool training, classroom instruction, and open-water dives. In resort areas, accelerated and intensive courses of several days or a week are given. On completing the training and several open-water dives, you receive a certification card, the open sesame to diving expeditions.

Snorkeling, on the other hand, is a carefree and much less expensive way to experience the euphoria of the underwater world. With mask, snorkel, and fins, you remain close to, often on, the surface of the water to view the exotic fish and colorful scenery. Hold your breath for a minute while you dive down 8 or 10 feet—easy to do with fins. Snorkelers peer under ridges to take a look at the creatures who live there, dive on underwater wrecks or reefs, then float back to the surface to breathe again. They swim alongside millions of tiny dazzling fish in schools and view sponges, sea grass, and coral. "Deeper is not necessarily better, it's only different," says one experienced diver.

Whether your choice is snorkeling or scuba, you'll view and mingle with a wondrous world.

GEORGIA

WILDERNESS SOUTHEAST, 711-AG Sandtown Rd., Savannah, GA 31410. Att.: Dick Murlless. (912) 897-5108.

Explore the tropical climes of the Keys and the Bahamas in a sailboat Wilderness Southeast's sailing/snorkeling programs. You experience both day and night sailing, calm and rough water. During the day, you dive in some of the most beautiful coral reefs in the world. "We swim along side millions of tiny dazzling fish in schools, and parade with brilliantly painted parrot fish," says Murlless. Time permitting, you also dive on wrecks. Choose from a 6-day trip to Pennekamp Reef on the Atlantic side of the Keys, limited to 9, $450. Or sail to the Dry Tortugas, 65 miles west of Key West, for 7 days of diving on patch reefs and wrecks encrusted with coral, limited to 6, $550. Or explore the Berry Island chain in Bahamas backcountry an

8-day trip, limit 14, $640. Jul.-Aug. No previous snorkeling or boating experience necessary, but you should be a confident swimmer. Snorkel gear provided. Bring your own sleeping bag and day pack. Minimum age: 15. (See also *Backpacking, Canoeing, Wilderness Living, Youth Adventures*.)

HAWAII

FATHOM FIVE PROFESSIONAL DIVERS, Box 907, Koloa, HI 96756. Att.: Terry O'Halloran. (808) 742-6991.

"Kauai is the home of the best diving in the Hawaiian Islands," Terry believes. "It's the oldest island, and because of that is has more interesting coral and lava formations than the other islands." A diver's journey with Fathom Five develops an environmental awareness. Fathom Five never takes more than six in a group, never overdives an area, never allows the taking of living creatures. Pre-dive instruction involves enthusiastic descriptions of what one is likely to see—turtles, rays, eels, myriads of tropical fish—and occasionally includes a lesson in marine biology. Both NAUI and PADI instruction are offered—basic through divemaster—with all open-water work. Courses also in photography, science, deep and cavern dives. Cave, reef, wreck, photography, and night dives from shore and boat.

CARIBBEAN

LA MER DIVING SEAFARI, INC., 823 U.N. Plaza, Suite 810, New York, NY 10017. (800) 348-3669 (outside NY) or (212) 599-0886 (in NY).

For the "last true virgin diving" in the Caribbean, fly from Miami (or Houston) to Cayman Brac to join Winston McDermot, owner of the *Little Cayman Diver*, for six full days of diving. "You visit dive sites where the reef walls start at 3 to 20 feet below the surface and plunge down thousands of feet," McDermot describes. "Sponges are up to 7 feet tall, gardens of sea fans and ships sway gently, schools of pelagics and clouds of brilliant tropical fish are so thick they compete with the 200-foot visibility. "You travel in style aboard his newly built, 65-foot luxury vessel. "With a 16-knot cruising speed, we spend minimal time traveling and maximum time at each dive site in Cayman Brac, Little Cayman, and reefs on the way to Cuba," McDermot adds. The limit of 16 guests ensures personalized service. Rate: $995/diver ($595 until Jun. '86) including 7 nights accommodation on board vessel, all meals, transfers from airport, backpacks, and weights. (Diving equipment not included.) Weekly departures: Feb.-Oct. & Dec.

TRIMARINE BOAT CO., LTD., Homeport, St. Thomas, V.I. 00801. Att.: Duncan & Annie Muirhead. (809) 494-2490.

"Because of our 12 years continuous exploration of the Virgin Islands underwater world and our extensive use of high-powered inflatables, we reach sites undiveable by any other means," says Duncan Muirhead. Trimarine dives "popular" sites, such as the Wreck of the Rhone, the Wreck of the Rocus, Santa Monica Rocks, and Ginger Island, as well as places undived for weeks. "Plus, we have our own list of over 100 dive sites, and may even discover a new one while you are on board," adds Duncan. Daily schedules allow morning, afternoon, and evening dives in three different locations. An instructor/guide is always on board. Sail and diving cruises are 7, 10, or 12 days, year round. Longer cruises can be arranged. Cost: $140/person/night. One diver describes a typical morning dive: "After a breakfast of eggs, pancakes, and bangers, I lazed through coral fields as unspoiled as I've seen, replete with sponges, gorgonia, and plenty of tropical. We swam with eagle rays and tweaked a nurse shark on the tail as she lay sleeping beneath a coral ledge." (See also *Charters/Cruises*.)

SCUBA CENTERS

California
: **Diver Den, Inc.,** 22 Anacapa St., Santa Barbara, CA 93101; (805) 963-8917. **New England Divers,** 398 5th St., San Francisco, CA 94107; (415) 434-3614.

Connecticut
: **Jack's Dive Center Inc.,** 466 East St., Rt. 10, Plainville, CT 06062; (203) 747-3170.

Florida
: **Biscayne Aqua-Center, Inc.,** P.O. Box 1270, Biscayne National Park Headquarters, Homestead, FL 33030; (305) 247-2400. **Capt. Slate's Atlantis Dive Center,** 51 Garden Cove Dr., Key Largo, FL 33037; (305) 451-3020. **The Diving Site & Coral Lagoon Resort,** 12399 Overseas Hwy., Marathon, FL 33050; (305) 289-1021. **Ginnie Springs,** Rt. 1, Box 153, High Springs, FL 32643; (904) 454-2202. **Plantation Inn Marina,** Hwy. 44 West, P.O. Box 1093, Crystal River, FL 32629; (904) 795-5797. **Reef Raiders Dive Shop,** U.S. Hwy. 1, Stock Island, Key West, FL 33040; (305) 294-3635.

Hawaii
: **Aloha Dive Shop,** Koko Marina Shopping Ctr., Honolulu, HI 96825; (808) 395-8882. **Maui Dive Shop,** P.O. Box 1018, Azeka Place Shopping Center, Kihei, HI, 96753; (808) 879-3388.

Illinois
: **Midwest Diving Specialists,** 203 South Linden, Normal, IL 61761; (309) 452-0222. **Underseas Scuba Center,** 626 N. Addison Rd., Villa Park, Ill 60181; (312) 833-8383.

Iowa
: **Divers Pro Shop, Inc.,** 628 South Dubuque St., Iowa City, IA 52240; (319) 338-9564.

Maine
: **Northeast Divers,** 395 South Main St., Brewer, ME 04412; (207) 989-4330.

Massachusetts
: **East Coast Divers, Inc.,** 280 Worcester Road, Rt. 9, Framingham, MA 01701; (617) 620-1176. **Inland Divers,** 100 S. Main St., Rt. 9, Leicester, MA 01524; (617) 892-3323.

Michigan
: **U.S. Scuba Center,** 822 South Rochester Rd., Rochester, MI 48063; (313) 656-0018.

Minnesota
: **Scuba Center,** 5015 Penn Avenue South, Minneapolis, MN 55419; (612) 925-4818.

New Hampshire   **Laporte's Skindiving Shop,** Box 53, Rt. 103, Newbury, NH 03255;
                 (603) 763-5353.

New York   **Central Skindivers of Nassau,** 2608 Merrick Road, Bellmore, NY
                 11710; (516) 826-8888. **Niagara Scuba Sports,** 2048 Niagara St.,
                 Buffalo, NY 14207; (716) 875-6528. **Westchester Dive Center,** 62
                 Westchester Ave., Port Chester, NY 10573; (914) 937-2685.

North Carolina   **Blue Dolphin Dive Shop, Inc.,** 1006 National Highway, Thomasville,
                 NC 27360; (919) 475-2516.

Pennsylvania   **Harrisburg Scuba Center, Inc.,** 991-A Peiffers Lane, Harrisburg, PA
                 17109; (717) 566-6552. **Mid-Atlantic Scuba Center,** 318 E. Butler Ave.,
                 Ambler, PA 19002; (215) 628-4935.

Texas   **Aquaventures Scuba Center,** 1614 Gessner, Houston, TX 77080; (713)
                 468-6211. **The Dive Shop,** 1426 Ranch Road 12, San Marcos, TX
                 78666; (512) 396-3483.

Washington   **The Deep End,** 5808 Summitview Ave., Suite 'A', Yakima, WA 98908;
                 (414) 921-4900. **Lighthouse Diving Center, Inc.,** 8215 Lake City Way,
                 Northeast, Seattle, WA 98115; (206) 524-1633.

Wisconsin   **Aqua Center,** 628 Bellevue St., Green Bay, WI 54302; (414) 499-6400.
                 Blue Waters Divers, Inc., 1724 North Clairemont Ave., Eau Claire,
                 WI 54703; (715) 834-0002.

DOG SLEDDING

"Hi! Ho!" the musher yells, and your team of huskies lurches forward while you hold on to the back of the sled for dear life. "There is nothing quite so exhilarating as skimming along in back of 12 panting, tail-wagging huskies," says one novice dog sledder.

Sledding across snowy landscapes is an adventure in unbelievable whiteness and silence—a silence broken only by the breathing of the dogs and the swish of the sled runners in the snow.

In the Colorado Rockies it is possible to sample dog sledding for a day or so, and in the meadows around Mt. Adams in Washington you explore on showshoes and skis as well as by dog sled.

But it's in the Far North—in Alaska and the Northwest Territories—that you feel you truly are answering the call of the wild. Here dog sledding has been and continues to be a classic means of wilderness transportation over the years. You can travel for a week without passing another human being. You will, however, pass Dall sheep, moose, caribou, and fox.

For some, the vast stillness of the 6-million-acre Denali National Park can be a bit frightening. It's you and your team against a wild and cold region, and the odds don't seem to be in your favor. You wonder how you'll survive if you're trapped by a blizzard, fall through the ice, or are chased by a grizzly. But the grizzlies are in hibernation, and your guide's expertise in winter survival and travel techniques puts to rest your fears.

Soon you relax and are ready to fully enjoy a superb adventure.

You rise early each day, feed the dogs first, then harness them up for the day's journey. The moon is still visible as you set off on the 14-foot sled across the frozen tundra. "If at all possible, plan to start the day going up hill," advises a recent adventurer. "The dogs love to run, especially in the morning when they're fresh, and they don't need the acceleration of a downhill slope."

You travel at a speed of four to eight miles per hour, covering less than 35 miles each day as you duck under the branches of black spruce and cross ice-covered bridges and rivers as slick as glass. You finish your day at dusk at one of the wilderness huts sprinkled through the area. Feed your dog team first—then settle down for your own dinner of caribou burgers and assorted sweets.

The hard working huskies bed down for the night outdoors, burying themselves in the snow with faces protected by their tails. The moon casts an eerie glow on the stark white snow as a fresh layer covers your tracks of the day.

After a snowy night, if your huskies appear to have broken away, worry not. Soon little mounds will rise up in the snow—and under each, a dog.

Certainly very little has changed here since the first great wilderness traveler passed this way. You think perhaps this part of the world is a better place for having stayed the same.

ALASKA   **BROOKS RANGE WILDERNESS TRIPS**, P.O. Box 40, Bettles, AK 99726. Att.: Dave Schmitz. (907) 692-5312.

Veteran Arctic explorer Dave Schmitz considers dogsledding through the Brooks Range Wilderness "a truly superlative Alaskan experience." It's a vast land of absolute silence in winter. "We never

In Denali National Park, musher on "gee pole" rig rides standing up—*Will Forsberg for Denali Dog Tours, AK.*

ALASKA

A loyal team awaits
their next command—
*Brooks Range Wilder-
ness Trips, AK.*

heard a man-made sound nor saw a human, an airplane, or even a jet's
contrail," comments one traveler, an airline pilot from Maine.
Participants meet in Bettles and spend the night at Dave's lodge. Then
it's off for seven days in the wild, with each one driving a dog team
much of the time. Besides careful training, Dave provides
expedition-class sleeping bag, parka, down pants, and boots and
counsels each on other equipment. His dogs are friendly and very well
trained—many of them veterans of the 1,000-mile Iditarod Race. You
spend nights in his trapline cabins, snug and warm. Excellent physical
condition recommended. Usually one guide for two people. 7-days,
$975/person with 4 in group. Feb.-Apr. Arrival: Bettles.(See also
Backpacking, Canoeing/Kayaking.)

DENALI DOG TOURS, Box 679, McKinley Park, AK 99755. Att.:
Will & Linda Forsberg. (907) 683-2644 or 683-2294.
    The Forsbergs spend five months each year covering over 2,000
miles of trails in Denali National Park with their dogs. They hunt for

their food supply and net salmon for their huskies. Their park concession gives them the sole right to conduct dog and ski tours within the old park boundaries and to use the system of backcountry cabins. They're ready to take guests anywhere in this 6-million-acre wilderness. "We stay in cozy log cabins for comfortable nights, though we are just as warm in wood-heated wall tents should you wish to visit remote areas," they say. Their "gee pole" rig on the dog sleds enables you to ride standing up, operating the brake and balancing—not just sitting in the basket bundled up. "We try to transmit to our guests some of the flavor of this unique Alaskan lifestyle," says Will. Both he and Linda are experts in winter survival and travel techniques. A former under secretary of the army, Norman Augustine, reports "a truly fantastic trip and incredible scenery" with the Forsbergs and their 16 superb dogs. Most exciting: "working our way through snowstorm and avoiding large holes in ice (dogs do this easily) when on rivers." Most interesting: "Personalities of the dogs—each a true individualist." Memorable: "When during lunch break team took off to chase caribou herd with passengers diving to board sleds!" Custom trips Nov.-Apr. Arrival: Denali Park. (See also *Ski Touring, Wilderness Living*.)

SOURDOUGH OUTFITTERS, Box 18-AT, Bettles, AK 99726. Att.: David Ketscher. (907) 692-5252.

You're a part of the wilderness, not an intruder, when you travel the traditional way with Sourdough through the Gates of the Arctic in the Brooks Range. "It involves a lot more than sitting on a sled," writes Dave Ketscher. "You help make camp, care for the dogs, and take turns showshoeing to break trail. It's an area of spellbinding beauty, snow-covered mountains, rocky peaks jutting out of an unmarked snowpack with majestic crowns that touch the Northern Lights." For a week you follow an old trail from Bettles to the North Fork of the Koyukuk River, spend nights in cabins or heated tent camps, and explore old timers' campsites. Return by ski plane. Scheduled for small groups by special arrangement; good physical condition a must. Fly to Sourdough's Walker Lake Wilderness Lodge (Apr.) for less strenuous dog sledding, x-country skiing, snowmobiling, ice fishing, and snow camping. Arrival: Bettles. (See also *Backpacking, Canoeing, River Running, Ski Touring*.)

COLORADO

KRABLOONIK, P.O. Box 5517, Snowmass Village, CO 81615. Att.: Dan MacEachen. (303) 923-3953.

"Come to Krabloonik for a traditional Alaskan dog sled ride in a handcrafted sled pulled by 13 huskies through beautiful woods and past magnificent views," Dan MacEachen urges. Bundle up! It's an unusual and exciting way to see the Snowmass area for 2 hours or for 1 or 2 days. Lodging and meals are provided on the longer excursion and luncheon on the day trip. Also 2-hour rides in morning or afternoon. The Krabloonik Kennels are in Old Snowmass Valley, a mile west of the village. Season: Dec.-Apr.

OREGON

WILDERNESS FREIGHTERS, 2166 S.E. 142nd Ave., Portland, OR 97233. Att.: John Simonson. (503) 761-7428.

A cozy Forest Service cabin in the foothills of Mount Adams is the headquarters for all-day and overnight dog-sledding excursions and 2- to 4-day hut-to-hut trips. Up to 8 participants meet at the Inn of the White Salmon (or in Portland), drive to the trailhead, and cover the last 2 1/2 miles on snowshoes, cross-country skis, dogsled teams, or by snowcat. Two tracksetters are used to set several miles of groomed ski trails. Then, riding luxurious sleds to which the dogs are harnessed, they whoosh through the timber and meadows of Peterson Prairie. It's an exciting way to see the snowy, scenic area. Hearty meals and sleeping quarters at the cabin. Day trip, $75; overnight, $140; hut-to-hut tours, 2 days/$140, 3 days/$275, 4 days/$375.(See also *Hiking with Packstock*.)

Fetching water for a hard worker—Will Forsberg for Denali Dog Tours, AK.

NORTHWEST
TERRITORIES

SUBARCTIC WILDERNESS ADVENTURES LTD., Box 685, Fort Smith, N.W.T., Canada, X0E 0P0. Att.: Jacques & Ruth van Pelt. (403) 872-2467.

"This winter or early spring, fly or drive into the subarctic's rugged landscape with us to experience the way a precious few native residents still cope with winter wilderness—in harmony, providing a 'life-on-the-land' experience with you being deeply involved," advises Jacques van Pelt. One of the many ways to do that is to partake in a dog sledding adventure, and Subarctic Wilderness offers quite a few. Choose a 3- to 5-day tour through the Tazan Highlands (caribou country), $150/day; a trek through Wood Buffalo National Park's forests and plains for 1-5 days, $140/day; ride the local trails, 2-12 hours, $120/day; or if you're experienced go solo overnight, $75. Your dogmobiles come complete with buffalo robes, mukluks, mittens, and hat. Your route passes panoramic views of the Slave River Rapids. Camp in a traditional wall tent, tipi, or cabin. End of Nov. to end of Apr. (except Jan.) (See also *Canoeing, River Running, Wilderness Living.*)

SKI TOURING/ SNOW CAMPING

It's about 20 degrees below zero with the wind-chill factor. And the wind is a big factor today, as it whistles right through your expensive down jacket and thermal long underwear while you wait your turn on the ski lift with a dozen other skiers.

Sound familiar? Probably, if you've ever taken a winter ski vacation of the downhill kind. But there's a happy alternative that is less tortuous, less expensive, and equally exciting. You won't get the rush of a fast, long run, but you'll have the chance to enjoy some scenic winter sights and exhilarating exercise.

Ski touring, more commonly referred to as Nordic or cross-country skiing, was born in the Scandinavian countries and often used as a form of winter transportation. It requires little more than a few inches of snow. Your equipment is inexpensive; a complete package (light touring skis, poles, low-cut boots, and loose bindings) can be purchased for under $100 or rented for just a few dollars. Complete your outfit with a parka, knickers, mittens, and wool or poly-propelene socks, and you're ready for your gliding expedition.

Of course, you can cross-country ski just about anywhere—in your backyard, at a golf course, or even in a parking lot. But you'll get the most enjoyment if you choose a spot with plenty of winter scenery. There's nothing like breaking a trail through a wooded wilderness where freshly fallen snow and glistening icicles create your personal winter palace.

Choose any terrain you like, perhaps a dense forest or an open field where animal tracks serve as your guide. Or follow a path specially groomed for touring. Cross-country centers maintain many miles of marked and groomed trails looping out in all directions, sometimes with huts and shelters strategically located.

There are good destinations all over the country—some where you're guaranteed snow all season long. You might choose a trip that combines cross-country with winter camping. If so, you'll have a chance to learn winter survival and more refined Nordic skiing techniques.

If you prefer to trek across deeper snow, slide into some snowshoes. Snowshoeing is probably the oldest form of winter travel, first used by nomads in northern Asia several thousand years ago and later discovered by the early American settlers. And it's still one of the best ways to get to hard-to-reach winter areas.

With snowshoes, you don't have the speed of cross-country, but you have more maneuverability. You can conquer snow drifts and steep winter trails without too much problem. Or, by using crampons, you can tackle more hazardous ice passes and even steeper snowbanks.

Once you master the techniques of snowshoeing, you'll be able to fish, camp, and backpack—all the things you love doing but thought had ended with the first snowfall. Now, with your snow-walking gear, you have all four seasons to enjoy the outdoors.

Gliding through an untracked wilderness in the Rockies—*Lone Mountain Ranch, MT.*

ALASKA

ALASKA DISCOVERY, INC., P.O. Box 26, Gustavus, AK 99826. Att.: Hayden & Bonnie Kaden. (907) 697-2257.

"Cross-country skiing on the Juneau ice field may be the biggest adventure you've ever embarked upon." predicts Alaska Discovery. "Conditions range from brillant blue skies with magnificent views of mountains, nunataks, and valleys to complete white-out necessitating travel by map and compass. Ultimately, the weather dictates the route and choice of campsites." You're led by a certified professional ski instructor who is also a certified wilderness guide. After guides issue top-quality skiing and glacier-travel equipment, you fly from Juneau to the 4,500-foot level ice field. The skiing is not difficult; daily cross-country (also Nordic) instruction and practice. (Prior skiing requisite, and ability to carry a 35- to 40-pound pack.) Rates: 6 days, $650; custom trips in Juneau area or St. Elias range, $100/person/day or less (group discounts). Jun.-Jul. (See also *Backpacking, River Running, Wilderness Living.*)

DENALI DOG TOURS, Box 670, McKinley Park, AK 99755. Att.: Will & Linda Forsberg. (907) 683-2466 or 683-2294.

With a park concession which gives them the sole right to conduct ski and dog tours within the old park boundaries and to use the system of backcountry cabins, the Forsbergs plan custom ski trips wherever you wish within Denali National Park. "Our trips can be as strenuous or relaxing as you wish," Will explains. "With over 12 cozy log cabins available to us, we can choose a location to fit your interests and experience," The Wonder Lake ski tour remains his most popular trip and is a challenge to all but the strongest skiers. "The varied terrain and flora make this an excellent trip to become familiar with Alaska's wildlife and scenery," Will says. "In a ski group of varied abilities we can assist slower skiers with a head start on the dog sled." He suggests coming in early March to see the start of the 1,000-mile Iditarod dog race, then tour with him for a week or so, and finally fly to Nome for "the incredible shindig as the racing teams finish their 2-week marathon. Arrival: Denali Park (by train from Anchorage or Fairbanks. (See also *Dog Sledding, Wilderness Living.*)

SOURDOUGH OUTFITTERS, Box 18-AT, Bettles, AK 99726. Att.: David Ketscher. (907) 692-5252.

Fairly high temperatures and long daylight hours make the wilderness of the Brooks Range a skier's paradise in April when winter scenery beckons and powder snow starts to firm up. "We can provide logistic support with a dogteam to allow skiers freedom from carrying heavy, bulky packs," writes David Ketscher, who describes his outfit as the oldest, most experienced resident wilderness guide in the area. Travel at your own pace, enjoying other recreational opportunities, such as ice fishing, and snow camping. Cost includes bush flights from Bettles and back. Arrival: Bettles, via Fairbanks, (See also *Backpacking, Canoeing, River Running, Dog Sledding.*)

CALIFORNIA

COFFEE CREEK RANCH, Dept. AG, P.O. Star Rt. 2, Box 4940, Trinity Center, CA 96091. Att.: Ruth & Mark Hartman. (916) 266-3343.

The Scott Mountains and surrounding national forest wilderness provide the setting for snowshoeing or ski touring at Coffee Creek Ranch. This is a small guest ranch, no more than 30 at a time. Skiers bring their own equipment for self-guided tours and use Coffee Creek's shuttle service to other ski areas with 5 miles of ungroomed trails. Accommodations with maid service: $25-$38/night for a double, plus $7 add'l./adult, $3 children/teen. No trail fee. Facilities also include a gourmet restaurant, snow playground, sleds, inner tubes, and ice skating. Nov.-Mar. Arrival: Redding, CA (See also *Pack Trips*—Trinity Trail Rides.)

MONTECITO-SEQUOIA CROSS COUNTRY SKI CENTER, 1485-A Redwood Dr., Los Altos, CA 94022. Att.: Dr. Virginia C. Barnes. (800) 451-1505 natl., (800) 227-9900 in CA, or (415) 967-8612. Sequoia Lodge, at 7,500 feet in Sequoia National Forests, is your base for touring some of California's most scenic trails, beginning right at the lodge door and ranging in length from an easy 2 1/2 to 20 miles. Marked trails lead to giant redwoods, open meadows, and majestic vistas. Lighted ice skating on Lake Homavalo, ski football, snowshoeing and moonlight tours are special attractions in this "winter wonderland". At the lodge, there are huge stone fireplaces, indoor recreation areas, guest rooms with private baths, hearty family-style meals. Equipment rentals, $16/2 days; tours $8 and up for half day to overnight. Instruction: half day/$8; full day/$14. Weekend, mid-week, and holiday festivities feature meals, lodging, use of trails, and "old-fashioned" hospitality beginning at $60/day. One skier sums up the ambience as "down home, relaxed easiness—no crowds, lines, or pressures.

SIERRA WILDERNESS SEMINARS, Box 707, Arcata, CA 95521. Att.: Marie Toombs or Tim Keating. (707) 822-8066. [Jul.-Sep.: Box 1048, Lone Pine, CA 93545. (619) 876-5384.]
    Crater Lake (southern OR) and Lassen National Park and Mt. Shasta (northern CA) are the scenic areas SWS has chosen for its courses in x-c skiing, snow camping, winter mountaineering, telemark, and snow survival. "We like to teach people the skills that bring self-confidence and satisfaction so they can enjoy the mountains on their own," say these experts who have been teaching 10 years. Adding to the enjoyment are their "Moonlight Ski Tours" through the silent night forest, and "Gourmet X-C Ski Weekends" which feature the best of skiing and eating. Their instruction is for all levels, from the beginner wanting to start at a leisurely pace, to the advanced x-c skier wishing to strengthen skills in more technical terrain. Most seminars are scheduled over weekends: $99/skier for 2 days, $125/3 days, $275 and up/5 days, $325/7 days. Rates include food, lodging, day packs. Jan.-May. (See also *Backpacking*.)

YOSEMITE NORDIC SKI SCHOOL, Yosemite National Park, CA 95389. Att.: Bruce Brossman. (209) 372-1244. [Jun.-Aug.: (209) 372-1335.]
    Yosemite offers everything in Nordic skiing, from groomed tracks to telemark lessons, and everything in between. Located at Badger Pass,

CALIFORNIA   the Nordic Ski School maintains groomed tracks to Glacier Point (21 miles round trip), has learn-to-ski packages (lesson & rental), daily lesson tours, hut skiing overnight tours to Glacier Point and Tuolumne Meadows, telemark rentals and lessons. Rentals are also available in Yosemite Valley on weekends and holidays, snow conditions permitting. Sample rates: Learn-to-ski package, $25. Rentals, $10/adult, $7.50/child. Nordic downhill, $31 with pass. Overnight ski tours to Glacier Point, $60/1 night, $85/2 nights (weekends). An annual Nordic Holiday Race, 15 km, is scheduled the first weekend in March. (See also *Mountaineering*.)

COLORADO   **COLORADO ADVENTURE NETWORK, INC.,** 194 S. Franklin St., Denver, CO 80209. Att.: Brooke & Eric Durland. (303) 722-6482.

A ski clinic in Steamboat over Presidents' Weekend each year,and hut-to-hut ski tours all winter from Vail to Aspen, are CAN's specialties. The 4-day ski clinic operating from a lodge perched above Steamboat Springs, offers beginning, intermediate, and telemark instruction each day. The program rounds out with tours on Rabbit Ears Pass, gourmet Scandinavian buffet meals, saunas, indoor-outdoor pool, square dancing evenings, and a moonlight ski tour to the local hot springs. For 40-60 participants, $150-$250 depending on room. The Vail-to-Aspen 5- or 6-day ski tour is for intermediates and up. Skiers follow the newly built 10th Mountain Division trail system with huts a day's ski tour apart. Enjoy panoramic views and endless telemark slopes by day, and a cozy hut with pot-bellied stove by night. Telemark experience and climbing skins desirable. Rate: $425. Custom winter adventures tailored to suit your skills. Both areas easily reached from Denver by car or plane. (See also *Backpacking*.)

OUTDOOR LEADERSHIP TRAINING SEMINARS, P.O. Box 20281-A, Denver, CO 80220. Att.: Rick Medrick. (303) 333-7831.

"Our winter courses are intense and spectacular" advises Rick. "We teach the basics of cross-country travel in high alpine valleys surrounded by famous Colorado peaks. You learn to ski with a pack; camp in tents, snowcaves on the Colorado hut system near Aspen and Vail; and share the tasks of cooking and camping. On ski mountaineering expeditions we attempt the ascent of a major summit rarely climbed in winter." Wilderness skiing course, 5 days, $275; Colorado Alpine Hut Ski Tour, 5 days, $395; ski mountaineering expedition, 7 days, $375. Also instructor's training workshops—"an intensive course for experienced backpackers, skiers and climbers"—10 days, $425. Dec.-Apr. Arrival: Denver. (See also *Backpacking, Mountaineering, River Running, Wilderness Living*.)

PARAGON GUIDES (The Mountaineering School at Vail), P.O. Box 3142-A, Vail, CO 81658. (303) 949-5682.

The magnificent Sawatch and Gore Ranges are the setting for Paragon's hut-to-hut backcountry ski tours. They operate high quality guided adventure on the Tenth Mountain Trail connecting Vail and Aspen, and trips to other central CO alpine huts. Trips are scheduled from 2-8 days with routes for beginners to advanced skeirs. Also snowcamp trips with alternate routes tied into the hut system. Or you can set out on your own snowcamp route with a guide. Tours include professional instruction in all aspects of winter travel, ski skills, and techniques to help you really appreciate the winter alpine environment; private and day lesson tour programs also offered. Rates from $60-$90/day, family and group rates. Paragon operates under auspices of U.S. Forest Service and Tenth Mountain Trail Association.(See also *Backpacking/Hiking, Mountaineering/Rock Climbing*.)

VISTA VERDE GUEST RANCH, Box 465, Steamboat Springs, CO 80477. Att.: Frank & Winton Brophy. (303) 879-3858.
    This 1,600-acre Rocky Mountain ranch, with 12 miles of marked and maintained beginner-to-expert trails, is the gateway to unlimited skiing over unmarked terrain as well as 30 miles of marked trails in the 1.1 million-acre Routt National Forest. "Happiness," the Brophys maintain, "is following a fox or coyote track up Hinman Creek, looking for beaver ponds, and glimpsing elk and deer...or skiing to the top of Kerry's Knoll where the view is fantastic and the downhill telemark a thrill." Winter fun includes horse-drawn sleigh rides, snowshoeing, use of spa and exercise center with whirlpool, sauna, and cold tub, and ice fishing; at night, sing-alongs, square dances. Guided half- and full-day tours, $10-$20; instruction, rentals extra. Cozy log cabins with kitchen, bath, and fireplace sleep 6 ($85/night/cabin, meals $25/day/person). Cook your own meals or enjoy fireside dining with homemade breads and pastries, pasture-fresh beef, and garden vegetables. Dec.-Mar. (See also *Ballooning*.)

MINNESOTA   **BEAR TRACK OUTFITTING CO.,** Box 51, Grand Marais, MN 55605. Att.: David & Cathi Williams. (218) 387-1162.
    "Tim and Janice each guided their loaded freighting sleds through the deep snow. Jim broke trail through Lizz Lake and Caribou Lake for the dogs to follow. I broke trail through Horseshoe until we found the campsite. Camp robbers eat out of your hand. Fell asleep about 10 p.m., waking every few hours to put wood on fire. Temperature is minus 18 degrees, and wind chill factor minus 30 degrees. Everybody relaxed and comfortable, preparing to ski. Saw otter, wolf and moose tracks..." So reads David's diary on a ski touring trek with dogsled support in the Boundary Waters Canoe Area. For winter camping enthusiasts, this can be the ultimate outdoor experience. Bear Track provides wood-heated tents and outpost tent cabins, and now has camp on the eastern end of North Shore Mountains Ski Trail, deep in Superior National Forest, with winterized rustic cabins, cedar sauna, and 125 miles of groomed, tracked trails. Lodge-to-lodge ski program. Group seminars to learn skiing, snowshoeing, ice fishing, camping techniques, first aid, and best choice of clothing and food. Rates: 3-day ski tour, $205; outpost cabin, $30/night (midweek) double, $7.50 each addl. Pickup charge for Duluth or Thunder Bay arrivals. (See also *Backpacking, Canoeing*.)

GUNFLINT LODGE, Box 100 GT-AG, Grand Marais, MN 55604.

Att.: Bruce & Sue Kerfoot. (800) 328-3325 nat'l. or (800) 328-3362 in MN.

In winter the Boundary Waters Canoe Area becomes a snowy wonderland for ski touring and showshoeing from December through April. For independent ski tourers and for guided trips, trails lead from the Kerfoots' lodge through the heavily forested wilderness on loops from 2 to 20 miles, with huts and shelters strategically located for noon stops. "They have great access to some tremendous wilderness areas," writes a satisfied guest. Ski-Through program for intermediates and experts operates among four resorts in the area which provide comfortable accommodations complete with fireplaces, saunas, and meal service as desired. (See also *Canoeing, Wilderness Living*.)

VOYAGEUR OUTWARD BOUND SCHOOL, P.O. Box 250, Long lake, MN 55356. Att.: Dee Dee Hull or Linda Larson. (800) 328-2943 (outside MN) or (612) 542-9255 (in MN).

Winter camping, cross-country skiing and dogsledding through the pristine beauty and quiet of the North Woods of Minnesota and Canada is a real pleasure for the adventuresome adult (18 and up). "Couple that with the unique group dynamics and opportunity for individual self-discovery in an adult Outward Bound course, and you've got a powerful experience that offers high adventure and guarantees personal renewal," says Hull. Eight-, 15-, 22-day courses require no experience; all equipment provided. Special courses for adults, corporate clients, the disabled, and a semester course (90 days) for those with greater interest. Rates: $600/8 days-$950/22 days. (See *Canoeing/Kayaking, Wilderness Living*.)

MONTANA   **LONE MOUNTAIN RANCH,** Box 69, Big Sky. MT 59716. Att.: Bob & Viv Schaap. (406) 955-4644.

One of the finest Nordic ski centers in the U.S., Lone Mountain maintains 47 miles of immaculately groomed trails from level to steep terrain and many wilderness trails. The ranch provides a guide for every 7 skiers and optional instruction ($10/lesson). Wooded trails, open meadows, exhilarating downhills, or flat track—all are here for beginner to advanced ability on a trail system radiating from the ranch. A wood-fired outdoor hot tub/Jacuzzi is an apre-ski attraction, and skiers gather at the main lodge for hot mulled wine, games, cards, conversation, and family-style meals. Lodging is in spacious log cabins with fireplaces, Franklin stoves, and electric heat. Twice a week the ranch arranges trips into Yellowstone Nationl Park to ski among the geyser and wildlife—"an experience not to be missed." On extended tours (up to 7 days) with snow camping, skiers encounter spectacular thermal areas and ice-shrouded waterfalls. Other ranch specials: sleighrides to North Fork cabin for dinner, and ski-to-lunch gourmet buffets—with blocks of snow as serving table for shrimp, fruit, roast beef, wines, homemade breads. Nordic holiday rate: $598/person/week double occupancy, with airport shuttle, meals, 7 nights lodging, trail fees, evening entertainment, horse-drawn sleighride dinner, and wonderful memories. Also short- and long-stay rates. Arrival, Bozeman, MT (See also *Pack Trips*.)

NEW
HAMPSHIRE

BALSAMS/WILDERNESS, Dixville Notch, NH 03576. (800)
255-0600 (in U.S.), (800) 255-0800 (in NH).

The Balsams maintains more than 50 kilometers of groomed touring
trails in the open terrain and scenic wilderness of its 15,000 acres in the
White Mountains. Used primarily by Balsams guests, the trails are
uncrowded. Special Sunday-to-Friday ski package includes a welcome
party, 6 days of alpine and Nordic skiing and 3 class lessons, nighttime
horse-drawn hayride, niteclub shows, 5 dinners, and breakfasts, 5
nights lodging—from $275, or a ski weekend package, Friday to
Sunday—from $150. Other snow activities at the Mobil-rated
four-star resort hotel—and four diamonds by AAA—include alpine
skiing, tobogganing, and ice skating. Indoor entertainment: dancing,
movies, game room, sing-alongs, congenial gatherings around a
roaring fire.

*Cross country back-
packing on groomed
trails—Lone Mountain
Ranch, MT.*

NEW YORK

COLD RIVER TRAIL RIDES, INC., Coreys, Tupper Lake, NY 12986,
Att.: John Fontana. (518) 359-7559.

"We ski several loops on our property and many miles of wilderness
logging roads in the Adirondacks," explain John and Marie Fontana.
"Our secluded lodge offers excellent cross-country skiing for novice to
expert, wonderful food, and a relaxing atmosphere." Complimentary
wine and beer with dinner, 3 fireplaces, and a heated ski preparation
room. "Although I reached my limit at four miles," reports an
exuberant first-timer, "I could envision the experienced skier being in
seventh heaven on these gorgeous trails." Rates: $40/person/day
including lodging with semi-private bath, hearty meals, and trail use

NEW YORK   (3 miles groomed trails, 17 miles maintained); B&B, $18. Guides, rentals, instruction, snow-shoeing, ice fishing. For 2-9 guests. Dec.-Mar. Arrival Saranac Lake, NY (See also *Pack Trips*.)

MOHONK MOUNTAIN HOUSE, New Paltz, NY 12561. (914) 255-1000 or (212) 233-2244.
   Mohonk's owners describe their century-old mountain resort as "a winter scene from *Dr. Zhivago*—the frozen lake, the horse-drawn sleighs, the icicle-laden trees, the deep, snowy inclines." Their 35-plus miles of marked, well-groomed trails—many color-coded for skill levels—range from virtually flat 1-mile beginner's loops to all-day wilderness jaunts that challenge advanced skiers. After-ski, hot cocoa by the fireplace. Equipment rentals, ski instruction $7.50/hour group, $15/hour semiprivate. Trail fee: $5/day. Other activities: ice skating and quick-paced hiking. Rates start at $90/person with private bath and 3 meals, ($70 with non-private bath). (See also *Backpacking*.)

PENNSYLVANIA   **THE INN AT STARLIGHT LAKE,** Box 27A, Starlight, PA 18461. Att.: Jack & Judy McMahon. (717) 798-2519.
   The McMahons' ski-touring guests send glowing reports about the terrain and hospitality: "Lovely scenery, good hills, and an easy beginner's trail. This is very much a family place, like a big friendly overgrown lake cottage, warm and homey." The touring center has 20 miles of marked trails over wooded huts and open farmland, 12 miles groomed and tracked. Professional instruction. $6/lesson; rentals $10/day; shop carries accessories. Inn accommodations (with 2 meals a day) start at ($82 for 2, Sun.-Thurs.; $97 Fri., Sat., & holidays). What else? "Great old movies on weekends, super home cooking, and an informal, relaxed atmosphere."

Helicopter ski touring in the North Cascades—Eric Sanford for Liberty Bell Alpine Tours, WA.

WASHINGTON **LIBERTY BELL ALPINE TOURS,** Mazama, WA 98833. Att.: Eric
Sanford. (509) 996-2250.

For the ultimate in ski touring Liberty Bell offers the
"Supertour"—helicoptering from the Mazama Country Inn each day
right into the heart of the North Cascades. "The views are absolutely
spectacular, and within minutes you and your group of 10 skiers and 2
guides are dropped off for an all-day tour down gentle, open slopes
and groomed logging roads to end up right back at the Inn," Eric
Sanford explains. He points out that it's easy enough for beginners yet
perfect for experts, too. ($55 including helicopter flight and use of
TRAK skis and boots.) Other Liberty Bell services: daily helicopter
downhill skiing in the North Cascades, an "Ultimate Powder Week"
(heli-skiing including instruction on powder), skiing downhill on
cross-country skis from the Mazama Country Inn, and a Ski
Mountaineering Seminar and Tour in the Cascades. (See also
Backpacking, Mountaineering, Cycling, Kayaking, River Running.)

VERMONT **BLUEBERRY HILL SKI TOURING CENTER,** Goshen, VT 05733.
Att.: Tony Clark. (802) 247-6735.

Take a loop around Hogback, race to Silver Lake, or just make
tracks in a snow world all your own at Blueberry Hill, located in
Vermont's tranquil Green Mountain National Forest. The Ski Touring
Center devotes itself to cross-country skiers of all ages and abilities
and has 75 km of both challenging and moderate terrain. Also retail
and rental departments, a repair shop, lessons, and an expert staff "to
see that our guests are skiing better with less effort." For skiing
enthusiasts, activities never cease: from seminars, waxing clinics, night
and guided tours, to the 60 km American Ski Marathon. The Inn,
built in the early 1800's gives a sense of traditional country living and
gourmet cooking—a good place to relax around the fire at night and
share the day's events.

GREEN TRAILS COUNTRY INN, Brookfield, VT 05036. Att.: Betty
& Jack Russell. (802) 276-3412.

From the Floating Bridge in historic Brookfield Village, 25 miles of
marked trails loop out over rolling meadows and frozen ponds,
through evergreen and maple woods, skirting marshes and the icy tips
of beaver houses. Nearby Allis State Park offers additional trails and
terrific views. The restored 19th century Green Trails Inn is a center
for x-country skiers, offering instruction and rentals, and 15 rooms,
most with private bath. Rates: B&B, $55-$61/couple; MAP,
$79-$85/couple. "Accommodations and trails are uncrowded,
unpretentious, and uncommonly good," according to a guest. A Mud
Season Festival every weekend in March is another Green Trails
specialty. "It's a chance to participate in the evolving season," explains
Jack Russell. You visit a dairy to see calves; go to a sheep farm to pet
lambs; observe the process of making fleece; sample the cheese of a
goat dairy; check out maple sugaring, an old Vermont tradition; and
celebrate with country entertainment at an old fashioned dinner.

WYOMING **GAME HILL RANCH,** Box A, Bondurant, WY 82922. Att.: Pete &
Holly Cameron. (307) 733-4120.

WYOMING   From the road it's a short ski trek into the ranch, which becomes your base for discovering isolated regions of high aspen groves, windswept ridges, and sun-filled valleys—ideal country for ski touring. With experienced guides you glide along untracked terrain, following partially frozen streams where moose and elk stop to drink. After an exhilarating day in the mountains, return to the snug comfort of the ranch and the welcoming aroma of Holly's gourmet meals and fresh-baked breads, or join Pete on his daily elk feeding chores. Dec.-Apr. Rates on request. (See also *Hiking with Packstock, Pack Trips.*)

SKINNER BROTHERS, Box 859-AG, Pinedale, WY 82941. Att.: Courtney Skinner. (307) 367-4506.

"Possibly no other mountain range in the contiguous United States can compete with the Wind River Mountains for winter trekking and camping." the Skinners say. On their 7- to 14-day trips, Jan.-Mar., you learn about building igloos and snow caves, skiing and high alpine touring, cooking, first aid, snowshoe travel, and other wilderness skills. "Good physical condition, patience, enthusiasm and a sense of adventure" are the only prerequisites. Equipment rentals and instruction. Altogether, the Skinner brothers boast 209 years of combined experience." (See also *Mountaineering, Pack Trips, Youth Adventures.*)

Setting up a tented home in the Tetons— Timberline Tours, WY.

TIMBERLINE TOURS, Box 855-A, Wilson, WY 83014. Att.: Peter Koedt.(307) 733-2565.

"We offer out-of-the-ordinary extended tours in spectacular, remote, alpine terrain," says Peter Koedt, who heads Timberline Tours. "Most overnights we build and sleep in snow shelters—often igloos. And we give the guests a great deal of personal attention before the trip as well as during." TT offers extended, customized tours in the Tetons. Tours vary in difficulty from low intermediate to advanced. Take a day trip for a taste of the wilderness or a little Nordic downhill, or sense the full power of the alpine environment on an extended expedition. For example, try the 9-day, 60-mile Teton Crest Tour which traverses the length of the range from Teton Pass to just south of Yellowstone. Koedt notes that spring touring in April and May is exceptional—"in many ways the most glorious part of the season." Dec.-May touring is also available. All communal equipment and food provided. Rental equipment in Jackson. Trip rates: $70/day/person, 2 person min. charge.

TOGWOTEE MOUNTAIN LODGE, Box 91-D, Moran, WY 83103. Att.: Dave & Judie Helgeson. (307) 543-2847.
   "We offer a long season, lots of powder, and no crowds," the Helgesons tell us. There are miles of marked trails, some groomed, winding through pine forests, across meadows and over gentle to steep slopes with machine-set track on most trails. Apre-ski activities center around the sauna/whirlpool spa and the Red Fox Saloon. Social Hour every evening features complimentary cocktails and hors d'oeuvres while exchanging "tales of the trails" and planning the next day's activities. Chef specials for ski appetites. Saturday "on-the-snow" cookout lunch. Rentals, guided tours, vacation packages ($130/person and up), and group instruction. Lodge sits on Togwotee Pass in full view of the Tetons, close to Yellowstone and Teton national parks. Arrival: Jackson, WY (See also *Pack Trips*.)

ALBERTA

SKOKI LODGE, P.O. Box 5, Lake Louise, Alta., Canada T0L 1E0. Att.: John M. Worrall. (403) 522-3555.
   At 7,200-foot elevation and 7 miles from the nearest access road, this rugged log lodge provides uncrowded skiing on scenic marked trails. Feb.-Apr. "Not recommended for absolute beginners, though the trails aren't difficult for intermediates," remarks John Worrall. Rentals and guided tours of the high alpine country in Banff National Park available on request. No trail fee. Overnight with 3 meals, $60, including transportation from the town of Lake Louise to the trailhead where you ski 7 miles to the lodge. Skoki Lodge welcomes up to 22 guests with "good food, good folk, and good times." (See also *Backpacking*.)

ONTARIO

KWAGAMA LAKE LODGE, 176 Manitou Dr., Sault Ste Marie, Ont., Canada, P6B 5L1. Att.: Mac & Grace MacEwan. (705) 253-3075.
   "We provide a unique cross-country wilderness ski adventure at the Kwagama Lake Lodge," Says Grace MacEwan. "You'll see signs of wildlife and may catch a glimpse of winter birds, grouse, marten, otter, fox, and rabbits in this world far away from civilization." Leave Sault Ste. Marie Sunday morning via the "Snow Train" for a 4-hour scenic ride through valleys, canyons, and around mountains. Baggage is transported by snowmachine and sled, while you ski the 9 miles to Kwagama Lake. After a hot toddy, settle into your wood-heated cabin 2, 3, or 4-bedrooms). A sauna and shower house is available at all

times. Nutritious, hearty meals are served family-style in the lodge's main dining room. Guests swap stories around the large stone fireplace. Monday to Friday, ski on a variety of groomed trails that wind through a pristine wilderness. Feature trails go to the Agawa Canyon and to Kwagama Mountain. Package includes train fare, all meals, use of trails, ski guide services. Price: Sun.-Sat. $452/person (Canadian). Late-Dec. to late-Mar. Says one repeat visitor: "The snow is always great, excellent terrain for skiing up to 2,100 feet, delicious meals, a fantastic sauna/bathhouse, and all the quiet and solitude your heart desires."

Enjoying a sleigh ride in a white wonderland—*Mohonk Mountain House, NY.*

WANAPITEI WILDERNESS CENTRE, 7 Engleburn Pl., Peterborough, Ont., Canada K9H 1C4. (705) 743-3774.

On touring skis or snowshoes, small groups follow abandoned logging roads and portages on both hilly and level terrain in the northern forests at Wanapitei's base in the Temagami area. There are over 100 miles of marked and 20 miles of maintained trails. Single and shared cabins (bring sleeping gear), meals and someone always on hand to lead tours. Best way to get there is from Temagami Village by ski-equipped plane or an 18-mile access road. Daily rates, $30 (Canadian dollars); New Year's & Mar. $27. Group rates. Jan.-Mar. (See also *Canoeing, Youth Adventures.*)

7 IN THE AIR

BALLOONING

Standing with several other adventurers inside a tightly woven wicker basket, you feel a bit like Dorothy attempting her first ill-fated return to Kansas from Oz. You hope at least *your* feet will leave the ground.

There's a crisp cold nip in the pre-dawn air. The wind is calm. "It's always at its calmest two hours before dawn and two hours after dusk," your pilot informs you. "There should be no problem filling the nylon balloon." He's right. In a short time the balloon is inflated to its full size—50,000 cubic feet—much bigger than a house, or two, for that matter. The ground lines are unhitched, the sandbag weights are tossed over the side, and you slowly rise.

Oddly, there's no sensation of motion. Rather than perceiving your movement sky-ward, you feel that the earth is dropping away below you. And it is, so to speak, at a pace of almost 500 feet per minute. It's quiet, very quiet. There's no rush of wind, since you are floating *with* it—your speed and direction entirely controlled by the breeze. In fact, there's no noise at all except for the occasional whoosh of the gas burner controlling your ascent.

The balloon pushes through powder-puff clouds. The backyards and highways below turn into a giant green and brown puzzle with animals, autos, and people forming its tiny moving parts. You wonder how the first hot-air balloonists—a duck, a rooster, and a sheep—enjoyed their flight back in 1783 over Annonay, France.

To gain altitude your aeronaut intermittently opens a blast valve, shooting more hot air into the giant rainbow-colored bubble that looms overhead. In the quiet of the morning people hear your voices and look up in amazement as you float by—participants in the "sport of the gods."

You continue upward perhaps to 8,000 feet or even higher, depending upon wind conditions and your pilot's judgment. As the air in the balloon cools, you descend gently, and the small specks that are earthlings become distinct again. You look for the chase car, hoping it will find roads that lead to your landing. There's no way to predict where it will be—only the wind knows.

Almost anybody can fly. The FAA, which regulates the sport, requires only that student flyers be at least 14 years of age and that aspiring private balloonists be 16. There are opportunities for rides at a number of balloon-dealer schools. They're not inexpensive. A typical one-hour sample flight may run from $100 per person and up (with champagne breakfast thrown in—a balloonist's landing ritual). Passengers often lend a hand with the take-off procedure—all part of the fun.

Getting a license is a bit more complicated. Requirements include a minimum of 10 hours of formal flight instruction, successful completion of a test, and check ride. It can take three months and cost from $1,000 to $2,000. Approximately 4,000 aeronauts are currently licensed in the U.S., but many more are enthusiasts of the sport as participants, spectators, or even take-off aides and chasers. The ballooning population has doubled in each of the past five years.

The group best equipped to get you off the ground is the Ballon Federation of America (BFA), a division of the National Aeronautic Association, formed in 1968 to promote, develop, and aid the art and science of free ballooning. It publishes a quarterly journal, *Ballooning*, available to pilot members for $30 a year and to associate members for $25 a year. Many clubs offer balloon instruction.

For a list of clubs in your area, write the BFA at P.O. Box 264, Indianola, IA 50125 (include a SASE) or call (515) 961-8809.

Listed below are a few of the multitude of balloon services now in operation. They can be called upon for availability of hot air balloons, flights, instruction, and other services.

ARIZONA

BALLOON ARIZONA, Box 64600, Tucson, AZ 85740. (602) 299-7744.

Fly in one of the world's largest hot air balloons among giant Saguaro cactus in Arizona's most beautiful desert terrain. Luxury flights include champagne breakfast and all transfers. Over 3,500 "adventurers" have taken this flight. Sep.-Jun., daily, weather permitting. $135/person. 10% discount for groups of 8 or more.

CALIFORNIA

BALLOON AVIATION OF NAPA VALLEY, P.O. Box 3298, 2299 Third St., Napa, CA 94558. (707) 252-7067.

"Trade in your earthbound cares for the most magnificent experience of your life," urges Chuck Foster. Breezes waltz you across the valley floor above the vineyards. The extra high basket sides are suede trimmed with a plush interior. "It sets standards for elegance and luxury in ballooning," says Chuck. His champagne balloon flight is $125/person, daily, weather permitting. Flights take place at sunrise; passengers receive fresh coffee and pastries at check-in. After a flight of nearly one hour, enjoy a poolside champagne celebration with French bread and cheeses, and take home your "Certificate of Aerostation."

COLORADO

BALLOON COLORADO, Box 1364, Dillon, CO 80435. (303) 468-2473.

Year-round flights amidst the splendor of the Colorado Rockies. Fly in one of the world's largest hot air balloons at the highest balloon port in the world. Luxury flights include champagne breakfast and all transfers. Over 3,500 "passengers" on these flights. Daily flights, weather permitting. $135/person. 10% discount for groups of 8 or more.

VISTA VERDE GUEST RANCH, Box 465, Steamboat Springs, CO 80477. Att.: Frank & Winton Brophy. (303) 879-3858.

Top off a week's ranch stay with a 1 1/2-hour champagne balloon flight down the Elk River Valley and over the surrounding mountains flanked by the Continental Divide and the Mt. Zirkel Wilderness Area. It offers a bird's eye view of elk, deer, fox, and other wildlife. The 1600-acre dude ranch, has log cabins, fine food, horseback riding and instruction, gymkhanas, a sauna/sports center, and more. $925/week with balloon flight. A "Balloon Ranch Package" also includes a crossing of the Continental Divide, an opportunity to do some flight training, and a third flight north of the ranch, $1,125. Open year round. (See also *Ski Touring*.)

CONNECTICUT

NEW ENGLAND HOT AIR BALLOONS, P.O. Box 706, Southington, CT 06489. Att.: Robert Zirpolo. (203) 621-6061.

Ready to sail away under a bubble of color—*Bob Zirpolo for New England Hot Air Balloons, CT.*

"Bring twice as much color film as you think you'll need!" says Robert Zirpolo, the company's aeronaut and flight instructor. "We've flown people from 5 to 99 years old!!" On daily Champagne Charters, Zirpolo flies over Meriden Mountain and across New England's lovely orchards, farmlands, and lakes. "We sometimes see deer in the cornfields." Year-round ballooning, morning and afternoon, 7 days a week, depending on wind and visibility. Special trips to see the colors of summer and flights over the Berkshires to view the spectacular New England fall foliage. Launch sites in Southington. Overnight lodging convenient to all launch sites.

MICHIGAN   **BALLOON CORPORATION OF AMERICA,** 2084 Thompson Road, Fenton, MI 48430. (313) 629-0040.

"On almost any day you will find up to 5 brightly colored balloons creating a carnival-like atmosphere and a photographer's paradise," comments Balloon Corporation of America. The outfit has been offering year-round ballooning adventures for 16 years "to carry forth old world traditions." Under the guidance of the First World Hot Air Balloon Champion, Capt. Phogg, BCA features a variety of ballooning experiences which are enhanced by its picturesque location and the abundance of lakes nearby (on the shores of scenic Lake Fenton). Introductory flights include a traditional champagne celebration, first flight certificate, and souvenir first flight balloon pin. Comprehensive training and all information regarding licensing, promotions, and sales provided. Bring only a free spirit! Rates: $200 for 1 person; $250 for 2 people; $325 for 3; $400 for four. Also group rates.

HANG GLIDING

It's man's age-long dream come true—stepping off a hill or mountain and flying like a bird. No instruments. No engine. Only the air. Free flight!

Skimming over hills and dunes, suspended beneath an ultralight hang glider, is indeed the oldest and newest way to fly, and its popularity is—well—soaring. Some 35,000 enthusiasts have taken up the sport in this country, and the numbers are ever increasing.

What attracts so many to the sport? Compared to sailplanes and small aircraft, hang gliders are relatively inexpensive. They are quiet and fumeless. And they are for all seasons and climates. But there's another drawing power. The very possibility of flying somewhat like a bird satisfies a yearning in the human spirit and excites the imagination of those who believe they can do it—can experience the exhilaration of unencumbered flight.

Although hang gliding actually started with the visionary but unfortunate flight of Icarus, its modern-day popularity came about thanks to Francis M. Rogallo, who invented and patented the flexible wing deltoid hang glider in the 1940s. Later NASA tested it as a spacecraft recovery system—and the art of man-flight had been altered. After 1969, when Australian Bill Bennett wowed Americans with his tow-gliding feats (using water skis and towed by a speedboat), hang gliding really started to catch on. And, it's catching on with everyone—young and old, men and women. "We have people as old as 82 flying hang gliders, they're called our 'Over the Hill Gang," says Joe Greblo, an instructor at Windsports International, Van Nuys, California.

Today most hang gliders are flexible wing aircrafts. One main asset of the modern-day hang glider is its lightness and compactness when folded. Unlike the rigid wing models, it can be handled by one person on the ground in a mild wind and solo launched. The pilot shifts weight to control the craft.

A standard new glider of the recreational variety costs $1,600 to $2,200. Used ones sell for much less, generally $800 and up for modern equipment in good shape.

Just about anyone with physical endurance and mental calm and confidence can pilot a hang glider. Muscle is helpful, as are large doses of instinct and dexterity. The best approach to hang gliding is first to read up on the subject, then visit a site, carefully observing how pilots take off and maneuver their gliders in the air by body shifting. If you feel ready to try it yourself, take lessons.

In a good course, certified instructors offer the fundamentals including ground instruction with films and lectures as well as training in the glider. You must comprehend wind conditions, aerodynamics, weather, and potential hazards. After several hours of classroom work and some time on a flight simulator, you're ready for your first flight, low and slow, progressing at your own rate. The aim is to teach safe techniques. Schools charge from $50 to $70 for a daily rate, including equipment. The rate generally drops if you take a package course. A 20-day lesson will cost about $625. (Rates vary depending on your location and the school you choose.)

Ideal beginner or intermediate slopes are long, wide, and sandy or grassy. There should be no obstruction and at least a 600-foot clearing ahead of take-off, plus a 100-foot clearing on the launching site itself. There should be no high brush or electrical power lines or wires ahead, and the prevailing wind should blow upward.

A relatively new technique in teaching is the use of tandem or dual instruction. With this method, a student goes into a high altitude flight with an instructor. The instructor handles all the difficult maneuvering moves while the student gets a taste of new heights.

Still, the sport is not without its dangers. Glider pilots have been killed. Many others injured. FAA investigation shows that most fatalities were caused by pilot error—taking off when the wind was too strong, failure to inspect the craft before take off and then experiencing a malfunction in the air, or attempting a maneuver that is too advanced.

The nature of the sport results in most pilots having a minor mishap while learning.

If you're sold on the sport, you may want to join the U.S. Hang Gliding Association (USHGA), Box 66306, Los Angeles, CA 90066. A $39 membership fee will bring you 12 issues of *Hang Gliding*, plus liability insurance and the association's directory of hang gliding clubs, schools, and flying sites. Or, you can write for a free directory.

In an attempt to reduce the accident rate, the USHGA has started to act as a sanctioning agency for meets, promoting and administering hang gliding contests, and certifying and regulating activities at these sites through its local chapters.

PARACHUTING

Me jump? Thirty years ago an invitation to throw oneself into the air with a parachute seemed as slaphappy as rolling over Niagara Falls in a barrel. Today, some 25 years after the first commercial parachute center was opened by French-American parachutist Jacques Istel, there are over 250 commercial jump centers, 450 parachute clubs in nearly all 50 states, and approximately 100,000 active jumpers in the United States (including students and experienced) who make more than 2 million jumps per year. And parachuting has developed into a popular intercollegiate sport. Annual national championships draw teams from more than 50 colleges and universities.

The first truly competitive parachutists were Russians. In the 1930s they conducted contests for amateur jumpers to see who could land closest to a selected ground target. The art of sky diving, however, was developed by the French, and Istel was responsible for introducing their techniques in the United States.

In the past decade parachuting has evolved into a complicated sport of skilled movement across the sky, quickness and accurate landings on a dime—literally. Some jumpers consider it an art form.

Learning to jump

The first jump requires the longest preparation and the greatest expense. To learn, sign up at a commerical center where the first-jump course may vary from $75 to $250. This includes equipment, instruction, and aircraft ride to the proper altitude. Succeeding jumps with instruction average $25 to $30, and without instruction $10 and up depending on the altitude desired.

It's not necessary to be a trained athlete to parachute. Nor does age make a difference, though above-average condition is required for jumpers past middle age. The novice receives four to six hours of pre-jump instruction. Basic points covered concern familiarity with equipment, how to exit from the plane and maneuver the parachute, how to land and roll, and emergency procedures in the plane, in the air and on the ground.

The student's first jumps are made from about 3,000 feet. These are "static line" jumps, with the chute's rip cord pulled automatically by a line attached to the plane. A reassuring jolt seconds after jumping indicates that the parachute has opened. It will take 15 to 25 jumps to get off "student status," which means you can then jump solo.

For information on commercial parachute centers and clubs in your area, call or write the U.S. Parachute Association (USPA), 1440 Duke St., Alexandria, VA 22314; (703) 836-3495. (No charge for this information.) Annual membership dues of $32.50 entitle you to a subscription to the monthly magazine, *Parachutist*, as well as to a third-party liability insurance policy. Each issue of the magazine lists active parachute centers and clubs around the country. USPA members are professionals, business people, pilots, and a cross section of those who simply love to jump.

First jump to freefall

After the first few jumps, the individual decides how far to pursue the sport--whether for the enjoyment of occasional successive jumps or for learning the techniques of freefall. For the dedicated parachutists, sky diving—plunging like a bird before pulling the cord—is the ultimate goal. *Freefall*—the very word connotes excitement.

The first freefall lasts just three seconds. Then you graduate to longer falls, using a stopwatch and altimeter and making controlled turns, loops, and maneuvers. On a freefall lasting 12 seconds you are moving at a speed of 100 to 120 miles per hour. But you have control over your body and can move across the sky at a ratio of two to one—that is, if you jump while two miles above the ground, you have time to move one mile across the sky. In formation flying, groups of jumpers follow one after another and meet in midair, forming stars, caterpillars, diamonds, or lines abreast as they drop at high speed.

A final step in sky diving, if you want to take it, is competition. The jumper is judged on a series of set maneuvers--individual style and accuracy, teamwork, and canopy work (building formations with parachute canopies).

As for safety, there's not too much to worry about. Jumping is safer than driving in an automobile. In 1985 for example, there were only 26 reported fatalities in over 2 million jumps, according to the USPA.

Accelerated freefall program

An alternative to the static-line jump as a teaching method is the recently developed accelerated freefall technique. Instead of jumping from 3,000 feet, the student's jumps are made at 10,000 feet with 50 seconds of freefall on each jump. The student is accompanied by two instructors (later by one) who hold on to his arms and parachute harness, helping him maintain stability.

The new technique enables the serious parachutist to learn and advance at a much faster rate. It generally takes 7 to 10 jumps to get off student status using the accelerated freefall method of instruction. Some jumps are accompanied by a parachuting video cameraperson who records the dive for ground review and evaluation. Costs for the accelerated freefall program are $200 to $250 for the first jump, $50 to $150 for each additional two- and one-instructor jump, until the levels of progression are mastered.

"Soft as a cat's paw"

A first-timer's emotions run the gamut from panic to sheer exhilaration, as described by one neophyte: "My turn came around, and I was frankly terrified. I jumped on cue, however, and 'whoom,' opening shock hit before I counted to three. The fright vanished, replaced by a feeling of peaceful other-worldliness. Earth sprawled below, no more real than a picture postcard, its problems reduced to the substance of the clouds on my right. I felt completely disengaged from the rules of both man and physics. The wind was soft as a cat's paw, brushing past my face and blowing me gently across the landscape. Camping, sailing, flying: They may get you away from the humdrum. But this is away from it *all*." *

*Lynde McCormick, *The Christian Science Monitor.*

PARACHUTING CENTERS

California	**The Perris Valley Skydiving Society,** 2091 Goetz Rd., Perris, CA 92370; (714) 657-8727. Perris Valley Airport.
Colorado	**Front Range Skydivers,** 165 Mikado Dr., Colorado Springs, CO 80919; (303) 598-8447.
Florida	**Paragators, Inc.,** Star Rt. 1, Box 462, Eustits, FL 32726; (904) 357-7800. Mid-Florida Airport.
	Skydive Deland Inc., P.O. Box 3071, Deland, FL 32723; (904) 738-3539. Deland Municipal Airport.

Learning to sail through the air with the greatest of ease—*Paragators, Inc., FL.*

Zephyrhills Parachute Center, P.O. Box 1101, Zephyrhills, FL 34283; (813) 788-5591.

Hawaii
Skydive Hawaii, 33 King St., No. 514, Honolulu, HI 96813; (808) 526-3020. Dillingham Airfield/North Shore.

Illinois
Skydive Sandwich, Rt. 34, Sandwich, IL 60548; (815) 786-8200 Sandwich Airport.

Indiana
Parachutes & Associates, Inc., State Rd. 28 W. Frankfort, IN 46041; (317) 654-6188. Frankfort Municipal Airport.

Kentucky
Greene County Sport Parachute Center of Kentucky, Rt. 2, Box 140, Bardstown, KY 40004; (502) 348-9531.

Massachusetts
Trojan Sport Parachute Center, 390 B Grant Road, Ft. Devens, MA 01433; (617) 772-2753 or 5999. Ft. Devons Military Base.

Minnesota
Minnesota Skydivers, 115 W. 47th St., Minneapolis, MN 55409; (612) 824-5985.

New Jersey
R.C. Paracenter Inc., Burlington County Air Park, Medford, NJ 08055; (609) 267-9671.

New York	**Albany Skydiving Center,** P.O. Box 131, Duanesburg, NY 12056; (518) 895-8140. Duanesburg Airport.
Pennsylvania	**AFF East,** 3506 Airport Rd., Chambersburg, PA 17201; (717) 264-1111. Chambersburg Airport.
Texas	**Skydivers of Texas Inc.,** 2553 Valley View Lane, Dallas, TX 75234; (214) 484-1234.
Utah	**Utah Sky Ranch,** 661 South 800 East, Salt Lake City, UT 84102; (801) 569-USPA or (801) 322-JUMP.
Washington	**Issaquah Parachute Center,** 2617 217st S.E., Issaquah, WA 98027; (206) 392-9010.

SOARING

An engineless plane sailing the heavens. Rising on currents of air. No means of staying up but by riding invisible air cushions. An exhilarating, silent world.

The earth's contours and substances reflect the sun's heat unevenly, filling the skies with ascending and descending waves of air. Part of the skill of a sailplane pilot is locating thermals—upward air currents on which to soar in endless spirals. "Sometimes we get on a hawk's tail and follow him right up," a pilot explains. "At 1,500 feet it's too high to spot a mouse. He's there for the same reason we are." As the thermal tops off, the sleek fuselage of the craft, with its long wings, moves through the atmosphere with a hiss of rushing air, gliding from one thermal to another, like stepping from cloud to cloud.

Much soaring in the United States is conducted on thermals, but lift is also obtained from waves of air produced by high velocity winds against a mountain range, or from winds hitting a perpendicular surface such as a cliff. This is called wave soaring and ridge soaring.

Pulled into the air by a powered towplane (or sometimes an automobile or winch), the sailplane runs along the runway on its single wheel before lifting up. It is aerodynamically designed to gain altitude on even slightly rising air, and can fly cross-country.

Today there are some 3,500 sailplanes in the United States, more than 12,000 licensed pilots, about 200 soaring clubs, and 175 commercial schools. The Soaring Society of America (SSA) was formed in 1932 to foster and promote all phases of gliding and soaring. A division of the National Aeronautic Association, it sanctions the annual National Soaring Championship contests and numerous regional races.

SSA has produced a soaring starter kit which will launch you on the adventure of motorless flight. The kit includes: a brochure, *How You Can Become a Glider Pilot*; a 36-page full-color booklet with a comprehensive overview of the sport, *Soaring in America*; a *Directory of U.S. Soaring Sites*, giving schools, flight operations, and SSA chapters; a current issue of its magazine, *Soaring*; and a SSA membership application. The entire kit may be ordered for $3 from SSA, Box 66071, Los Angeles, CA 90066.

Another source of information on clubs, schools, and other aspects of the sport is the booklet, *Start Soaring* ($2), put out by the leading U.S. manufacturer of sailplanes, Schweizer Aircraft Corporation, Box 147, Elmira, NY 14902.

A few of the larger soaring centers in the United States are listed below.

Arizona	**Arizona Soaring, Inc.,** P.O. Box 27427, Tempe, AZ 85282; (602) 568-2318. Estrella Sailport. Sailplane demonstration rides, tows, rentals, instruc., hangar, Overnight $10/person.
California	**Calistoga Soaring Center,** 1546 Lincoln Ave., Calistoga, CA 94515; (707) 942-5592. Calistoga Airpark. All yr., daily. 10 sailplanes, 4 towplanes. Instruction. Thermal, ridge, wave.

Sailplane Enterprises, P.O. Box 1678 Hemet, CA 92343; (714) 658-6577. Hemet-Ryan Airport. All yr., daily. 15 sailplanes, instruction, 4 towplanes. Thermal, shear-line, wave.

Skylark North Gliderport, P.O. Box 918, Tehachapi, CA 93561; (805) 822-5267. Fantasy Haven Airport. All yr., daily exc. Tues. 14 sailplanes, instruction, 4 towplanes. FAA test examiners. Camping facilities and restaurant at soaring airport.

Colorado

Black Forest Gliderport, 9990 Gliderport Rd., Colorado Springs, CO 80908; (303) 495-4144. 7 mi. NE of Colo. Springs. All yr., daily exc. Mon. 10 sailplanes, instruc., 2 towplanes. Thermal, wave.

The Cloud Base, Inc., 5117 Independence Rd., Boulder, CO 80301; (303) 530-2208. Boulder Municipal Airport. All yr., daily. 6 sailplanes, instruc., 2 towplanes. Thermal, ridge, wave.

Florida

Lenox Flight School, Rt. 4, Box 4639, Arcadia, FL 33821; (813) 494-3921 or 735-1132. Farwell Airport. Gardner, FL. All yr., by appt. 3 sailplanes, 1 towplane, instruc., airplane rides. Thermals. Nearby camping in Arcadia and at Peace River Resort in Zolfo Springs. Motels in Arcadia-Wauchula.

Seminole Flying & Soaring, 1600 West Hwy. 419, Chuluota, FL 32766. (305) 365-3201. Flying Seminole Ranch Airport. 12 miles NE of Orlando. All yr., daily. 4 sailplanes, 2 towplanes, instruc., rentals, rides. Thermal.

Illinois

Hinckley Soaring, Inc., Hinckley Airport, U.S. Hwy. 30, Hinckley, IL 60520; (815) 286-7200. Apr.-Nov., daily exc. Mon. 6 sailplanes, 2 towplanes, instruc. Thermal.

Nevada

Desert Soaring, 1499 Nevada Hwy., Boulder City, NV 89005; (702) 293-4577. Boulder City Airport. 30 min. from Las Vegas. All yr., daily exc. Mon. Instruc., rentals.

New Hampshire

Northeastern Gliderport, Brady Ave., Salem, NH 07938; (603) 898-7919. Daily, Jun.-Oct., wkends Apr.-Dec. 20 sailplanes, instruc., demon., 3 towplanes, FAA test examiners.

Pennsylvania

Kutztown Aviation Service, Inc., R.D.4, Box 52, Kutztown, PA 19530; (215) 683-3821 or 8389. Kutztown Airport. All yr., daily. 14 sailplanes, instruc., 3 towplanes. Thermal, wave.

Posey Aviation, Inc., P.O. Box 41, Erwinna, PA 18920; (215) 847-2770. Van Sant Airport. All yr., daily. 12 sailplanes. instruc., rentals, 4 towplanes. Thermal, wave.

Virginia   **Warrenton Soaring Center, Inc.,** R.R.#616, Warrenton, VA 22186;
(703) 347-0054. Warrenton Airpark, Apr.-Dec., Sat., Sun., Wed. 4
sailplanes, instruc., rentals, 3 towplanes.

8 STILL MORE...

WILDERNESS/ NATURE EXPEDITIONS

How would you like to watch whales migrate off the Nova Scotia coast? Or photograph a pelican nest in the Northwest Territories? Or watch loggerhead sea turtles come ashore to lay their eggs on Little St. Simons Island off the coast of Georgia?

These are but a tiny sampling of the world of wilderness and nature expeditions. Whether your interest is natural history, marine biology, anthropology, or geology—whether you wish to concentrate on photography, sightseeing, or backwoods exploration—there's a tour for you.

The expeditions described in this chapter are extremely varied. You can rough it, camping each night, or take day trips and spend nights in comfortable lodges. Or perhaps you'll build an igloo for a cozy night.

Not all of these adventures give you an intense physical workout. On some, you become an observer, working side-by-side with scientists and scholars. On others the hiking, trekking, and wilderness exploration present more of a challenge.

Whatever criteria you use to select your expedition, several factors should not be overlooked. Consider the weather, season, and migratory patterns in the region. All of these conditions will affect the quantity and variety of your sightings for both wildlife and plantlife. Most expedition teams include at least one biologist, botanist or zoologist—leaders who provide information which you'll savor as much as your photographs.

If your travels include camping, most likely everything except a sleeping bag will be provided. But don't forget other essentials: pen and paper for note taking during sightings and at seminars, a tape recorder to save exotic bird whistles or dolphin conversations, binoculars, and a camera with a long distance lens. You'll want to record every sight and sound—there surely will be an eyeful and an earful!

ALASKA

ALASKA DISCOVERY, INC., P.O. Box 26, Gustavus, AK 99826. Att.: Hayden & Bonnie Kaden. (907) 697-2257.

The rapid ice recession in Glacier Bay has created a spectacularly dynamic fjord system in southeast Alaska. Twelve fortunate people will study the area for 2 weeks in June through informal discussions, background readings, and field observation. Some travel is by seaplane, power boat, or hiking—but most is in kayaks, with no previous experience required. Co-sponsored by the University of Alaska (Juneau), the exploration unveils a world of glacial geology; mammal and bird identification; marine, plant, and animal succession; humpback whale and sea bird ecology; and more. Biologist/naturalist/certified wilderness guides. All-inclusive price: $750; $15 extra enrollment fee for 3 credits. Arrival: Gustavus. (See also *Backpacking, River Running, Ski Touring.*)

Earning your gold the old-fashioned way—*Camp Denali, AK.*

ALASKA   **CAMP DENALI,** Box 67CA, Denali National Park, AK 99755. Att.:
Wally & Jerri Cole. (907) 683-2290. [Winter: (907) 683-2302.]
    To the wilderness seeker, Denali National Park means wildlife
(caribou, grizzly, moose, mountain sheep, wolf, fox, wolverine,
beaver, marten, lynx, to name a few), and birdlife (ptarmigan, golden
eagle, and at least 130 other species); and it means rivers, braided
streams, taiga trails and lakes which reflect the magnificent beauty of
the Alaska Range and the "Great One"—Denali, highest mountain in
North America at 20,320 feet. This is the environment of Camp Denali

A caribou bull magnifi-
cently silhouetted
against Mt. McKin-
ley—*Camp Denali,
AK.*

located near Wonder Lake, at the end of the road 90 miles from the
park entrance. The Coles, hospitable owners of Camp Denali, provide
programs designed to acquaint you with the plant, bird, and animal
life that abounds, and interpret the phenomena of the tundra world.
Cabins with Yukon stoves, propane lights, and private privies, have
full views of the snow-capped mountains. Family-style meals are
served at the lodge, and evening slide shows and talks interpret the
Alaskan environment. Activities include wildlife viewing, panning for
gold, hiking, photography, fishing, and overnight camping or
backcountry exploring. Minimum stay: 4-5 nights,
$160/person/night. (See also *Backpacking/Hiking.*)

DENALI DOG TOURS AND WILDERNESS FREIGHTERS, Box 670,
McKinley Park, AK 99755. Att.: Will & Linda Forsberg. (907)
683-2644 or 683-2294.

The wilderness in which the Forsbergs travel and live covers 6 million acres. "We rarely encounter other travelers during our tours," they say. "It gives you the feeling of having this vast wilderness all to yourself." Their park concession gives them the sole right to use 12 log cabins in the park, and they plan wilderness trips with dog sleds and skis in winter, and on foot in summer. They plan each trip according to the interests and experience of their guests. Their goal is to give you some of the flavor of their unique Alaskan lifestyle and to introduce you to the flora, fauna, and remarkable beauty of the area. Linda is a recognized expert on the park's mammal population with special expertise in the wolves. They know the park well-covering over 2,000 miles of trails each year. (See also *Dog Sledding, Ski Touring.*)

HUGH GLASS BACKPACKING, CO., P.O. Box 110796-AT, Anchorage, AK 99511. Att.: Chuck Ash. (907) 243-1922.

"There is an inner peace, a tranquility, to be found in the wilderness that is attainable in but few other settings," remarks founder Chuck Ash. Choose from 8 wilderness trips and live amid beauty and grandeur, witnessing the ageless rhythm of life above the Arctic Circle. The regions for his trips are Wrangell—St. Elias National Park; Denali National Preserve; Lake Clark National Park; Aniakchak National Monument; Noatak River National Preserve; Prince William Sound; Kenai Fjords National Park; Gates of the Arctic National Park; and Katmai National Park (Valley of 10,000 Smokes or Bay of Islands). Most involve hiking/trekking; some include rafting, canoeing or kayaking; others combine modes of travel. Pass from alpine tundra to bottom land spruce forest, viewing volcanic peaks, pristine waters, majestic fjords and glaciers, and glacial mountains. Observe how bear, wolves, moose lynx, fox, salmon, trout, eagles, songbirds, waterfowl, and wildflowers are all interlocked in a timeless embrace. Trips: 7-10 days. Average cost: $125/day. Start from Bettles, Anchorage, or King Salmon. (See also *Canoeing/Kayaking, Backpacking/Hiking.*)

MOUNTAIN TRAVEL, 1398-AG, Solano Ave., Albany, CA 94706. (800) 227-2384 or (415) 527-8100.

"Led by professional or amateur naturalist guides, our wildlife trips encourage a greater understanding of the world's wild places," says Mountain Travel. They offer an Alaskan wildlife safari to see caribou migration. The trip features day hikes from a tented camp in the Arctic National Wildlife Range, deluxe cabin camp, and an optional visit to Pribilof Islands. (17 days, $2,390, Jun.) Or explore a marine wilderness on a 10-day cruise through the Inland Passage in Southeast Alaska. Numerous islands support sea bird and marine mammal colonies, and the waters team with fish, dolphins, porpoises, and whales. It is the most intensive feeding area for humpback whales in the entire eastern Pacific. Explore secluded coves and bays from the cruise boat, the *Delphinus,* and go ashore for hikes, berry-picking, "botanizing," and beachcombing. ($1,490, Jun. & Jul.) (See also *Backpacking, Canoeing—AK, River Running—AK, Mountaineering.*)

COLORADO

COLORADO OUTWARD BOUND SCHOOL, 945 Pennsylvania St., Denver, CO 80203. (303) 837-0880.

Programs take place on the high alpine terrain of the Colorado Rocky Mountains; the rapids of the Green, Yampa, and Colorado Rivers; the deserts and canyonlands of southeastern Utah. You start with a backpack and work your way up to major peak ascents. The summer session, May-Nov., gets into basic campcraft, mountaineering, gorge crossing, whitewater rafting, rock climbing, rappeling, wilderness travel, and emergency care. In winter it's ski mountaineering or cross-country skiing, ice climbing, glissading, and winter campcraft in Colorado's Collegiate Range. (For Outward Bound's headquarters, See CT.)

Hiking and picnicking in a mountain meadow—*Camp Denali, AK.*

OUTDOOR LEADERSHIP TRAINING SEMINARS, P.O. Box 20281-A, Denver, CO 80220. Att.: Rick Medrick. (303) 333-7831.

ON an OLTS intensive 7-day Outdoor Adventure Course, you learn the basics of rock climbing, paddle the fast and exciting rapids of the Arkansas River, and attempt to scale a 14,000-foot peak in the Sangre de Cristo Range. With a primitive 3,000-acre working ranch as your base, you stay in tents or tepees and share camping duties with 6 to 12 other participants and instructors. The $350 tuition covers food and group equipment; backpacks and sleeping bags available for rental. Meeting personal expectations, cooperative activities, and sharing responsibilities are the goals. Jun.-Aug. Arrival: Denver or Colorado Springs. (See also *Backpacking, Mountaineering, River Running, Ski Touring.*)

UNIVERSITY OF THE WILDERNESS, P.O. Box 1687, Evergreen, CO 80439. Att.: DAT Trips. (303) 674-9724.

Within the Medicine Bow National Forest, the University's Snowy Range Campus lies 35 miles west of Laramie (WY) at 9,000 feet. It's 50 historic buildings are dispersed over the wooded 13-acre site, divided by two tumbling trout streams and surrounded by spectacular peaks, tundra country, and shortgrass prairie. This is base camp for backpacking, canoeing, and rafting expeditions into the area. Sample trips: Snowy Range High Country, Sheep Mountain Wildlife Refuge, Wyoming's Beautiful Wildflowers, and Rocky Mountain Mushrooms—all 5 days, $275-$285. Also wilderness photography workshops and skiing/snowshoeing in winter. Bring or rent sleeping gear. Some university credits. (See also *Backpacking*—CO.)

CONNECTICUT   **OUTWARD BOUND, INC.**, 384 Field Point Rd., Greenwich, CT 06830. Att.: Pat Lyren. (800) 243-8520 or (203) 661-0797.

This is the headquarters for a nonprofit organization that began during World War II as a training school for British seamen and has spread to five continents. Today, it offers a year-round schedule in schools located in 5 distinct parts of the U.S.—the Colorado Rockies, Hurricane Island off the coast of Maine, North Carolina's Great Smoky Mountains, Pacific Crest in Washington's and Oregon's Cascade range, and Voyageur in the Minnesota Boundry waters. All schools offer standard 18- to 28-day courses that teach self-discovery in the wilderness. Other training includes emergency first aid and rescue, map and compass reading, ecology, rock climbing and rappeling, food planning and cooking, final expedition, solo, and a marathon event. There are shorter courses for those with limited time; semester-length courses for those over 18; intensive courses for adults, as well as specialized management development programs for business executives. Tuition for the standard course of 3-4 weeks is $950 to $1800, which includes food, equipment, and instruction. Special courses for 4-18 days range in price from $310-$1,100. (See also *Mountaineering/Rock Climbing, Canoeing/Kayaking, Youth Adventures.*)

FLORIDA   **EVERGLADES CANOE OUTFITTERS, INC.**, 39801 Ingraham Hwy., C-6, Homestead, FL 33034. Att.: Sheri M. Leach. (305) 246-1530.

Explore the Everglades, one of the most exotic wilderness areas in the world. "Our naturalist guides have an in-depth knowledge of the unique ecological balance of the Everglades as well as practical backcountry camping experience," says Sheri Leach. Choose from several exciting trips. A 9-day, 100-mile backcountry paddle exploration lets you canoe and camp along winding trails, through creeks, rivers and open bays in the mangrove wilderness. (Feb., $549.) Or stargaze in the Cape Sable area with its isolated beaches many miles from the distraction of city lights. On this 7-day paddling trip you see more than 100 bird species, pass mangrove forests, and spend time fishing or photographing the sights. (Dec., Mar., Apr., $445.) Both trips limited to 9 canoeists; no canoeing or camping experience needed. Or design your own custom guided exploration, concentrating on your field of interest, whether it's fishing, plants, birds, wildlife or photography. Cost: $60-$115/person/day, depending on group size and the length of the trip. "These are trips for doers," Sheri reminds travelers, "folks who'd rather paddle than ride, who enjoy working together and sharing camp chores." (See also *Canoeing/Kayaking*.)

GEORGIA

LITTLE ST. SIMONS ISLAND, P.O. Box 1078-AG, St. Simons Island, GA 31522. Att.: Laura Gibbens. (912) 638-7472.

Birders may spot up to 200 species on the sand beaches, and in the salt and freshwater marshes, tidal flats, and pine and oak forests of this privately owned, unspoiled barrier island off the Georgia coast. "The place was very restful with wonderful birding—we saw 110 species in two weeks," reports one satisfied couple. Among the other sights and sounds: bottlenose dolphins, bellowing alligators, and loggerhead sea turtles who come ashore in the summer to lay their eggs. Explore the 10,000-acre secluded and undeveloped island in the company of professional naturalists. This intriguing hideaway offers the luxury of charming accommodations, excellent meals, ocean and pool swimming, horseback riding, canoeing, and other activities to enjoy small groups (up to 24). Rates: $112-$145/person, 2-night minimum, including room, meals, activities. Discounts available. Air taxi or van shuttle from nearby airports arranged. No charge for island ferry with reservation. Open year round.

WILDERNESS SOUTHEAST, 711-AG Sandtown Rd., Savannah, GA 31410. Att.: Dick Murlless. (912) 897-5108.

This base camp trip, called Coastal Incredible Edibles, features collecting, preparing, and eating the freshest of seafood—crabs, oysters, mussels, whelk, periwinkles, shrimp, and fish. "We have delicious recipes but we encourage participants to share their culinary skills and ideas," says Murlless. "There's so much food that we usually eat supper right through until midnight." Primitive camping; all equipment provided except sleeping gear (3 days, $130; 4 days $180). Additionally, camping on wild, little-known and beautiful Sapelo Island offers the chance to explore beaches, dunes, a live oak forest, and the rich salt marsh ($40/day). Or add another 2 days based out of R.J. Reynolds' old mansion to study the historical aspects of the island ($50/day). Costs include everything except day pack and sleeping gear.(See also *Youth Adventures, Backpacking, Canoeing, Scuba—FL.*)

WOLFCREEK WILDERNESS, Rt. 1, Box 1190-A, Blairsville, GA 30512. Att.: Alan Sentkowski, Exec. Dir. (404) 745-6460.

This private nonprofit organization focuses on wilderness adventure education. Its seminars and courses, given all year, center around leadership training, backpacking, rock climbing, and canoeing trips. They work with classroom teachers and administrators to develop programs in environmental outdoor education that are specifically applicable in each school situation. They also contract with corporations for "Team Challenge" programs—a 3-day ropes course and team building seminar for executives. Rates for various courses range from $30 to $50 per day for each participant. (See also *Youth Adventures*.)

MASS.   **EARTHWATCH,** 680 Mount Auburn St., Box 403, Dept. AG,
Watertown, MA 02172. (617) 926-8200.

Would you like to excavate dinosaurs in Colorado—or mammoths
in South Dakota? Help biologists understand the ecology of the
Everglades? Work to save the endangered leatherback sea turtles in St.
Croix? These and some 90 other research expeditions taking place in
20 states and 40 countries are sponsored around the world by
EARTHWATCH, a non-profit organization. You are invited to work
side-by-side with scholars and scientists for two or three weeks in
search of knowledge. No experience is necessary—just a willingness to
work hard and sometimes rough it under primitive field conditions in
exchange for a unique learning experience. As part of a team each
participant shares field chores—recording natural sounds, gathering
ethnographic data, conducting oral history interviews, surveying
flora and fauna, observing animal behavior, assisting in diving
operations. 2-week expeditions, $500-$2,000 plus, and travel expense
to research area.

Getting a whiff of
wildflowers—*Paul
Fraughton for
Canyonlands Field
Institute, UT.*

MAINE   **CHEWONKI FOUNDATION,** R.F.D. 3, Wiscasset, ME 04578. Att.:
Tim Ellis. (207) 882-7323.

A participant cites the highlights of Chewonki's weeklong natural
history of the Maine coast workshops: "An all-day canoe trip to an
island of magnificent pine forests; hiking in the Camden Hills and
seeing schooners on Penobscot Bay; going down through fields and
woods at dawn to watch birds waking and mists rising from the salt
marshes; dragging a pond to study its creatures; salt-water swimming
after a day's field trip; enjoying the friendships that develop and the
hidden talents that come to light. An ideal vacation for families." The
workshop is for anyone of any age interested in the coastal
environment. Evening lecture-discussions complement field trips led
by trained naturalists around the Chewonki Peninsula. Cost is $250,
$175 for children 12 and under. Also family wilderness trips—about

10 participants, 2 leaders—7 days of Downeast sailing, rowing, sea kayaking, and camping, $400; or 6 days hiking and camping in Baxter State Park, $400. (See also *Canoeing/Kayaking*.)

MINNESOTA   **GUNFLINT NORTHWOODS OUTFITTERS,** Box 100, GT-AG, Grand Marais, MN 55604. Att.: Bruce & Sue Kerfoot. (800) 328-3325 nat'l. or (800) 328-3362 in MN.

With emphasis on learning the skills of wilderness living, the Kerfoots send small groups—never more than 9—into the vast Boundary Waters Canoe Area on the Minnesota/Canada border with a guide and complete equipment. "We blend together with paddling and portaging, the features of the northwoods," they explain—"wild animals and birds, berry picking, wilderness cooking and camping, photography, and outstanding fishing." It's a nature-oriented fun trip, not a test of endurance—well-suited for families. The 6-day adventure starts Sunday morning and ends Friday afternoon in time for sauna baths before a farewell dinner and overnight at the lodge. For adults $295, children 12 and under $150. (See also *Canoeing, Ski Touring*—Gunflint Lodge.)

VOYAGEUR OUTWARD BOUND SCHOOL, P.O. Box 250, Long Lake, MN 55356. Att.: Dee Dee Hull, or Linda Larson. (800) 328-2943 (outside MN) or (612) 542-9255 (in MN).

You'll find high adventure and experiences that open up self-discovery in the year round activities of this Outward Bound School. Courses for youth (14 and up) and adults range from canoe expeditions in the North Woods of Minnesota and Canada, to backpacking and mountaineering in the Montana Rockies, or whitewater canoeing and desert exploration along the Rio Grande River on the Texas/Mexico border. In winter, develop your showshoeing, dogsledding, and cross-country skiing skills in the sparkling white beauty of the North Woods. Each course provides a learn-by-doing approach to help you discover the great outdoors on a personal level. No experience necessary and all equipment provided on these 8-, 15-, 22-day and semester-long courses. Rates: $600/8 days-$1,800/28 days. (See also *Canoeing/Kayaking, Ski Touring/Snowshoeing*.)

NEW MEXICO   **SOUTHWEST SAFARIS,** P.O. Box 945, Dept. AG, Santa Fe, NM 87504. Att.: Bruce Adams. (505) 988-4246.

Bruce Adams has solved the problem of how to cover the vast distances of the magnificent Southwest: he transports visitors by air, hopping from one spectacular scene to another. At one spot you'll continue by jeep, at another by foot or by river raft. One-day and lodging tours available. The emphasis is on geology, archaeology, ecology, and history. The aircraft doubles as a portable classroom from which to study huge geological landforms and grasp the relationships among widely separated Indian ruins. "And yet, to fully appreciate the southwest today," Bruce adds, "one must climb into a cliff dwelling, raft down the San Juan, and jeep through Monument Valley. Or, to see the Grand Canyon and the Four Corners Region in a day, do it by plane" (from Santa Fe, NM). He offers day excursions for $299, and 3- to 5-day safaris from $895-$1,595.

OREGON

NATURE EXPEDITIONS INTERNATIONAL, 474 Willamette Ave., Box 11496, Dept. AGN, Eugene, OR 97440. (503) 484-6529.

Natural history highlights the exceptional trips offered by this organization to Alaska, the Southwest, Hawaii, and other regions. An Alaskan wildlife expedition is specially designed for the first-time visitor who wants to see the magnificence of Glacier Bay, Katmai, and Denali national parks and observe the diverse wildlife. It's a land of spectacular glaciers, fjords, high peaks, and wolves, moose, grizzlies, mountain goats, Dali sheep, whales, seals, thousands of birds and wildflowers. (16 days, $2,790.) On an Indian country exploration in the Southwest the highlights include natural wonders such as Monument Valley and Canyon de Chelly, and Navajo, Hopi, and Anasazi sites in New Mexico, Colorado, and Arizona. (16 days, $1,790.) On a natural history expedition in Hawaii, be prepared for a fascinating tale of the "real" Hawaii-humpback whales, helicopter flights to difficult-to-reach wonders, active volcanoes, marine biology, reef ecology, tropical birdlife, flora, culture, and more. (15 days, $1,590.) Expert naturalists accompany all trips.

Soaking in the sights from cliffside—*Susan Voorhees for Special Odysseys, WA.*

O.R.E. INC., 30493 Lone Pine Dr., Junction City, OR 97448. Att.: Bob Doppelt or Peggy Bloom. (503) 689-6198.

"Through our natural history program, you can experience the fun of rafting a river while gaining insights into the natural and social world around you," notes Bob Doppelt. "The joys and thrills of rafting

OREGON

are still the primary focus, while informal education about natural history, photography, geology, or environmental issues is available for those interested." This year, O.R.E. offers four wildlife and birding trips on the Owyhee, John Day, or Rogue rivers in May, in cooperation with the Audubon Society. In addition, the outfitter has three photography workshops on the Klamath (Jul.), Salmon (Aug.), and the Rogue (Sep.). Geology trips scheduled May-Jul., and river clean-up trips in Jun., Aug., and Sep. A "resource person"—someone especially trained in geology, botany, photography, etc.—accompanies each trip. College credit offered on some workshops sponsored by colleges and universities. (See also *River Running, Youth Adventures*.)

UTAH

CANYONLANDS FIELD INSTITUTE, Professor Valley Ranch, P.O. Box 68, Moab, UT 84532, Att.: Karla J. Vanderzanden. (801) 259-7750.

The goal of this non-profit educational organization is to help people *understand*, not just see, the natural wonders of Canyonlands and Arches national parks. "Explore with us in a spirit of learning and discovery," they urge. Their programs involve three types of trips: First, 2- to 3-day field trips with day excursions on natural history, geology, archaeology, and local lore, with leisurely hikes and carpooling to reach destinations. Participants make their own motel/camping arrangements ($35/person/day). Second, 3- to 7-day vacations by horseback, raft, jeep, and leisurely hiking or backpacking with qualified outfitters and instructors. Accommodations, most meals, transport and instruction included ($50-$95/person/day). Third, workshop seminars, 3-7 days, utilizing indoor and outdoor classroom settings, custom-arranged for management development and other groups ($50-$70/person/day). CFI is well aware of the extraordinary features of this amazing country and conveys enthusiasm to guests on trips by raft, canoe, bike, jeep, horse, and on foot. As stated by a women's magazine editor, "It definitely ranks among the most exciting, and personally satisfying vacations I've ever taken." Mar.-Nov. Arrival: Moab or Grand Junction.

WASHINGTON

JACKSON MOUNTAIN EXPLORATIONS, P.O. Box 2652, Renton, WA 98056. Att.: Bob Jackson. (206) 255-6635.

Geologist Bob Jackson wants to take you to the spectacular Cascade Range to find crystals, fossils, and even gold. Bob's main business is collecting mineral specimens for museum collections, but on the side he introduces people from all over to the wonders of the geology of the Northwest. "About a third of my clients are fossil and mineral collectors," he says, "and the rest are just interested in the beauty of nature." You can collect quartz and pyrite crystals on a 1-day trip or over a weekend, including camping out at a wilderness hot spring. Other 1-day trips are amber collecting, fossils, or gold panning. Since Bob has thoroughly explored the geology of the areas you'll visit, he can guarantee you'll find specimens of minerals, fossils or gold. Prices from $10-$29. Also a 2-day collecting trip, $85/person, and 2- to 8-day helicopter-supported trip, $280/person. Special rates for groups. Jun.-Oct.

Constructing an igloo to guard against the elements—*Mary Sterling for Special Odysseys, WA.*

SPECIAL ODYSSEYS, P.O. Box 37, Medina, WA 98039. Att.: Susan or Skip Voorhees. (206) 455-1960.

For more than 10 years Skip and Susan Voorhees have been leading adventurers into the awesome vastness and spectacular beauty of the Arctic—a region which they well understand. (Susan, in fact, was the first woman to lead an expedition to the North Pole.) With justifiable pride in their out-of-the-ordinary adventures, they offer five separate Arctic itineraries and two to Atlantic Canada. Journey to Resolute Bay across the immense barrenlands. See beautiful Northern Baffin Island or Grise Fjord on Ellesmere Island. Visit Inuit villages and see ancient stone bear and fox traps. Stand on top of the world at the North Pole. Visit the land of the midnight sun in Greenland with its majestic glaciers and icebergs. Or trek in the old-world mode of travel—by dog sledge. You are guaranteed breathtaking scenes: sparkling glaciers, rolling tundra, frozen seas, and soaring peaks. View polar bears, caribou, and Muskox herds, Beluga whales, narwhals, and Eskimo villages, where knowledgeable Inuit guides introduce their culture and art. Trips range from 7-12 days; $2,350-$7,000. Or visit Atlantic Canada: Newfoundland in July when the whale migration is in progress (13 days, $1,990) or Nova Scotia in September during fall foliage time (7 days, $965). Each is an in-depth Canadian experience.

NORTHWEST TERRITORIES

SUBARCTIC WILDERNESS ADVENTURES LTD., Box 685, Fort Smith, N.W.T., Canada, X0E 0P0. Att.: Jacques & Ruth van Pelt. (403) 872-2467.

"If you've been thinking of getting away from the urban life to the peace of the land, our personalized small-group experiences could be just the way to have an unforgettable adventure in Canada's unspoiled north," says Jacques van Pelt. Subarctic Wilderness offers several warm weather tours and treks that let you explore the forests and clear waters—far from the city. On a 2 1/2-day "pacey" journey, you stay in the comfort of a guest home, and enjoy brief strolls and fascinating experiences: a meeting with the Mayor of Fort Smith, a small group community exploratory trip, a visit to the Northern Life Museum, and a view of the world's northernmost white pelican nesting site. Weekly departures. Rates: 1-2 persons, $251/person; 3-12 persons, $151/person. Or take a 6-day adventure in the spring, summer or fall in Precambrain Granite country and the Interior Plains. Here you meet the region's finest representation of people, landscape, flora, and fauna. Among the sights: a white pelican rookery, portage wagon trails, cliff views over the Salt Plains, Pelican Rapids mid-river sunrise. Among the activities: a game migration trail foot safari, stream paddling and bathing, river rafting. Rates: 2 persons, $570/person; 3-7, $450/person. Departures for both trips from Fort Smith. (See also *Canoeing, River Running, Dog Sledding*.)

YOUTH ADVENTURES

Whatever your age, if you're young of heart and strong of mind and body; this chapter is for you. The activities, many with a wilderness angle, will teach you new skills or show you how to hone some old ones.

Learn emergency care—survival and rescue techniques. Discover how to patch a bicycle tire, what tools you need for ice climbing, and the motion to use when glissading. Your spirit will soar and your physical stamina will improve as you tackle unbelievable new challenges—whether you're rappeling in the Rocky Mountains, cycling across the country, or canoeing in Quebec.

Best of all, you'll have plenty of fun as you discover great adventures all over North America.

ARIZONA **EXPEDITIONS INC./GRAND CANYON YOUTH EXPEDITIONS,** R.R. 4, Box 775, Flagstaff, AZ 86001. Att.: Dick & Susan McCallum. (602) 774-8176 or 779-3769.

The McCallums' 18-day oar-powered trip in the Grand Canyon ($1,200) is their specialty. "It's designed for young adults from 16 to 25 and older people." Dick explains. Participants learn whitewater river navigation, camping skills, wilderness survival, river rescue techniques, physical conditioning, and safety training. "We also run charter trips to fit the needs of any special youth group," he adds. "Just let us know what type of adventure your group is looking for." (See also *River Running*.)

CALIFORNIA **TREK AMERICA,** P.O. Box 1338, Gardena, CA 90249. Att.: Mark Sheehan. (800) 221-0596.

"We'll custom tailor an itinerary for any group—schools, colleges, boy scouts, girl scouts, or the local YMCA," says Mark Sheehan of Trek America, an outfitter who specializes in van camping expeditions. "It's a great way to combine education with a vacation," adds Sheehan. Groups are small, with 13 passengers and a professional leader in each van. Trek America's destinations include Washington, D.C., Williamsburg, Carlsbad, Mesa Verde National Park and the wet 'n' wild Orlando, Disneyland, and Panama City Beaches, or wherever your group wants to go. They'll cater to your group's individual needs or interests en route, whether you'd like to plan a windjammer cruise, river rafting or horseback riding. There is no minimum age. Prices range from $275 to $1,550, or about 20 percent less than individual rates for trips from 11 days to 9 weeks. (One free seat is provided for the organizer.) Accommodations vary. Year-round departures. (See also *Van Camping*.)

COLORADO

C BAR T TRAIL RANCH, P.O. Box 158, Idledale, CO 80453. Att.: Quentin K. Felch. (303) 674-5149.

C Bar T's two coed sessions with 15 young people in each focuses on horseback riding and pack tripping in national forest lands of the Colorado Rockies. After gathering in Denver, the group drives to the base ranch in the foothills for several days of learning riding and wilderness camping skills. Each participant learns to handle, care for, and feed his or her own horse. Then it's off to remote areas of the high mountains for 12 to 18 days of riding, camping, trail blazing, and backcountry adventure. "Prepare to enjoy a real rough-it wilderness experience," advises one young equestrienne. Hearty meals from the chuckwagon kitchen. For boys 11-16, girls 13-17; Jun.-Aug.; 3 weeks, $1,050; 4 weeks, $1,300; 7 weeks, $2,250.

DELBY'S TRIANGLE 3 RANCH, Box 14, Steamboat Springs, CO 80477. Att.: Delbert Heid. (303) 879-1257.

Del Heid specializes in pack trips to a base camp in the Mt. Zirkel Wilderness Area, 114 square miles with over 40 lakes and miles of streams and beautiful trails. Young people 8 to 18 learn about riding and packing, woodmanship, animal and plant life, forest-fire prevention, and outdoor survival. Also hours of trout fishing.

Rafters learning what it means to go downriver—Theodore F. Whitmoyer for Expeditions Inc./Grand Canyon Youth Expeditions, AZ.

"Qualified instructors will be with the groups at all times." says Del whose had more than 20 years of experience with young people. "There's a lot—an awful lot—of riding. We teach kids how to care for their horses." One-day trip, $50; 3 days, $125 (for groups of 5-10; $195 if fewer than 5 participants). Jun.-Oct. (See also *Pack Trips*.)

DVORAK EXPEDITIONS, 17921-AG U.S. Hwy. 285, Nathrop, CO 81236. Att.: Bill Dvorak. (303) 539-6851 or (800) 824-3795 (in CO May-Sep.). [Oct.-Apr.: 1-A, Blue Mtn. Rd., Lyons, CO 80540. (303) 823-5126.]

Through instructional clinics on the Green River (UT), more than 500 students have learned whitewater techniques from this highly qualified outfitter. Among the trainees are youth groups from camps, churches, scouts, and schools as well as those in the program offered by NOLS in Lander, WY. "We specialize in training on wilderness rivers," Bill Dvorak states, "and we pride ourselves in turning out well-rounded boaters. They learn sound technical kayaking, rafting, and canoeing skills, the ability to read the river, the principles of minimum impact camping, dutch oven cooking, the history and geology of the rivers they run, and river rescue and evacuation techniques." His 6-day clinics on the Green River, Jun.-Aug., cost $520 (or $470 with your own kayak gear). A special program teaches those with lower extremity disabilities how to kayak. (See also *Canoeing and River Running*.)

CONNECTICUT **OUTWARD BOUND, INC.,** 384 Field Point Rd., Greenwich, CT 06830. Att.: Pat Lyren. (800) 243-8520.

"We believe that most young people, by the age of 14, are ready to take on more responsibility along with the challenges and excitement that come with it," states Outward Bound. The program for 14-, 15-, and 16-year-olds is designed to give young people the chance to get out of their usual summer routines, try new things, and meet new people in a challenging environment. Junior courses are similar to the standard courses, though they're geared to the energy and developing abilities of younger students and led by instructors trained to work with this age group. Students backpack, canoe, rock climb, sail or raft on the same terrain as on standard Outward Bound courses. They learn low-impact camping, route finding, outdoor nutrition and cooking, shelter construction, navigation, first aid and search and rescue techniques. In all courses, participants partake in group expeditions, a solo period, and a mini-marathon. Course costs range from $850-$1,800 for 2-3 weeks. Jun.-Aug. (See also *Mountaineerng/Rock Climbing, Canoeing/Kayaking, Wilderness Nature Expeditions*.)

GEORGIA **WILDERNESS SOUTHEAST,** 711-AG Sandtown Rd., Savannah, GA 31410. Att.: Dick Murlless. (912) 897-5108.

Wilderness Southeast offers two unique summer enrichment programs—both featuring camping but not your typical summer camp—as well as customized, year-round programs for youth groups. On a charter basis, Dick Murlless designs adventures such as river canoeing and wilderness backpacking, sea island base camps, or a tropical ecology program in the Florida Keys. His "Coastal Experience" summer camp is for academically gifted 7th to 8th graders on a wild island off the Georgia coast. It features marine biology, ecology, astronomy, wilderness camping, and foraging for seafood in three 11-day sessions—$340, bring day pack and sleeping gear. Each session is for 18 students with 3 instructors. The other "camp" is a

mountain backpacking program for teens, ages 13-17. This trek
features experiences in self growth, wildlife ecology, interpersonal
communication, and survival skills, as well as physical challenges.
Three 12-day sessions each summer for 12 students with 2 instructors;
$400, bring sleeping gear. (See also *Backpacking, Canoeing,
Scuba*-FL, *Wilderness Living*.)

WOLFCREEK WILDERNESS, Rt. 1, Box 1190-A, Blairsville, GA
30512. Att.: Alan Sentkowski, Exec. Dir. (404) 745-5553.

With an individualized approach to wilderness adventure (8
participants to 2 instructors), this private nonprofit educational
organization teaches the basic skills of backpacking, whitewater
canoeing, and rock climbing. The goal—to develop self-confidence
and the freedom to appreciate a wilderness environment. Each 21-day
program is entirely mobile, leaving from Wolfcreek Lodge for the
backwoods of Georgia, North Carolina, and Alabama. "The
challenge and excitement of these activites are real and involving,"
they explain. "It's day-to-day living on a meaningful basis with others
and yourself." The 3-week coed programs, Jun.-Aug., are for
14-year-olds and up. For middle school children, 12-14 years, 2-week
adventure camps offer ropes course, hiking, canoeing, and rock
climbing. Courses for adults, too. (See also *Wilderness Living*.)

MARYLAND   **AMERICAN YOUTH HOSTELS, INC.,** Travel Dept., P.O. Box
37613, Washington, D.C. 20013-7613. (202) 783-6161.

Would you like to join a group of teenagers (13-18) or college
students (18-25) for cycling or hiking trips in various parts of the
country—East, Midwest, West, Alaska, Canada? Trips are scheduled
from 9 days to several weeks—with a transcontinental cycling trip
lasting 70 days. Most trips average $150 (plus)/week in cost and are
year round. It's a great way to explore so many parts of the
country—historic spots in New England, salt-sprayed Cape Cod, the
Amish region, Wisconsin's lakes, the spectacular Pacific coast and
Alaska, and mountainous gorges from the Cascades to the
Appalachians. Depending on your choice of trip, extra activities may
include canoeing, snorkeling, sailing, horseback riding, rafting, or
beachcombing. (See also *Cycling*.)

NORTH COUNTRY MOUNTAINEERING, INC., 1602 Shakespeare
St., Historic Fells Point, MD 21231. Att.: Steve Schneider. (301)
563-4309.

NCMI is a professional guide service that sponsors climbing trips
for teenagers (14 to 20) to Colorado, Washington, South Dakota,
Wyoming, and California. With no more than 3 participants per
guide, trips last from 1 to 6 weeks and cost $395 to $1,895. Most (an
ascent of Mt. Rainier, for example) require stamina and
determination, "but no one will be pushed beyond his or her abilities."
Steve Schneider promises. He has made many rock and ice ascents,
has taught rock climbing and winter mountaineering, and is co-author
(with his sister, Anne) of *The Climber's Sourcebook*, and *Backpacking
on a Budget*; and author of *High Technology: the Guide to Modern
Mountaineering Equipment*. (See also *Mountaineering*—DC.)

MAINE   **MAINE WATERWAYS CAMPS,** Box 62, Deer Isle, ME 04627. Att.:
             Carl W. Selin. (207) 348-2339. [Winter: (305) 743-4676.]
             With canoeing headquarters on Pleasant Lake in the Maine
             Wilderness and a sailing center on Deer Isle in Penobscot Bay, Capt.
             Selin offers both fresh- and salt-water sports for 10- to 18-year-olds.
             They have a choice of camping, canoeing, sailing, cycling,
             backpacking, and kayaking in separate or combined programs. A
             camper/counselor ratio of 5-to-1 insures thorough instruction. Most
             programs are for 2 weeks ($450), others up to 6 weeks ($1,300), or 8
             weeks ($1,725), with frequent starting dates throughout the summer.
             Also for young people: sailing and biking programs in Prince Edward
             Island and Nova Scotia. Since 1949 Capt. Selin has guided groups on
             wilderness trips in Maine and on waterfront activities in MN and CA.
             He's a former Director of Physical Education at the U.S. Coast Guard
             Academy in New London, CT. (See also *Sailing Schools,
             Canoeing*—Maine Wilderness Canoe Basin.)

Climbers tackle a cliff
in unison—*Pacific
Crest Outward Bound,
OR.*

MAINE

SUNRISE COUNTY CANOE EXPEDITIONS, INC., Cathance Lake, Grove Post, ME 04638. Att.: Martin Brown. (207) 454-7708.

Participants spend the first few days of these 3-week sessions at Cathance Lake learning the basics of canoeing, camping, and northwoods living. (An abbreviated 10-day trip is also offered.) Then they're off to remote and wild rivers of eastern and northern Maine, such as the St. Croix and Machias, for an uninterrupted wilderness experience. A more challenging expedition in north central Quebec on the Chamachuane River has been added for older teens (15-17). With each group of 15 are at least two Registered Guides, experts in wildlife biology, forestry, survival, and youth leadership training. "Teaching whitewater technique is our specialty," Marty Brown explains. "But there are also layover days for hiking, fishing, and relaxing. We hope to establish skills and standards for future outdoor travel." Adds an enthusiastic paddler, "It's almost a training trip for guides." The Jun.-Aug. coed program is for 12- to 17-year-olds; $565-$870 covers all but a fishing license. Arrival: Banogor, ME, and Quebec City. (See also *Canoeing/Kayaking*—ME, TX & Quebec.)

MONTANA

DOUBLE ARROW OUTFITTERS (AG), Box 495, Seeley Lake, MT. 59868. Att.: Jack Rich. (406) 677-2411, 2204 or 2317.

At its Wilderness Horsemanship Camp for 9- to 16-year-olds (coed), the Double Arrow teaches according to individual experience and ability in weeklong sessions. "We have qualified counselors," says Jack Rich, "and provide excellent wall-type camp tents on wood frames, great campfood, top horses and equipment, and experienced instructors and guides. "It's a real wilderness experience," For those wishing to take more than one session, training and instruction are progressive. For 7-day session, $235; discounts for additional sessions or more than 1 child per family. Jun.-Jul. Arrival: Missoula. (See also *Hiking with Packstock, Pack Trips, River Running.*)

NEW HAMPSHIRE

THE BIKING EXPEDITION, INC., Box 547 AG, Henniker, NH 03242. Att.: Tom Heavey. (603) 428-7500. (800) 245-4649 (in east).

Tom and Susan Heavey, co-authors of *25 Bicycle Tours in New Hampshire*, have developed their favorite mode of travel into a program for teenagers with summer trips in New England, the Canadian and U.S. Rockies, and abroad. The bicycle, they feel, provides the most satisfying opportunities for educational and adventurous travel. Outings of 20 to 30 days are led by two experienced adults. Teenagers from 13 to 18 pedal through varied scenes, attend summer theaters and festivals, ride a lobster boat or coastal ferry, explore museums and cheese factories, visit historic spots and picturesque villages, view spectacular mountains and wilderness wildlife, and sometimes combine biking with canoeing, hiking, cruising, or train rides. Costs vary: 20 days, $1,012; 30 days, $1,865.

OREGON

O.R.E., INC., 30493 Lone Pine Dr., Junction City, OR 97448. Att.: Bob Doppelt or Peggy Bloom. (503) 689-6198.

"Our youth group trips are 'hands-on' adventures where group

members are involved in all activities. Your group has the opportunity
to row the rafts and share the fun and excitement of the rapids," says
Bob Doppelt, who has 14 years of experience in directing camps and
outdoor programs for youths. O.R.E. starts each trip by teaching
participants the basics of river rafting and safety. En route, you hike
and explore the beautiful side country and do lots of swimming and
relaxing. Youth trips are offered on the Oregon's McKenzie, North
Umpqua, Grande and Deschutes rivers, Idaho's Salmon, and
California's Klamath rivers. Trips range from 1-6 days, with rates
based on date, group size, and river chosen. Special mid-week and
low-season rates. All youth groups eligible, including church and
scout groups and YMCA's. Guides carefully trained in youth
leadership and group dynamics are licensed river guides with Red
Cross certification. Reports one Boy Scout leader and youth trip
participant, "all of us feel that if we could each pick a
once-in-a-lifetime experience, an O.R.E. trip would be it. But the
highest praise we can give is that all 14 boys want to go again next
year." (See also *River Running, Wilderness Living*.)

Youngsters take com-
mand of campfire
cooking chores—*Zan
Mautner for Kootenai
Wilderness Recreation,
B.C., Canada.*

OREGON

PACIFIC CREST OUTWARD BOUND SCHOOL, 0110 S.W. Bancroft, Dept. AT86, Portland, OR 97201. (800) 547-3312 or (503) 243-1993.

Teens 14 years and older have fun learning backpacking, rock climbing, and whitewater rafting while they learn even more about themselves outside traditional school walls. They increase their self-confidence, self-esteem, and teamwork skills in highly supervised, structured small groups. Outward Bound gives each student an opportunity to grow and achieve in a supportive environment. "They experience the challenge and adventure of backcountry travel during a most memorable summer," reports Outward Bound. "They also learn they can do almost anything—if they really try." Coed courses are 12-28 days in California, Oregon, and Washington. Special course offered for leadership training and youth-at-risk (15- to 17-year-olds). Financial aid available. Trips scheduled year round. Outward Bound is the oldest and largest non-profit wilderness school in the country. (See also *Backpacking, River Running.*)

VERMONT

KEEWAYDIN WILDERNESS TRIPS, Box 521, Middlebury, VT 05753. Att.: Abbott T. Fenn. (802) 545-2538 or 352-4247.

This is the oldest tripping camp in America, established in 1894. In summer, Indian guides join groups of boys, 9 to a trip with 2 adult leaders, for 29 days of canoeing and 8 training and travel days in northern Quebec in the trapping grounds of the Cree Indians. Trips start with training at Lake Dunmore in Vermont before paddling the 350-mile wilderness route from the Hudson's Bay Post on Lake Mistassini. You bake your own bread, catch fish, paddle and pole on rivers and lakes, and are resupplied midway by plane. Minimum age is 15; cost $1,650.

VIRGINIA

INNER QUEST, 220 Queen St., N.E., Leesburg, VA 22075. (703) 478-1078.

Inner Quest offers safe, challenging outdoor adventure trips geared for young adults (ages 10-16). Each year they arrange programs for 8,000 students, cooperating with over 200 schools, colleges, and businesses, with an emphasis on personal growth and development and outdoor skills. Their Appalachian trips for 10-12 years olds combine backpacking, caving, rockclimbing, and canoeing and, depending on skill level, take place in either the Harper's Ferry area or Shenandoah National Park (VA). Rate for 7 days, $295, Jun.-Aug. On West Virginia adventures 13- to 16-year-olds rappell, rockclimb, explore caves, and backpack the Otter Creek Wilderness Area. The more advanced version gives more time to each activity including canoeing on the Cheat River headwaters. Family discounts for 2 or more applicants. Jul.-Aug., 12-19 days, $495-$745.

WYOMING

SKINNER BROTHERS, Box 859-AG, Pinedale, WY 82941. Att.: Monte Skinner. (307) 367-2270.

Since 1956 the Skinner brothers have offered 30-day wilderness exploration sessions during the summer months in the Gannett Peak region of the Rocky Mountains. Primarily for ages 10 through college, limited to 40 campers per session, the sessions emphasize whitewater rafting, riding, climbing, trout fishing, and survival training. They also feature learning about animal habits and habitats, shelter construction, use and preparation of edible wild plants, and overland travel. Each camper has his or her own horse, learns to ride and care for it, and takes a 3-day pack trip. Campers build a log raft before the session ends and float down a section of the Green River for 7 days. Jun.-Aug., coed, $1,575. Video brochure explains all. (See also *Mountaineering, Pack Trips, Ski Touring.*)

WILDERNESS VENTURES, P.O. Box 2768-AG, Jackson, WY 83001. Att.: Mike & Helen Cottingham. (307) 733-2122.

"For me the turning point was Mt. Rainier, when I decided to go to the top," one student recalls. "When I got there, I wrote a message to myself in case I forget: 'I can do anything I want—remember.'" The Cottinghams have designed a series of wilderness encounters in the Rockies, the Northwest, and Alaska for small groups of students 13 to 20 years old. The emphasis is on exploring, learning, and cooperating in a variety of wild environments. Their 6-week Northwest Expedition, for example, includes hiking in the Rockies; backpacking in the Cascades, Olympic National Park, and Yellowstone backcountry; rafting the Deschutes; and snow climbing in Mt. Rainier National Park. Each program is fun, exciting, enlightening—and possible for any young person in average physical condition willing to participate and learn. Rates: $1,500 and up for 27 days, to $2,400 for 44 days. Jul. and Aug.

BRITISH
COLUMBIA

KOOTENAI WILDERNESS RECREATION, Argenta, B.C., Canada V0G 1B0. Att.: Zan Mautner. (604) 366-4480 or 4287.

Crossing a creek—
without the greatest of
ease—*Zan Mautner for
Kootenai Wilderness
Recreation, B.C.
Canada.*

"Unique adventures in outdoor living await young people 8 to 14 years," Zan Mautner writes. "We spend some time at camp learning specific skills, then go out right away and put them to use." Emphasis is on backpacking and campcraft, with outings from 2 to 5 days to alpine meadows, glacial lakes, and dense river valleys. The base camp is near the north end of Kootenay Lake in the beautiful Kootenay Mountains. Coed groups limited to 12, with 2 staff members per session, Jul.-Sep.; 10 days, $385; 14 days $539. (Canadian dollars.) Also sessions for 15- to 18-year-olds as well as a training session for aspiring counselors. Bring pack and sleeping gear. Arrival: by air to Castlegar, bus to Nelson, B.C. (See also *Backpacking, Mountaineering*.)

ONTARIO

WANAPITEI WILDERNESS CENTRE, 7 Engleburn Pl., Peterborough, Ont., Canada K9H 1C4. (705) 743-3774.

Wanapitei is a small coed youth camp offering unique wilderness canoeing and camping experiences in the Canadian North. Campers 8 to 18 share an active in-camp and wilderness preparation program with experienced, dedicated leaders and then participate in wilderness canoe trips ranging in length from 1 to 6 weeks. A vibrant, sensitive community atmosphere warms Wanapitei's spectacular wilderness setting on Lake Temagami. Sessions run from 2-8 weeks. Rates (Canadian funds) are $650/2 weeks, $1,225/month, $2,100/8 weeks. "All the things I've seen, all the things I've done, and all the people I've met through Wanapitei—it boggles my mind," says one university student. "I most strongly suggest the Wilderness Centre for anyone who wants to see Canada in a unique and rewarding way, and at the same time, learn about and enrich themselves—a 5-star rating here." (See also *Canoeing, Ski Touring*.)

COMBOS

Your pack trip has ended, and you wish you could board a raft and run a river. And after that, you'd like a jeep and camping trip—or you want to backpack then do some skin diving or ballooning.

Well—combinations like this are possible. More and more outfitters are expanding their own expertise and equipment or else they are coordinating their trips with other experts to offer a variety of activities and extra fun in a single trip.

There are combo ideas sprinkled through this book. But here are a few special ones worth noting.

For most combos, the Adventure Guides office, (212) 355-6334, maintains departure dates and rates and can handle your reservations.

COLORADO   **ULTIMATE ESCAPES, LTD.,** M-115 S. 25th St., Colorado Springs, CO 80904. (800) 992-4343 or (303) 578-8383.

Within the spectacular setting of the Sangre de Cristo Range, Gary Ziegler of Ultimate Escapes has designed a potpourri of activities guaranteed to excite anyone who likes adventure. In a 7-day trip he has you riding horseback in the Wet Mountains for 2 days, spending a day on introductory rock climbing techniques, then 2 days of cycling, and an overnight rafting trip through Brown's Canyon of the Arkansas River. You'll have 4 nights of camping at an 1890s ranch and 2 nights at a comfortable mountain resort. Departures twice monthly, May-Sep., $555. Another Ziegler specialty is a 3-day horsepack trip followed by 2 days rafting the Arkansas. Departures from Colorado Springs every Monday, May-Sep., $465. (See also *Hiking with Packstock, Pack Trips, River Running.*)

FAR FLUNG ADVENTURES/TELLURIDE RAFTING, P.O. Box 685, Telluride, CO 81435. Att.: Bill White. (303) 728-3895.

With headquarters in Telluride, once a thriving mining community and now a tourist mecca, Bill White is prepared to send you hiking, climbing, horsepacking, fishing, rafting, and jeeping—with whatever combination you want. You can ride horseback into a sandstone canyon and desert country to see Indian sites and wild horses—as well as antelope, elk, deer, bald and golden eagles—then raft the Dolores River. Or pack into the high country and run the Black Canyon of the Gunnison. Or try some climbing in the San Juan and Uncompahgre mountains. (See also *River Running.*)

Involved with Far Flung's trips are:

FRENCHY'S MOUNTAIN, P.O. Box 646, Naturita, CO 81422. Att.: Bill Koon. (303) 728-3895. (See also *Cattle Drives, Pack Trips.*)

248

FANTASY RIDGE MOUNTAIN GUIDES, P.O. Box 1679, Telluride, CO 81435. Att.: Michael Covington. (303) 728-3546. (See *Mountaineering*.)

HAWAII **SOBEK EXPEDITIONS,** Dept. AG, Angels Camp, CA 95222. (209) 736-4524.

"Hawaiian Dreams" is the newest offering of Sobek Expeditions, an outfitter headquartered in California but running rivers throughout the world. This 8-day adventure features an overview of the natural wonders of Hawaii. You hike along Kauaki's rugged Na Pali coast, watch the sun rise at Haleakala Crater, dive into swimming pools and waterfalls on Maui, and continue to other off-the-beaten-track destinations. Then—add some sailing, skin diving, and windsurfing before heading home. Including air fare from the West Coast: $995 plus add ons. Or consider several combos Sobek arranges in Alaska, such as hiking in Danali National Park, sea kayaking in Glacier Bay, wildlife sighting in the Kenai and Katmai regions, and more. (See also *River Running*-CA.)

IDAHO **MACKAY BAR—IDAHO'S WILDERNESS CO.,** 3190 Airport Way, Boise, ID 83705. (800) 635-5336 or (208) 344-1881.

Your smorgasbord of wilderness adventures arranged by Mackay Bar start with a wine-and-cheese orientation and first-night accommodations in Boise. Combos include flying to a historic wilderness ranch for a few days, then on to the put-in for 6 days on the Middle Fork; or ride horseback from the ranch on an overnight pack trip to the Main Salmon put-in for two days of rafting, then up to an enchanting river lodge before flying back to Boise. Their own Mountain Air Serivce links these top-quality adventures. Most trips are customized. At the rustic Stonebraker Ranch in the Idaho Primitive Area, cabins are lighted by kerosene lamps and meals cooked on a woodburning stove. With extra days you pack to high mountain lakes to camp and fish. The lodge on the Salmon River features well-appointed cabins, candlelight dining, horseback riding, and redwood hot tubs. Most packages average $150/day including charter flights.

SALMON RIVER LODGE, P.O. Box 348, Jerome, ID 83338. Att.: Dave Giles. (208) 324-3553.

Dave Giles' lodge, at the end of the river road, is strategically located to combine his three specialties—rafting down the Main Salmon, jetboating back upstream to the lodge, then saddling up for packing high into the Salmon River Breaks Area of the Salmon National Forest. It's a region of beautiful meadows, lush forests, and rocky buttes, with scenic glimpses of the Salmon River far below. Some scheduled trips, but most are customized for your own group. (See also *Pack Trips, Jet Boating, River Running*.)

OREGON **HELLS CANYON ADVENTURES,** P.O. Box 159, Oxbow, OR 97840. Att.: Gary Armacost. (800) HCA-FLOT or (503) 785-3352.

Hells Canyon of the Snake River separates Idaho and Oregon, and outfitters in both states combine rafting with riding. Gary Armacost is one of them. First you spend 3 days with Gary on his deluxe trip in Hells Canyon. You raft downriver in 18-foot rafts through Wild Sheep Rapids, Granite Creek, and perhaps walk around Suicide Point! Then you meet Cal Henry for 3 days of horsepacking in the Wallowa Mountains—the way the early explorers did it. (If you're staying with the river instead of taking the riding combo, it's a 6-day trip that ends with jet boating back upriver to the starting point.) May or Jun., $520. Gary also combines 3 days of backpacking from Black Lake to Emerald Lake, then down Granite Creek to meet a jetboat that takes you to the put-in for 3 days of rafting Hells Canyon. Jun.-Sep., $460. (See also *Jet Boating*.)

Other outfitters who combine rafting Hells Canyon with riding in the Wallowas and Eagle Cap Wilderness are:

CAL HENRY, Box 26-A, Joseph, OR 97846. (503) 432-9171. (See also *Hiking with Packstock* and *Pack Trips*.)

LUTE JERSTAD ADVENTURES, LJA, INC., P.O. Box 19537, Portland, OR 97219. (503) 244-4364. (See *Pack Trips* and *River Running*.)

WALKER RIVER EXPEDITIONS, Rt. 1, Box AG, Enterprise, OR 97828. Att.: Jim Walker. (503) 426-3307. (See *River Running*.)

MONTANA   **GLACIER RAFT COMPANY,** P.O. Box 264-J, West Glacier, MT 59936. Att.: Darwon Stoneman. (406) 888-5541.
For a horseback and rafting combo, you could hardly pick a more scenic region. It's a 5-day adventure, starting with a drive along the south edge of Glacier National Park, cross the Continental Divide, and reach a ranch where you get horses and camp overnight. Then ride over scenic trails, catch cutthroat, and camp for 2 days before reaching the Middle Fork of the Flathead for rafting out. Jun.-Aug., $450. Another option is hiking and rafting. For five days you raft the Middle Fork of the Flathead, stopping each day for hikes to seldom visited points accessible only with a raft for crossing the river. Jun. & Jul., $395. (See also *River Running*.)

UTAH   **TAG-A-LONG TOURS,** P.O. Box 1206, 452 N. Main St., Moab, UT 84532. Att.: Paul M. Niskanen. (800) 453-3292 or (801) 259-8946.
Tag-A-Long calls its rafting/jeeping combo "the ultimate wilderness adventure." In 7 days (starting in Moab) you raft Cataract Canyon of the Colorado River then drive and camp through the spectacular red-rock region of Canyonlands. "One day you're poised above the Big Drop on the river, and another day you are holding tight as the jeep inches up a seemingly impassable incline," they say. Departures every Sunday, May-Oct., $825. (See also *Jeeping, Van Camping, River Running*.)

UTAH

ADRIFT ADVENTURES, P.O. Box 81032, Salt Lake City, UT 84108. Att.: Myke Hughes. (801) 485-5978.

Combine an overland safari with hiking, riding, and whitewater rafting in the Canyonlands and you have an unbeatable combo. Start this 7-day trip driving from Grand Junction to Durango for a day's hike in the San Juan Mountains. Your continuing route leads to Mesa Verde National Park and through Canyonlands National Park to the Arches National Park for an evening horseback ride and cowboy cookout. Next morning start a 3-day run on the Colorado River through Cataract Canyon, ending with a scenic flight back to Grand Junction. May-Sep., $795. Another combo route winds from Salt Lake to the Arches and Canyonlands and Cataract Canyon; $840. For spring skiers AA offers skiing at Snowbird followed by a wild ride through Cataract Canyon when the water is high—Apr. & May, 7 days, $639. (See also *River Running.*)

VERMONT

VERMONT BICYCLE TOURING, Box 711-BV, Bristol, BT 05443. Att.: John S. Freidin. (802) 453-4811.

You can cycle circles around a windjammer on a 5-day combo recently launched by John Freidin. Board the Schooner *Homer W. Dixon* on Lake Champlain on Sunday afternoon for five nights of shipboard life. Each day a van meets you and your bike at a different port, and lets you off at a bicycle trail for circling the area—then it's back on the schooner in time for a swim, sail, and dinner. (5 days, $535-$595.) For a Friday-to-Sunday combo with meals and overnights, cycle one day and canoe the Connecticut River the next. (2 days, 2 nights, $169-$189.)

MEXICO

FAR FLUNG ADVENTURES, Box 31, Terlingua, TX 79852. Att.: Mike Davidson. (915) 371-2489.

There's adventure south of the border for anyone who likes to raft and ride. Far Flung has teamed up with Marcos Paredes of Desert Trails for horse trips into the Sierra del Carmen combined with rafting the Rio Grande in Big Bend country. The mountain range offers "the most impressive scenery in northern Mexico," and Paredes leads you through it on 2- to 4-day trips. Riding to a high camp at 8,500 feet you're rewarded with a 100-mile view. After a few days in the saddle, bask in the comfort of a 2-day river trip through Mariscal Canyon or 3 days in Boquillas Canyon. It all adds up to a great week's adventure.

RIVER RUNS/OUTFITTERS

The following pages list nearly 130 different river runs in North America and the professional outfitters who are equipped to take you on them. For information about each of their services, please turn to the *River Running* chapter, page 145.

Alaska (central)—Alatna, Chickaloon, Koyukuk, and Yukon rivers:
   NOVA Riverrunners of Alaska, AK; Sourdough Outfitters, AK.

Alaksa (northern)—John, Kobuk, Nigu, Noatak, and Wild rivers:
   NOVA Riverrunners of Alaska, AK; Sourdough Outfitters, AK.

Alaska (southern)—Copper, Deshka, LionsHead, and Matanuska rivers:
   NOVA Riverrunners of Alaska, AK; Far Flung Adventures, TX.

Alaska (southeastern)—Alsek, Stikine, and Tatshenshini rivers:
   Alaska Discovery, AK; Mountain Travel, CA; Sobek Expeditions, CA.

Arizona—Grand Canyon of the Colorado River:
   American River Touring Association, CA; Arizona Raft Adventures, Inc., AZ; Canyoneers, Inc., AZ; Del E. Webb Wilderness River Adventures, AZ; Diamond River Adventures, AZ; Expeditions Inc./Grand Canyon Youth Expeditions, AZ; Grand Canyon Dories, CA; Grand Canyon Expeditions, UT; Henry & Grace Falany's White Water River Expeditions, Inc., CA; O.A.R.S., Inc., CA; Outdoors Unlimited, CA; Sierra Western River Guides, UT; Sobek Expeditions, CA; Southeastern Expeditions, Inc., GA; Steve Currey Expeditions, Inc., UT; Western River Expeditions, Inc., UT; Wild & Scenic, Inc., AZ; William McGinnis' Whitewater Voyages, CA.

California—American, Calif. Salmon, East Carson, Eel, Kern, Kings, Klamath, Merced, Sacramento, Scott, Smith, Stanislaus, Trinity, Tuolumne, and Yuba rivers:
   Action Adventures Wet 'n' Wild, Inc., CA; All-Outdoors Adventure Trips, CA; American River Touring Association, CA; Eagle Sun, Inc., OR; ECHO: The Wilderness Company, CA; Kern River Tours, CA; Klamath River Outdoor Experiences, CA; Libra Expeditions, CA; Orange Torpedo Trips, OR; O.R.E., Inc., OR; Outdoor Adventures, CA; Outdoors Unlimited, CA; River Trips Unlimited, Inc., OR; Sierra Western River Guides, UT; Sobek Expeditions, CA; Sunrise Scenic Tours, OR; Tributary Whitewater Tours, CA; Turtle River Rafting Co., CA; William McGinnis' Whitewater Voyages, CA; Zephyr River Expeditions, CA.

Colorado—Arkansas, Cache La Poudre, Colorado (upper), Gunnison, North Platte, Rio Grande, Roaring Fork, and San Miguel rivers:
   Adventure Bound, Inc., CO; Colorado Adventures, Inc., CO; Dvorak Expeditions, CO; Echo Canyon River Expeditions, CO; Four Corners Expeditions, CO; Outdoor Leadership Training Seminars/Arkansas River Tours, CO; River Runners Ltd., CO; Roaring Fork River Company, CO; Sierra Western River Guides, UT; SilverCreek Expeditions, CO; Ultimate Escapes, Ltd., CO; Wilderness Aware, Inc., CO.

Colorado—Dolores and Gunnison rivers:
   Dvorak Expeditions, CO; Echo Canyon River Expeditions, CO; Far Flung Adventures/Telluride Whitewater, CO; Four Corners Expeditions, CO; Outdoor Leadership Training Seminars/Arkansas River Tours, CO; Roaring Fork River Company, CO; Wilderness Aware, Inc., CO.

Idaho—Blackfoot, Lochsa, Snake (not Hells Canyon) and Teton rivers:
   Adrift Adventures, UT; Glacier Raft Company, MT; Great Adventures West, MT.

Idaho—Hells Canyon of the Snake River:

ECHO: The Wilderness Company, CA; Grand Canyon Dories, CA; Hells Canyon Adventures, OR; Idaho Adventures River Trips, ID; Lute Jerstad Adventures, LJA, Inc., OR; Walker River Expeditions, OR.

Idaho—Salmon River (lower):
Grand Canyon Dories, CA.

Idaho—Salmon River (Main and/or Middle Fork):
American River Touring Association, CA; Barker-Ewing Idaho, Inc., WY; ECHO: The Wilderness Company, CA; Grand Canyon Dories, CA; Happy Hollow Camps, ID; High Adventure River Tour Inc., ID; Holiday River Expeditions, UT; Idaho Adventures River Trips, ID; Mackay Bar, ID; Middle Fork Rapid Transit, ID; Middle Fork River Company, ID; Middle Fork River Expeditions, ID; O.A.R.S., Inc., CA; O.R.E. Inc., OR; Orange Torpedo Trips, OR; Outdoor Adventures, CA; Salmon River Lodge, ID; Sierra Western River Guides, UT; Western River Expeditions, Inc., UT.

Idaho—Selway River:
Steve Currey Expeditions, Inc., UT.

Kentucky—Cumberland River:
Mountain River Tours, Inc., WV.

Maine—Allagash, Kennebec (upper), Penobscot (West Branch), Rapid, and Dead rivers:
Downeast Rafting Co., Inc., NH; Eastern River Expeditions, ME; Maine Whitewater, Inc., ME; Northern Outdoors, Inc., ME; Rolling Thunder River Co.; ME; Unicorn Rafting Expeditions, Inc., ME.

Maryland—Upper Youghiogheny River:
Appalachian Wildwaters Inc., WV; North American River Runners, Inc. WV.

Montana—Blackfoot, Clearwater, Flathead, Smith, Upper Missouri, and Yellowstone rivers:
Adrift Adventures, UT; Double Arrow Outfitters, MT; Glacier Raft Company, MT; Great Adventures West, MT; Great Northern Rafting, MT.

New Hampshire—Swift, and Pemigiwasett rivers:
Downeast Rafting Co., Inc., NH.

New Mexico—Rio Chama and Rio Grande rivers:
Arizona Raft Adventures, Inc., AZ; Echo Canyon River Expeditions, CO; Far Flung Adventures, TX; New Wave Rafting Co, NM; Rio Grande Rapid Transit, NM; Taos Whitewater, NM.

New York—Upper and Lower Hudson, and Moose rivers:
Adventures En Eau Vive, Ltee., P.Q., Canada; Eastern River Expeditions, ME: Northern Outdoors, Inc., ME; Pocono Whitewater Rafting, PA; Unicorn Rafting Expeditions, Inc., ME; Whitewater Challengers, Inc., PA; Whitewater World, Ltd., PA.

North Carolina—Chattooga, French Broad, Nantahala, and Nolichucky rivers:
Mountain River Tours, Inc., WV; Nantahala Outdoor Center, NC; Southeastern Expeditions, Inc., GA.

Oregon—Bruneau, Crooked, Deschutes, Grande Ronde, Illinois, John Day, McKenzie, and Umpqua rivers:
Grand Canyon Dories, CA; Lute Jerstad Adventures, LJA, Inc., OR; Middle Fork River Company, ID; O.R.E. Inc., OR; Orange Torpedo Trips, OR; Pacific Crest Outward Bound School, OR; Sundance Expeditions, Inc., OR; Sunrise Scenic Tours, OR; Walker River Expeditions, OR; William McGinnis' Whitewater Voyages, CA.

Oregon—Owyhee River:
ECHO: The Wilderness Company, CA; Grand Canyon Dories, CA; Lute Jerstad Adventures, LJA, Inc., OR; Middle Fork River Company, ID; Steve Currey Expeditions, Inc., UT; Turtle River Rafting Co., CA; Walker River Expeditions, OR; William McGinnis' Whitewater Voyages, CA.

Oregon—Rogue River:
Action Adventures Wet 'n' Wild, Inc., CA; American River Touring Association, CA; Eagle Sun, Inc., OR; Lute Jerstad Adventures, LJA, Inc., OR; O.A.R.S., Inc., CA; O.R.E. Inc., OR; Orange Torpedo Trips, OR; Outdoors Unlimited, CA; Pacific Crest Outward Bound School, OR; River Trips Unlimited, Inc., OR; Rogue Excursions Unlimited Inc., OR; Sobek Expeditions, CA; Sundance Expeditions, Inc., OR; Sunrise Scenic Tours, OR; Turtle River Rafting Co., CA; William McGinnis' Whitewater Voyages, CA.

Pennsylvania—Lehigh, Pine Creek, and Youghiogheny rivers:
Canyon Cruises, PA; Pocono Whitewater Rafting, PA; White Water Adventurers, PA; Whitewater Challengers, Inc., PA; Whitewater World, Ltd., PA.

South Carolina/Georgia—Chattooga River:
Wildwater Ltd., SC.

Tennessee—Hiwassee, Nolichucky, and Ocoee rivers:
Nantahala Outdoor Center, NC; Ocoee Outdoors, Inc., TN; Outland Expeditions, TN; Southeastern Expeditions, Inc., GA; Sunburst Wilderness Adventures, TN; Wildwater Ltd., SC.

Texas—Rio Grande, and Guadelupe rivers:
Far Flung Adventures, TX; New Wave Rafting Co., NM; Outback Expeditions, TX; Outdoor Leadership Training Seminars/Arkansas River Tours, CO; Southeastern Expeditions, Inc., GA.

Utah—Cataract Canyon of the Colorado River:
Adrift Adventures, UT; Adventure Bound, Inc., CO; American River Touring Association, CA; Colorado Adventures, Inc., CO; Holiday River Expeditions, UT; Tag-A-Long Tours, UT; Western River Expeditions, Inc., UT.

Utah—Desolation and Gray canyons (Green River Wilderness) of the Green River:
Adventure River Expeditions, Inc., UT; American River Touring Association, CA; Colorado Adventures, Inc., CO; Fastwater Expeditions, UT; Holiday River Expeditions, UT: Tag-A-Long Tours, UT: Western River Expeditions, Inc., UT; Wild & Scenic, Inc., AZ.

Utah—Dinosaur National Monument on the Green, and Yampa rivers:
Adventure Bound, Inc., CO; American River Touring Association, CA; Holiday River Expeditions, UT.

Utah—San Juan River:
Fastwater Expeditions, UT; O.A.R.S., Inc., CA; Wild & Scenic, Inc., AZ.

Utah—Westwater Canyon of the Colorado River, also Labyrinth/Stillwater canyons:
Adrift Adventures, UT; Adventure Bound, Inc., CO; Tag-A-Long Tours, UT; Western River Expeditions, Inc., UT; Wild & Scenic, Inc., AZ.

West Virginia—Dry Fork, Gauley, New, North Branch, Upper Potomac, and Tygart rivers:
Appalachian Wildwaters Inc., WV; Cheat River Outfitters, WV; Class VI River Runners, Inc., WV; Eastern River Expeditions, ME; Mountain River Tours, Inc., WV; North American River Runners, Inc., WV; Sobek Expeditions, CA.

West Virginia—Cheat River:
Appalachian Wildwaters Inc., WV; Cheat River Outfitters, WV; North American River Runners, Inc., WV; White Water Adventurers, PA; Whitewater World, Ltd., PA.

British Columbia—Chilcotin, Fraser, and Thompson rivers:
Frontier River Adventures, B.C., Canada; Whitewater Adventures, B.C., Canada.

Manitoba—Berens, Bloodvein, Gods, Hayes, and Pigeon rivers:
North Country River Trips, Man., Canada.

Northwest Territories—Coppermine, Nahanni, and Slave rivers:
Sobek Expeditions, CA; Subarctic Wilderness Adventurers, Ltd., N.W.T., Canada; Whitewater Adventurers, B.C., Canada.

Ontario—Ottawa River:
Wilderness Tours, Ont., Canada.

Quebec—Rouge River:
Whitewater World, Ltd., PA.

Costa Rica—Pacuare, Reventazon, and Chirripo rivers:
New Wave Rafting Co., NM.

Mexico—Balsas, Rio Antigua, Rio Grande de Santiago, Rios Moctezuma, and Usumacinta Rivers:
Far Flung Adventures, TX; New Wave Rafting Co, NM; Outback Expeditions, TX.

INDEX